IMAGES
of America

GLENS FALLS PEOPLE AND PLACES

On the cover: A group botany students from the Ridge Street School are shown on a nature outing from school. (Courtesy of the Chapman Historical Museum collection.)

IMAGES
of America

Glens Falls People and Places

Bob Bayle, Lillian Casola,
Stan Malecki, and Gwen Palmer

ARCADIA
PUBLISHING

ISBN 978-0-7385-6295-7

Published by Arcadia Publishing
Charleston, South Carolina

Printed in the United States of America

Library of Congress Catalog Card Number: 2008930908

For all general information contact Arcadia Publishing at:
Telephone 843-853-2070
Fax 843-853-0044
E-mail sales@arcadiapublishing.com
For customer service and orders:
Toll-Free 1-888-313-2665

Visit us on the Internet at www.arcadiapublishing.com

*This book is dedicated to the prosperous
and preposterous citizens of Glens Falls from the past.
Without their stories, this book would not have been possible.*

Contents

ACKNOWLEDGMENTS

The content of this book would not exist without the total cooperation and support of the Chapman Historical Museum. The archives of the museum contain information about people and places in the city of Glens Falls. As volunteers in this education center, the Corners Group became fully aware of the material contained therein and felt that it should be shared with the public. Secondly, recognition should be given to the four authors who immersed themselves in the researching of material for this publication. It has taken almost four years to gather, edit, prepare, and edit again the information found here. Commitment, dedication, and congeniality have led to the completion of *Glens Falls People and Places*. Finally, thanks must be given to those citizens of Glens Falls from the past whose lives enriched the community. The prosperous and the preposterous contributed to its economy, development, and expansion. Their stories had to be told.

INTRODUCTION

Glens Falls is a small city on the Hudson River about 50 miles north of Albany, the capital of New York State. It presently has a population of about 14,000 people but flourished with over 20,000 at one time. Its economy previously featured several paper mills, quarries, and the world-famous Glens Falls Insurance Company. During World War II, it was designated as "Hometown U.S.A." thanks to its native son Robert Patterson, secretary of war. Patterson suggested Glens Falls for the honor, it was accepted, and a publicity campaign showing what the towns back home were doing for the war effort was developed for *Look* magazine in 1943. However, now most of the mills are gone. One lone paper mill, a cement company, and a limestone quarry still exist. The area is home to several catheter medical supply companies but none located directly in Glens Falls.

Serving as a gateway to the Adirondacks, Glens Falls gains from the summer tourism industry centered in Lake George to the north and Saratoga Springs with its racetrack to the south and the local ski areas in the winter. Its many festivals provide activities for visitors to the area. Located approximately halfway between New York City and Montreal, Canada, it is a natural stopping off point for travelers. Cultural activities abound with the Hyde Collection, a world-class art museum, the Glens Falls Symphony Orchestra, a community theater group, and numerous sports venues.

In the mid-1700s Glens Falls was simply referred to as "the Corners," as it existed only as a bend in the road between major British forts in Fort Edward and Lake George. As Quaker settlers moved in, it began to be called "Wing's Falls," after Abraham Wing, one of the first men to own property here. However, due to some unpaid debts of Wing, a man named Johannes Glenn stepped in and ended up with naming rights to the village, hence, Glenn's Falls. Pearlville and Pearl Village were tried as names also, but they never really established themselves. Later the Glens Falls Insurance Company was responsible for dropping one *n* and the apostrophe, so Glens Falls remains the correct name today.

In the 1700s, when the original patent was being divided, the village fathers felt they should settle at the northern limits of today's city. However, at the southern end of the settlement was the Hudson River where a drop in elevation provided a natural falls. These provided inexpensive waterpower to turn waterwheels, so mills developed in this area and men settled there. Therefore the village developed from the south to the north. Included near the river were granaries, lumber mills, and limestone quarries, all operated by waterpower. With increased employment opportunities came immigrant workers, and the area prospered.

The mill owners became millionaires who invested in banks, insurance companies, the canal system, and other businesses that created community pockets with individualized names such as Fountain Square, Union Square, Monument Square, and the East End. Family names such as Crandall, Sherman, Finch, Spier, Ordway, Lapham, Morgan, McEchron, Colvin, Pruyn, and Hyde all reflect wealth in the Glens Falls area. Most of these earned their money through some form of the lumbering industry. In addition, more colorful characters who contributed to the community were Broncho Charlie Miller, alleged to be the youngest Pony Express rider; Daniel Sickles, a Civil War general who carried a tiny coffin containing his amputated leg for display; Estelle Palmer, community activist; Helen Foulds, who lived her last years as a "guest" in the Glens Falls Hospital; Billy Joe Clark, founder of the first temperance society; and James Morgan, who died mysteriously in a barn fire.

The medical community was enriched by the names of doctors Annie Hull and Annetta Barber, two of the first women medical professionals in the area; Edgar Bemis, with questionable medical techniques; Lemon Thomson, who ran an early hospital on Warren Street; and Edgar Birdsall, responsible for introducing radiology to the area. Glens Falls contributed two governors to New York State, John Alden Dix and Charles Evan Hughes. Hughes was also chief justice to the U.S. Supreme Court and a presidential candidate. A record-breaking world champion bicycle racer, Harry Elkes, came from here.

The research found the rich marrying the rich, with family dynasties being created. Their elegant homes with exquisite gardens on large expanses of land graced the main streets of the village. These men, with their women usually in the background, became the backbone of the community, demanding amenities that provided culture, entertainment, and social structure. As soon as things became available, telephone and electrical services were installed, doing away with gaslights. Sewer and water lines allowed for indoor plumbing, eliminating outhouses. Trolleys allowed the village to grow away from the center of town. As progress evolved, the trolleys made way for buses and trains were responsible for goods from local industries being sent to far-reaching areas. Opera houses, vaudeville stages, and theaters provided world-famous entertainers a venue for their performances in Glens Falls. The performers stayed in the elegant American, later the Hotel Ruliff, and Madden Hotels with their horse barns and carriage houses nearby.

The development of Glens Falls started before the Revolution, but it was really an evolution over a longer period of time. The nearness to the beautiful Adirondack Mountains and Hudson River allowed for the development of one of the richest cities in the region in a previous era.

The photographs in this book will feature these people, the prosperous and preposterous, their properties, and the areas of the city that developed due to their efforts. The story of Glens Falls is the story of these people and places. In some cases, portraits of individuals were not available, but their story was important so in some instances, only photographs of their homes or businesses may appear. Unless otherwise noted, photographs from the collection of the Historical Society of Glens Falls and Queensbury, at the Chapman Historical Museum, will be used to tell this saga.

One

THE SOUTH

The Hudson River played a major part in the way Glens Falls was settled. With the drop in elevation at the bend in the river, rapids and falls were prominent. This caused the topography to be constantly changing. Whirlpools and eddies formed and allowed for erosion to create caves and hollowed-out spaces in the rock. For the early Quaker settlers, the river held control of the way things were to develop. The knowledge of using moving water for power came with them, so it was natural that the people established mills along this stretch of the river. By the middle of the 1800s, there were numerous mills capable of grinding grain, cutting lumber, and eventually making paper. Since this is where employment opportunities existed, it made sense for citizens to build their homes within walking distance of their work. With the development of the Feeder Canal alongside the river, prosperity abounded. The river, or south end of town, features businesses and the following people living near the Hudson River and the Feeder Canal: Col. John Cunningham, George Finch, John Keenan, James Morgan, Daniel Sickles, and Calvin Robbins. In addition, there will be material on Cooper's Cave, the Feeder Canal, Glens Falls Coal Company, Imperial Wall Paper, Jointa Lime, Portland Cement, and logging on the Hudson River.

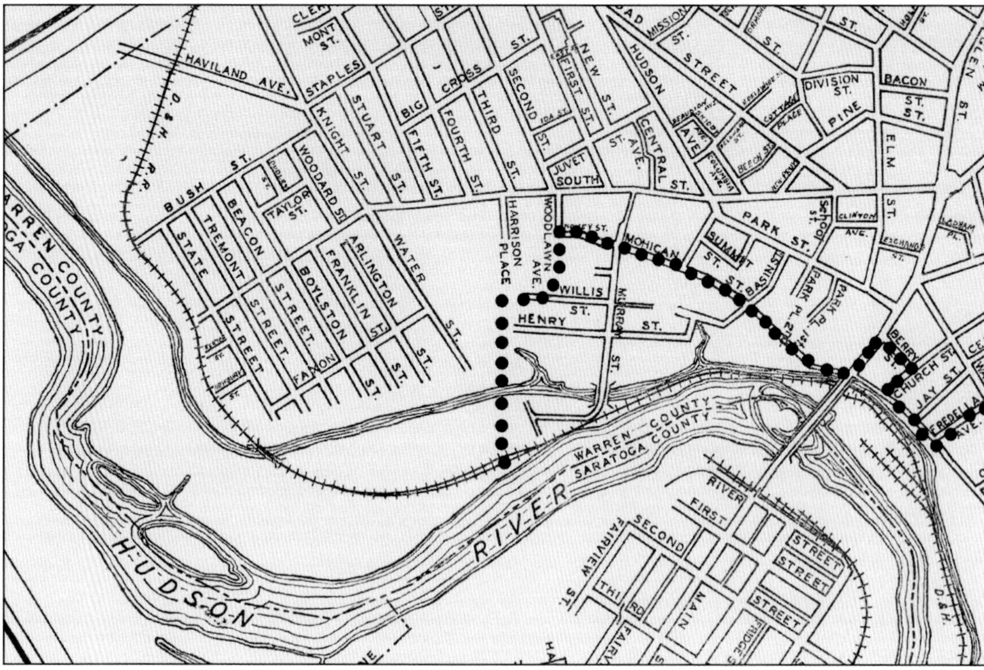

For the purpose of this book, the south or "river" will refer to the area along Mohican Street, going to Glen Street and up to Berry Street, and then down Church Street and along Oakland Avenue to Fredella Avenue. The people in this section were connected with businesses along the river and canal.

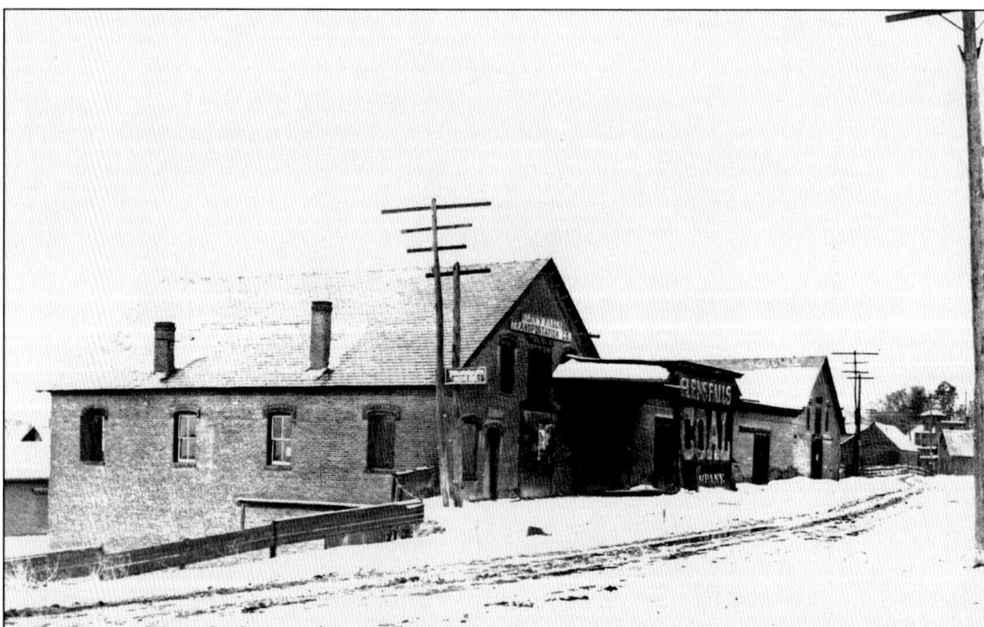

The Glens Falls Coal Company had facilities along the canal. When lumber barges were unloaded in New York City ports, they were loaded with coal to be brought back to Glens Falls. The majority of homes in the area were heated with wood or coal, and the canal allowed for the easy import of this important raw material.

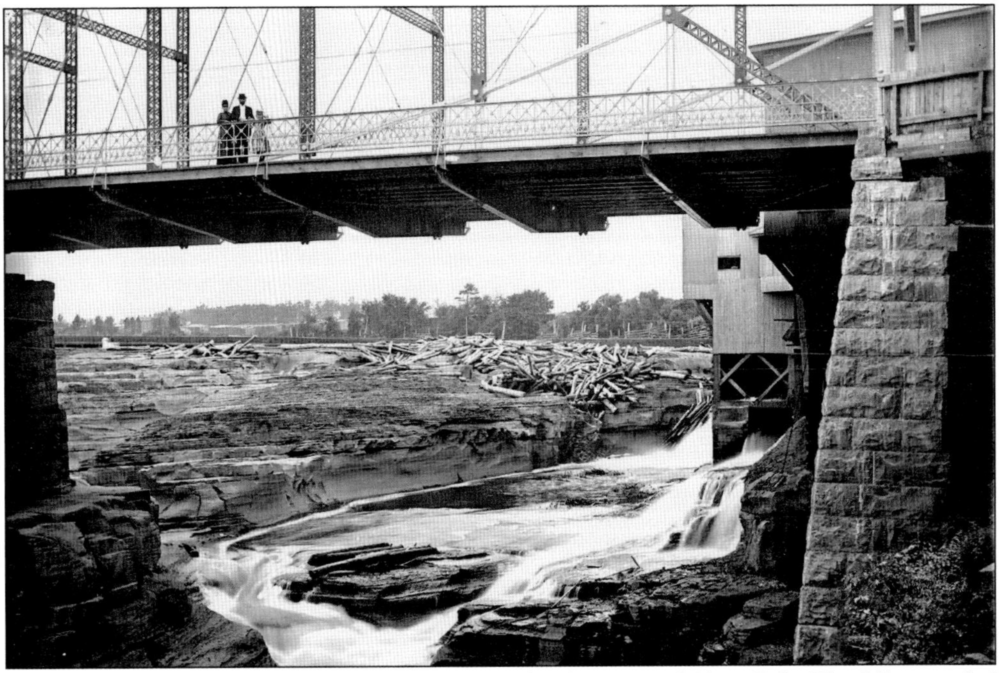

The Hudson River was the important piece in the development of Glens Falls. The falls provided cheap power, so as the mills developed, the workers settled near them. Logs from the Adirondacks were floated down the river to the many mills that were established there. At times there were so many logs in the river, men could actually walk from shore to shore without getting wet.

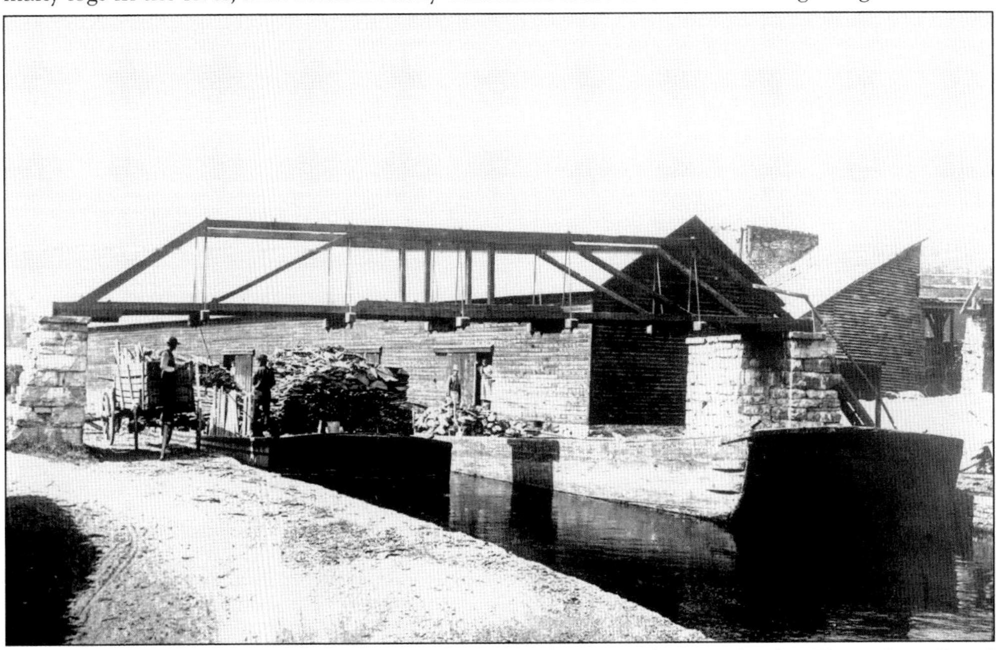

Alongside the river, the Feeder Canal was established to provide water for the Champlain Canal to the east of town. The canal also provided a staging area for sorting logs to go to the various mills and a way to get products to the Champlain Canal and on to the Hudson River route south to New York City. This opened Glens Falls to the world and unlimited wealth.

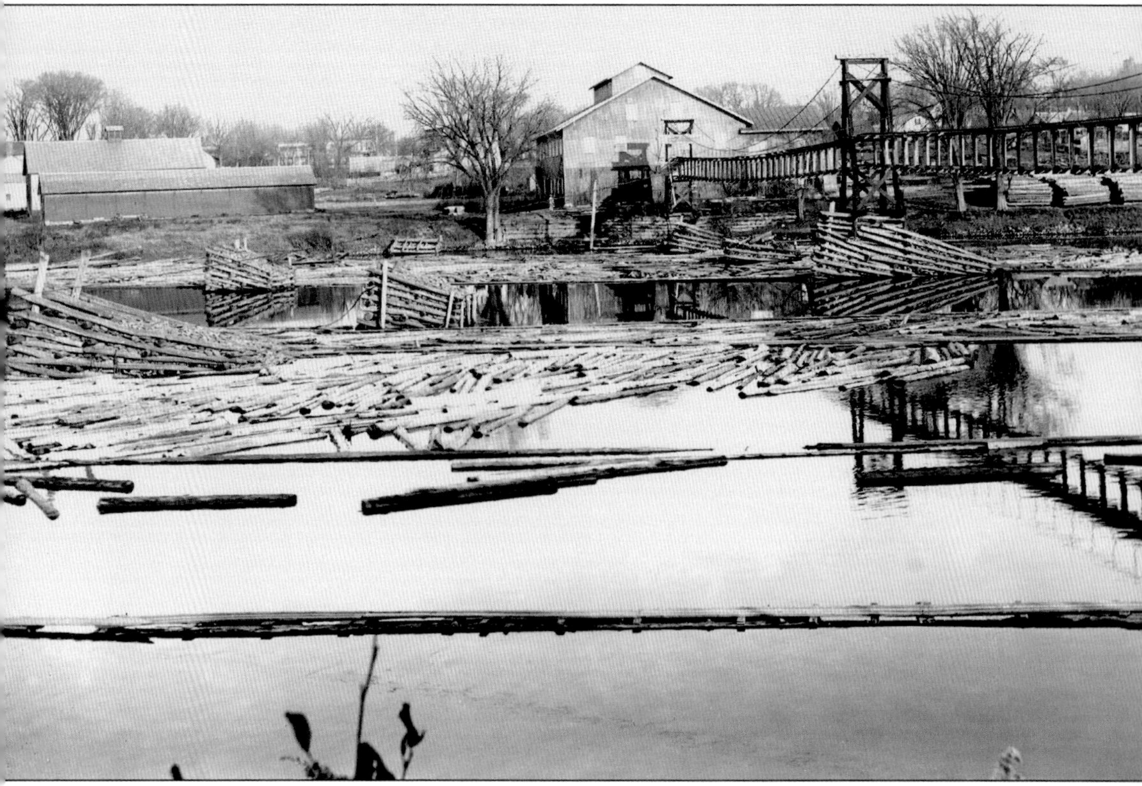

When Abraham Wing settled in Glens Falls, he recognized the value of the falls and established a sawmill on the north side of the Hudson River. With the completion of the Feeder Canal in 1832, mills abounded as there was now an easier way to get logs to their places of business. Piers were placed in the river to allow the sorting of marked logs. Each spring with high water levels, the river drives brought hundreds of thousands of logs to the area, earning Glens Falls the reputation of being the lumber capital of the United States. The bend in the river allowed for the logs to slow down in their travel downstream, and the sorting could begin. Large chains were strung across the water, and logs were held until needed by the various mills. The picture shows the piers in the water and logs floating to the end of their travels.

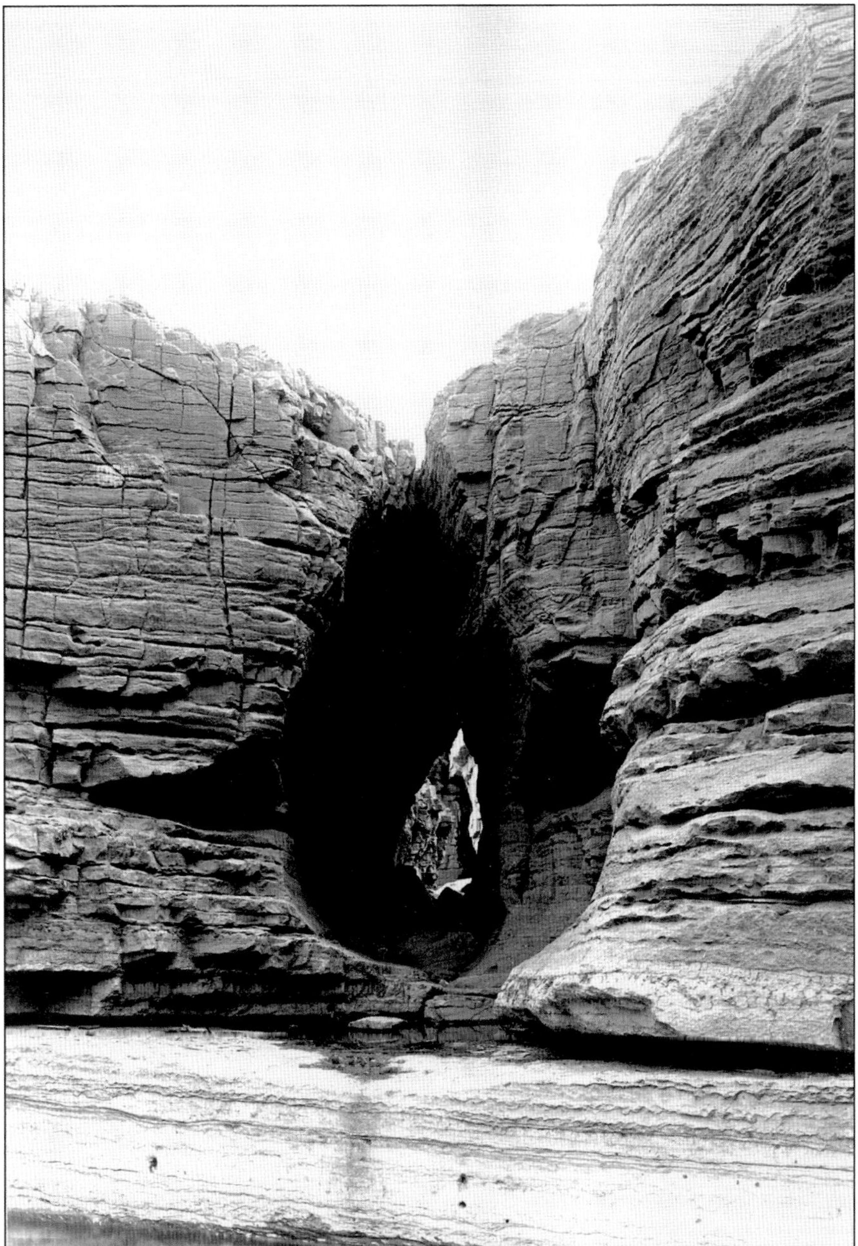

In 1825, after returning from a trip through the Adirondacks, James Fenimore Cooper began his famous novel *The Last of the Mohicans.* What appeared to be a cave on an island in the middle of the Hudson River between Glens Falls and South Glens Falls inspired him to create a story where two young daughters of a commander of the fort in Lake George were traveling to Fort Edward. They were about to fall prey to a band of marauding natives when they were secreted into a limestone cave and were saved. At one time a spiral staircase led down to Cooper's Cave, named after the author, but in the early 1960s, it was dismantled for safety reasons. In 2007, a visitors' platform was established on the South Glens Falls side of the river for viewing, but going into the cave is no longer allowed.

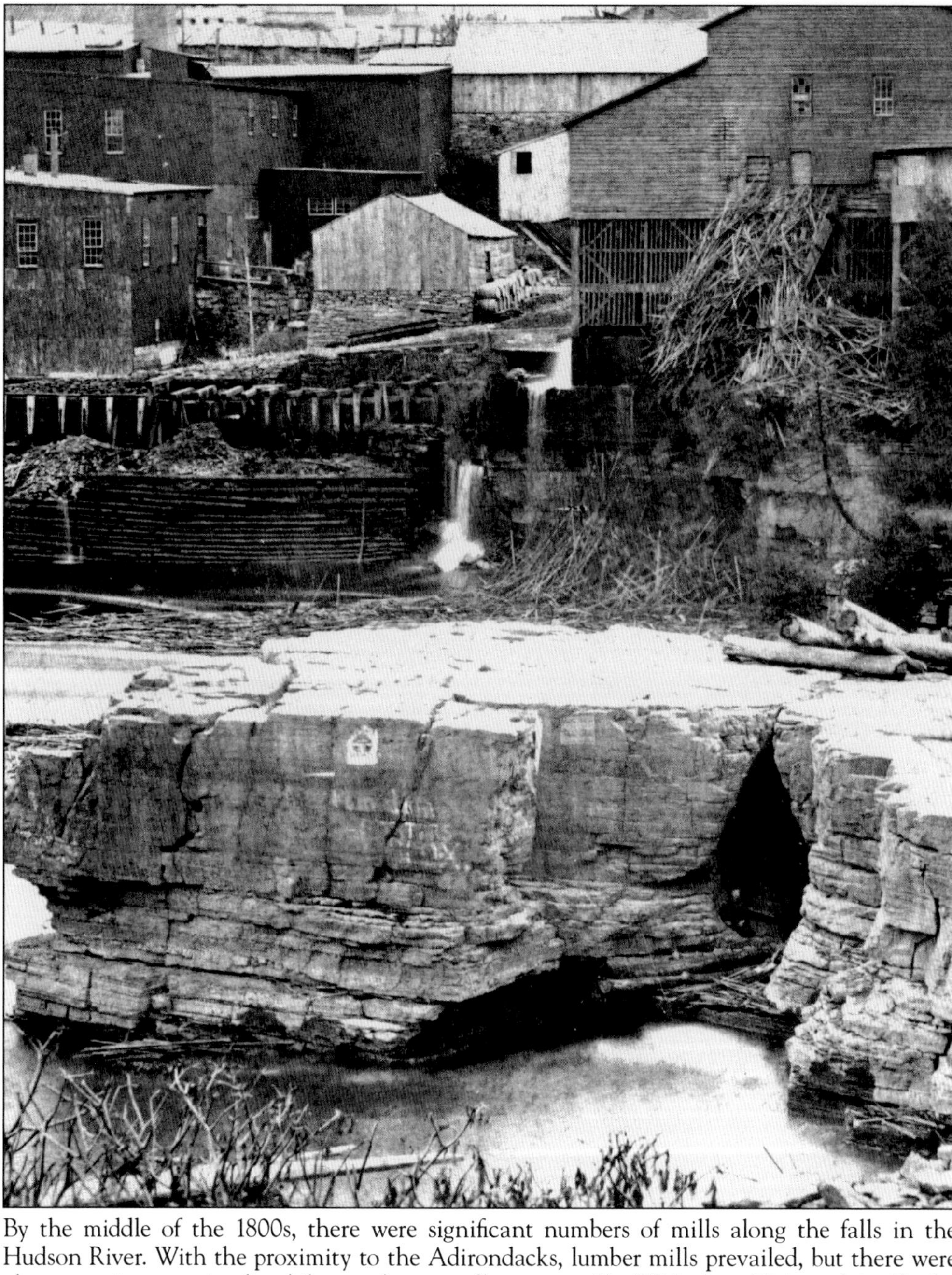

By the middle of the 1800s, there were significant numbers of mills along the falls in the Hudson River. With the proximity to the Adirondacks, lumber mills prevailed, but there were also granaries, quarries, limekilns, and eventually, paper mills. With the addition of the Feeder Canal, industries that took advantage of the available transportation developed between it and the river. The falls provided inexpensive power, and the men who owned the mills owned the wood lots in the mountains, invested in the canal, and owned the canal boats that ran on it. All this development produced a large number of millionaires for such an isolated community. It was only natural that these same men became directors of local industries, banking institutions, and cultural foundations. This early view of Cooper's Cave, looking north, shows how the mills' owners took advantage of the space along the river.

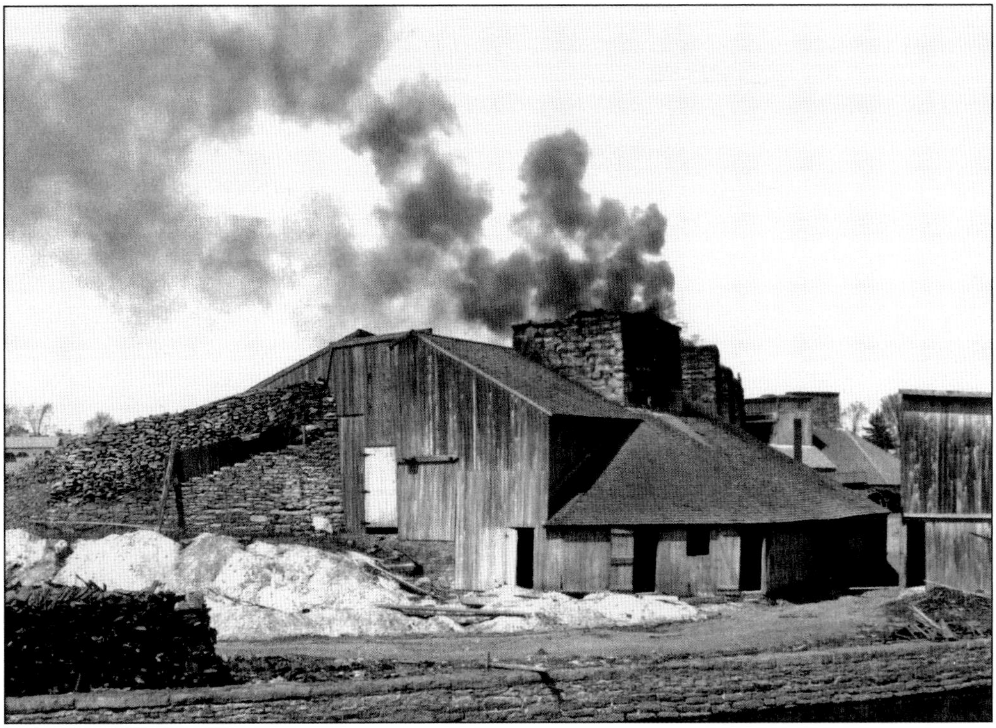

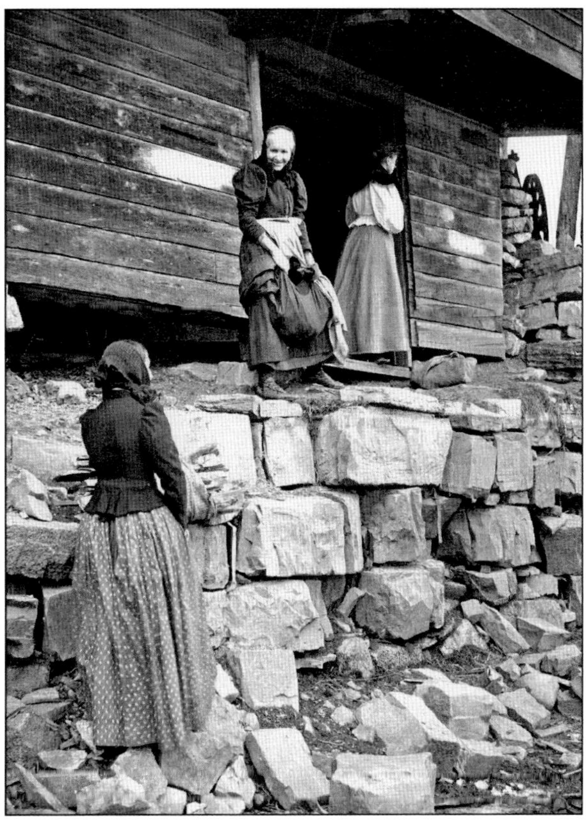

By the mid-1800s, Jointa Lime was producing between 120 and 140 barrels of the finest-quality lime daily (shown). Limestone was burned for use in agriculture and the building trades. The main kilns were located between the canal and river near present-day Oak Street. After it was burned, it was loaded on canal boats and transported to Troy where John Keenan peddled it throughout the streets. As the business grew, Keenan became an extremely influential man in Glens Falls. There were extremes between classes in society at this time, and many of the less fortunate were reduced to scavenging for coal, charcoal, wood, and limestone for use in their everyday lives. It was not unusual to find local immigrant women searching the area of the kilns for scraps that could improve the quality of their lives.

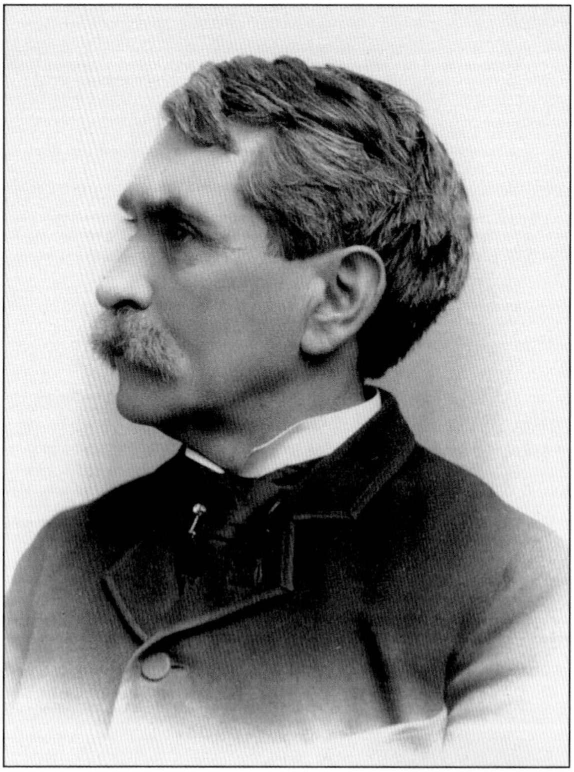

John Cunningham, 1840–1924, graduated from Union Law School in 1860. Cunningham served for three years with the 118th Regiment of the Union army during the Civil War, enlisting when he was 22 years old. He rapidly advanced through the ranks, and when he made brevet lieutenant colonel, he earned the right to be called Colonel Cunningham. From 1892 to 1924, he served as president of the Glens Falls Insurance Company. Under his leadership, the company's assets grew greatly. In addition, he was the collector of internal revenue for Clinton, Essex, and Warren Counties. In 1873, Colonel Cunningham married Elizabeth Fowler, and they made their home on Berry Street in Glens Falls (shown). At age 80, he self-published a memoir entitled *Three Years with the Adirondack Regiment* for private circulation. He was well known and respected by the community.

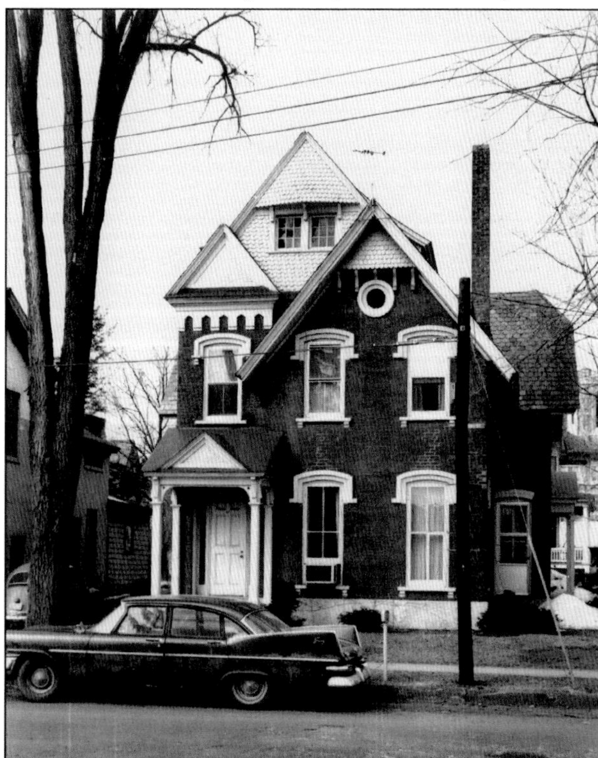

George Finch, 1856–1906, was the son of Jeremiah Finch. He attended the Glens Falls Academy and Riverside Military Academy in Poughkeepsie. Together with William Rice, he founded the *Glens Falls Morning Post* newspaper. He was identified largely with Adirondack interests. He served as president of Imperial Wallpaper as well as Finch Pruyn and Company. He was also vice president of the National Bank of Glens Falls.

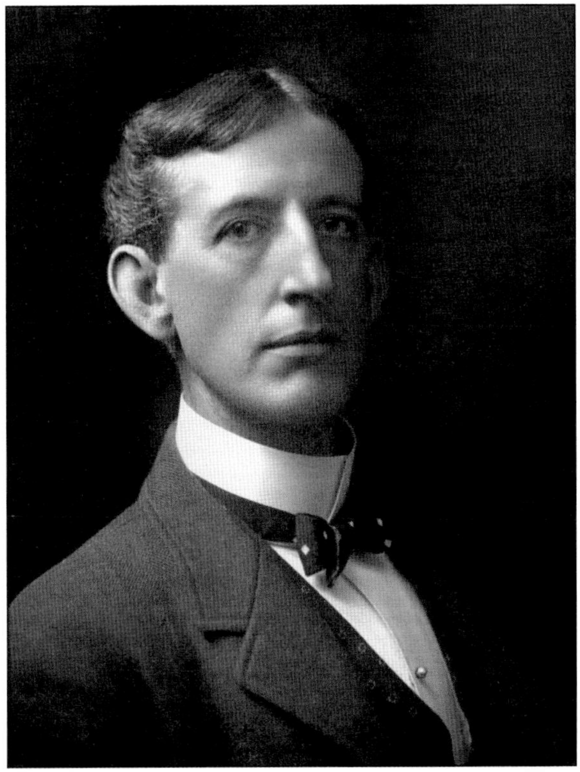

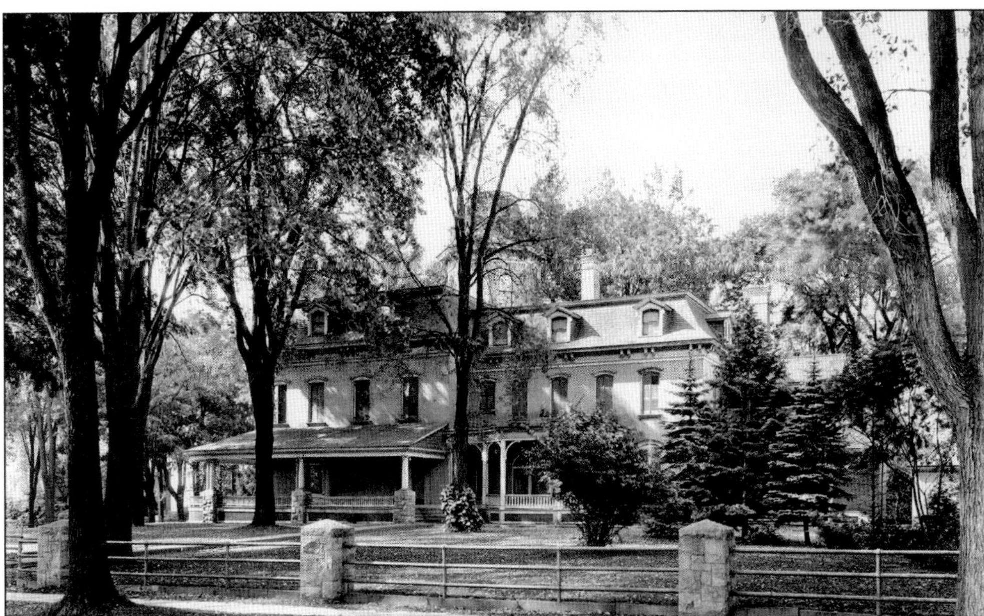

George Finch married Harriet Smith of Northville in 1894. They owned a stately home at the corner of Warren and Prospect Streets in Glens Falls. Noted for its stone and iron-rail fencing and wraparound porches, it had well-manicured gardens, huge barns, and a carriage house to accommodate the horses needed for transportation at the time. He died at the age of 50 during an emergency appendectomy.

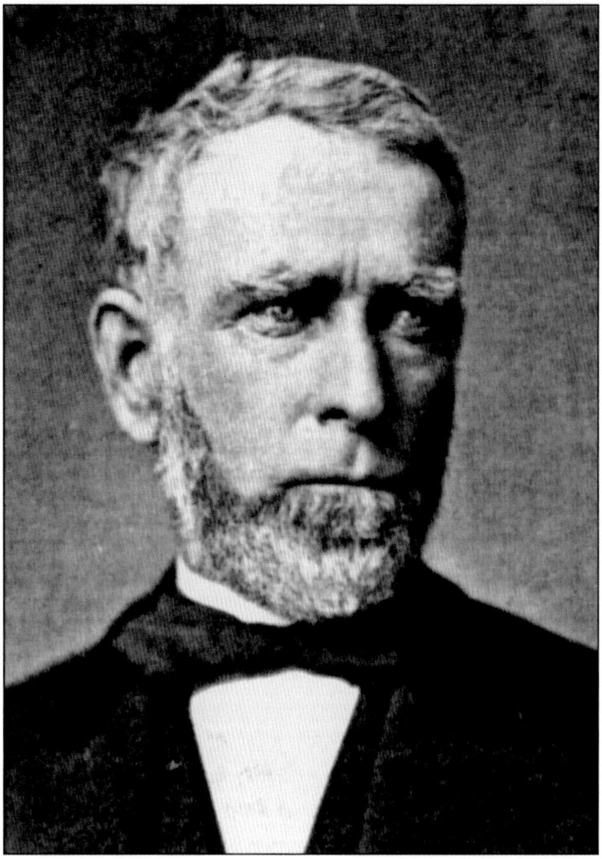

John Keenan, 1809–1885, arrived from Ireland in 1831 and settled in Queensbury in 1847. He manufactured lime in Smith's Basin and used the Champlain Canal to transport limestone to markets out of the area. He partnered with several men, including Halsey Wing in 1851, to form other companies. The limestone industry flourished because of the pure form of limestone, a huge supply of wood providing abundant fuel, and the Feeder Canal for cheap transportation. Keenan served as a village trustee and four terms as president. He was largely responsible for the railroad coming into the area and forming a community water system. Keenan's interest in Jointa Lime was bought out for a considerable amount of money. However, he held a patent for a specific limekiln, and all companies using his brand of kiln paid him royalties.

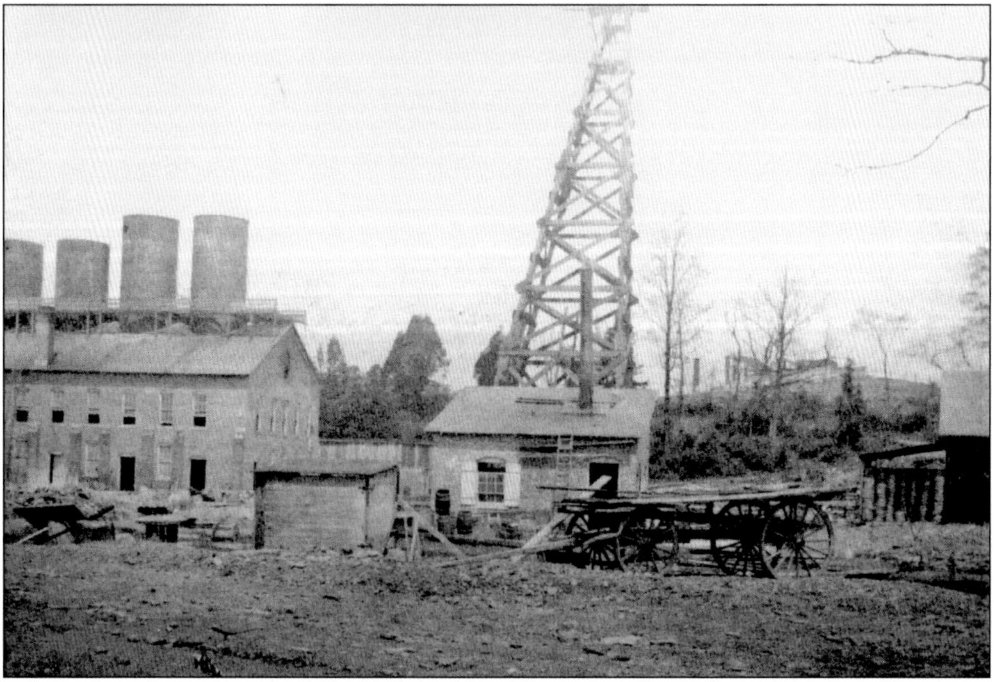

Samuel Kendrick, 1845–1917, was born in Wolcott, Vermont, and was self-educated but did attend one term of college. He called 8 Berry Street his home for a number of years. Active in politics, Kendrick served as treasurer and three times as Democratic president of the village. He was also the second mayor of the city of Glens Falls from 1910 to 1912. He was part owner of the Kendrick and Brown Lumber Company located between Cooper and Warren Streets, incorporated in 1895. The employees of the company are shown at the plant. In addition to finished lumber, his company supplied other building supplies, including glass, hardware, plaster, and paints. He employed carpenters who custom-built cabinets, window sashes, and blinds. The business offices were located on Lawrence Street from 1911 until 1944. He also served as vice president of the Glens Falls Savings and Loan.

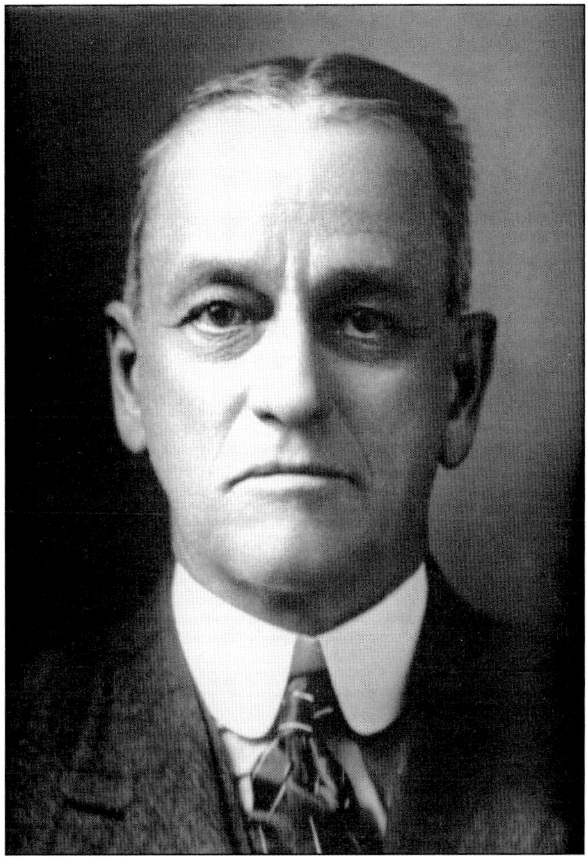

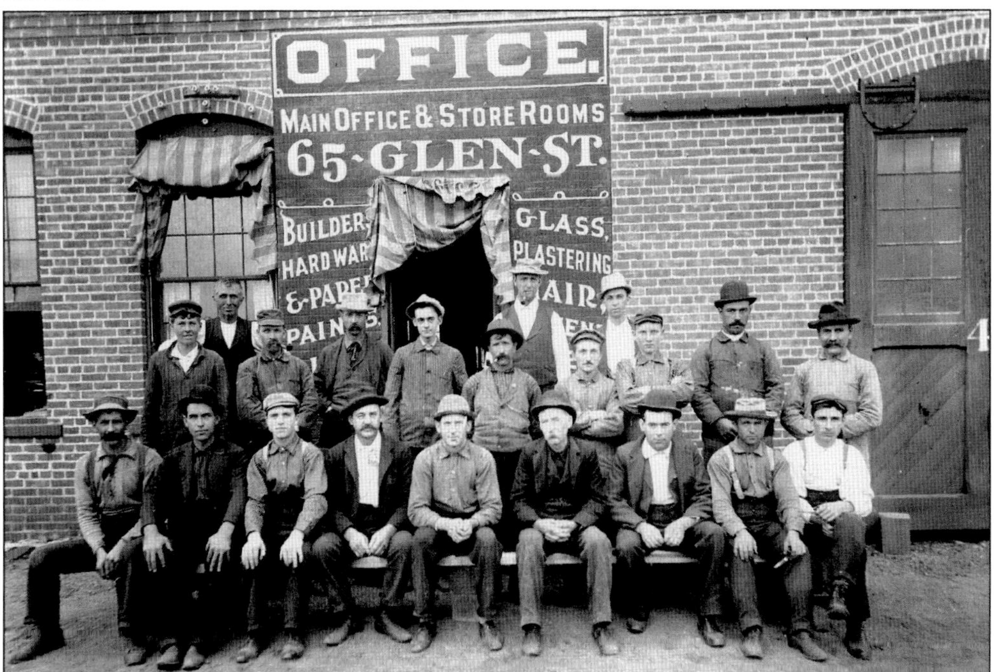

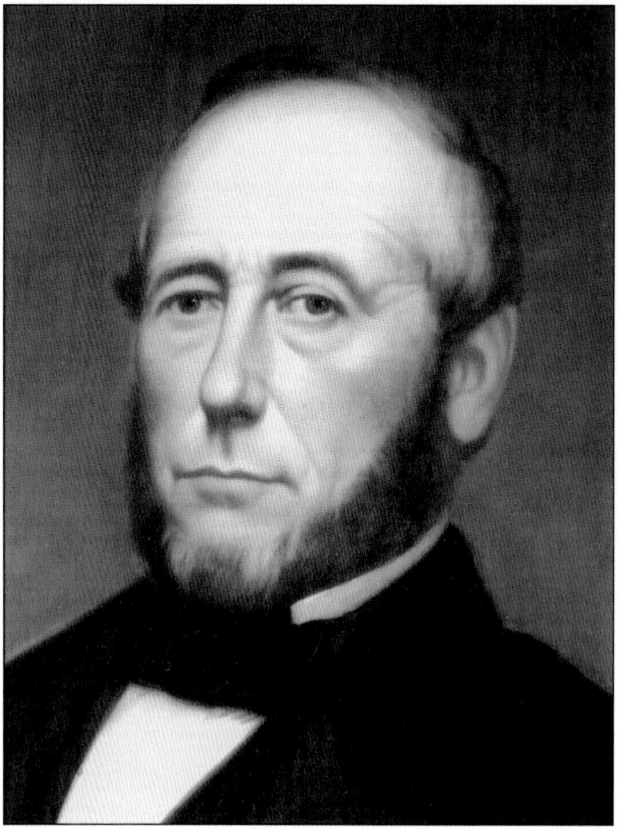

James Morgan, 1814–1873, was born in Bolton as the third child of nine. During his early years he worked on a farm for $8 a month. He was known for his hard work and perseverance. Morgan was apprenticed at the Cheney Mill, and as he saved money, he kept adding to his properties. He owned the largest lumber business on the Hudson River and by 1841 was considered extremely wealthy. It was reported that his company had two years worth of logs on hand at all times (shown). Morgan was considered kindhearted, but he had enemies. After a lawsuit with prominent families in the area, the courts established that he indeed owned parts of the river, but he was forced to allow logs to go downstream to the various mills. Soon after, he died mysteriously in a barn fire.

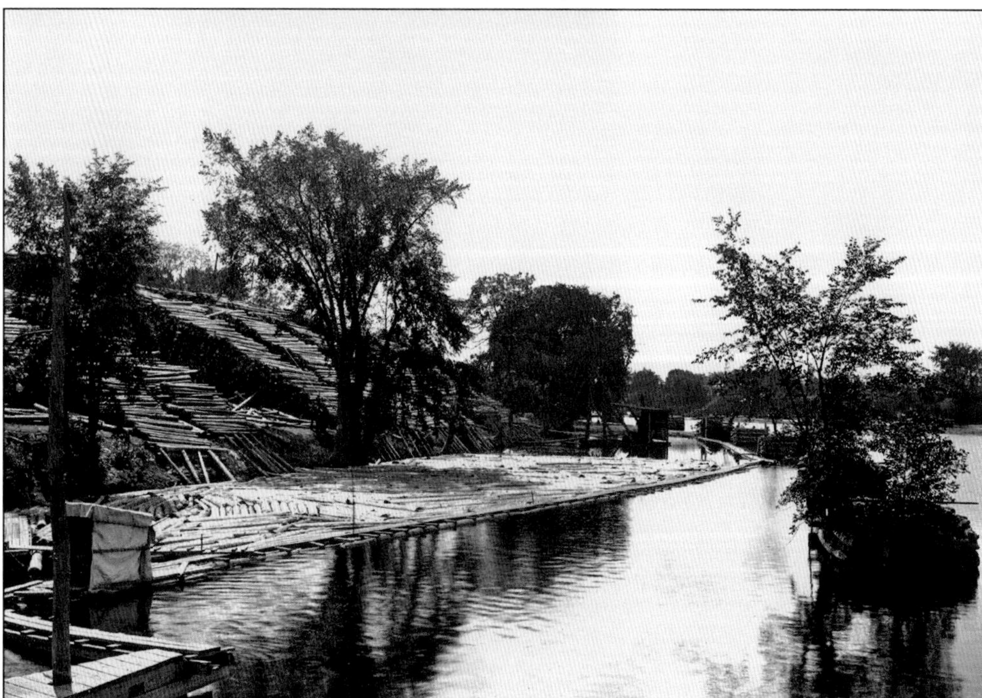

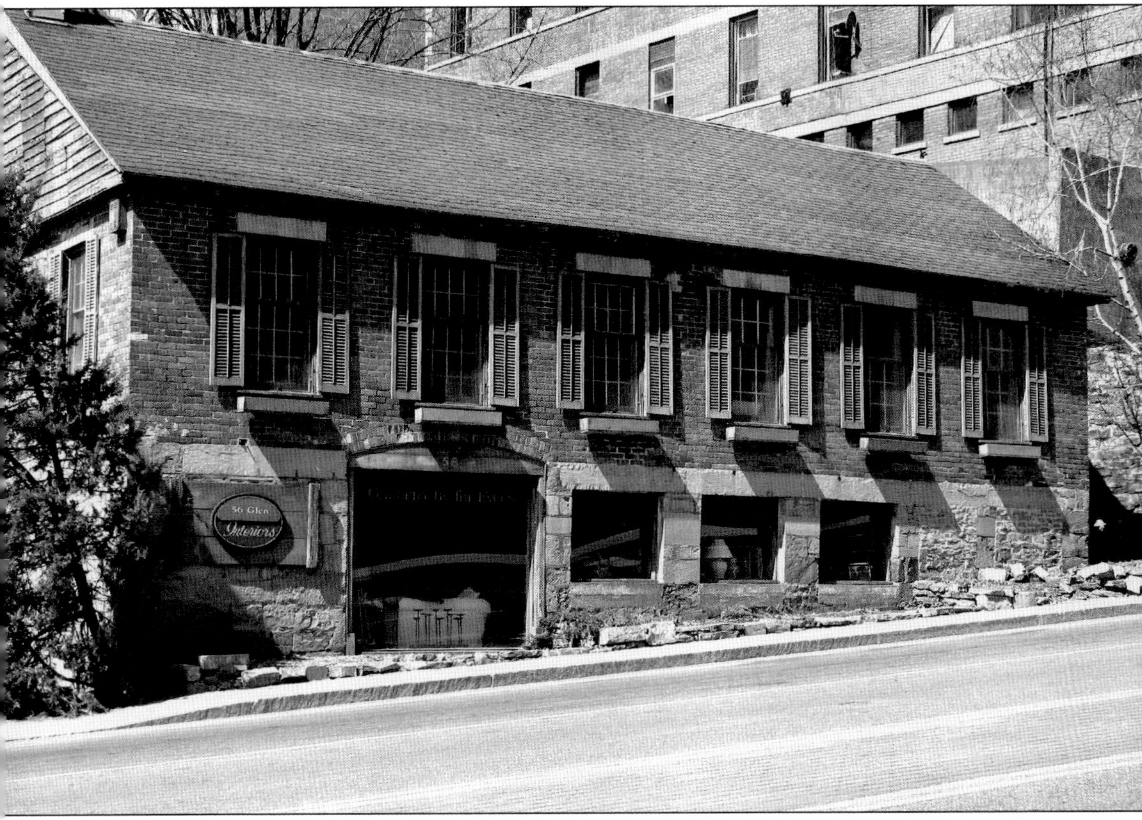

Calvin Robbins, 1801–1864, was a blacksmith when he came from Connecticut to Glens Falls. By 1835, he had his own shop, and the building still exists as one of the oldest buildings in the city. As a blacksmith, Robbins would have made horseshoes, hinges, barrel bands, and wheel rims. He was an assessor, a member of the first village board of trustees, and a pound keeper, a person who kept an enclosure for stray animals found in the village. This would have included cows, sheep, pigs, and poultry. Robbins and his wife Polly had seven children while living over the blacksmith shop on the Glen Street Hill (shown). Insects, the smell of horses, heat, soot, and danger of fire were constant threats to their health. In addition, his kind of work often left a smithy with impaired hearing. His daughter Marion married Darwin Sherman, son of millionaire Augustus Sherman.

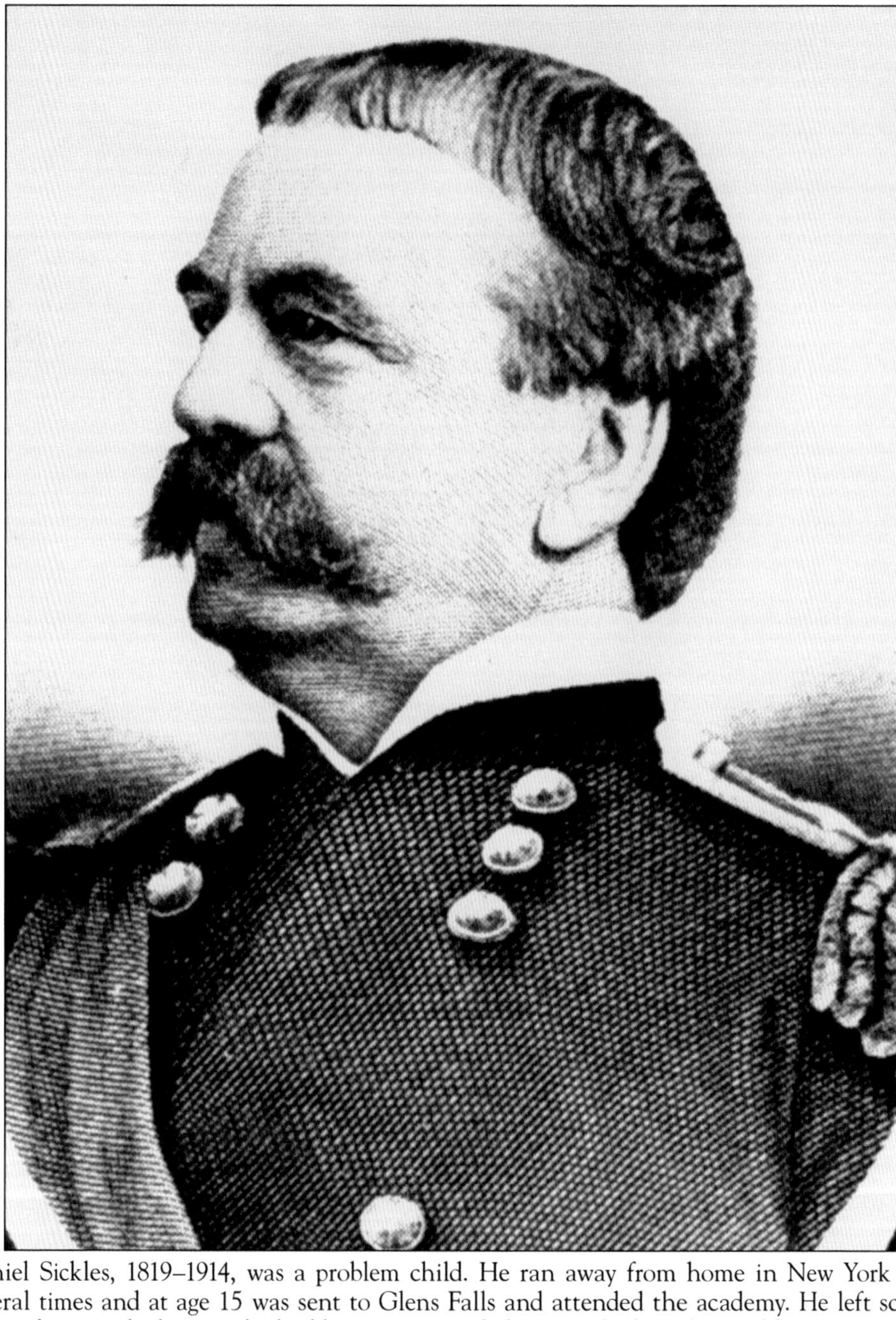

Daniel Sickles, 1819–1914, was a problem child. He ran away from home in New York City several times and at age 15 was sent to Glens Falls and attended the academy. He left school after a few months because he had been reprimanded. He worked on the weekly newspaper the *Glens Falls Messenger* and learned the necessary skills to be successful. Sickles saw fighting at Gettysburg during the Civil War and was partially responsible for winning the battle by not following orders. He lost a leg during the war and carried it around in a small coffin for all to see. It was later given to the Army Medical Museum. Sickles was acquitted of murder charges after shooting the son of Francis Scott Key. He maintained a friendship with Mary Todd Lincoln and allegedly had an affair with the queen of Spain. Although his time in Glens Falls was short, he certainly was a colorful character and can be considered a preposterous citizen.

Two

The Center

The center of town is usually referred to as the business district. However, in its early development, Glens Falls's center of town also contained stately homes along with the many individually-owned businesses. Small mercantile stores sold household items ranging from oil lamps to chamber pots. The business district also included places to buy hay and animal feed. Of course, at a time when water was considered suspicious, bars and taprooms abounded. As the town grew, so did technological improvements. Paved streets, village water, a sewage system, and a trolley line all added to the quality of life. Belowground cisterns provided a supply of water for the first volunteer fire departments. As the wealth of the community grew, so did service industries such as banking and insurance. The banks had clocks on the sidewalk in front of them to indicate their presence. This chapter will concentrate on the families who lived in the main part of town as well as some of the businesses that prevailed, including the Crandall Block, Crandall City Park, the downtown business district, and Monument Square. The people included are Fred and Juliet Chapman, Marion Chitty, Addison Colvin, Daniel Cowles, Henry Crandall, Cutler DeLong, Zopher DeLong, Orange Ferris, Jeremiah Finch, Helen Foulds, A. W. Holden, Louis Juvet, Jerome Lapham, George Little, Russell Little, William McEchron, Ernest Miller, Patrick Moynehan, and Ephraim Potter.

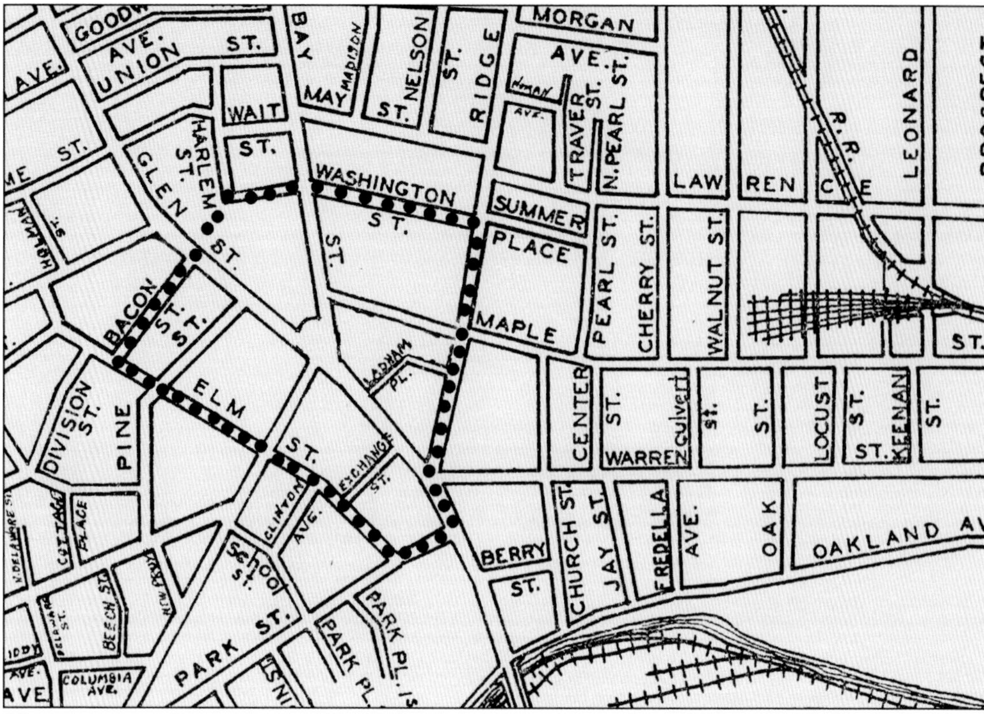

This chapter will concern itself with the area beginning with Park Street in the south, up Glen Street going up Ridge Street in the north as far as Washington Street, west to Glen Street, south to Bacon Street, and west to Elm Street and turning south, ending back at Park Street. This circle encompasses almost the entire present-day main business district.

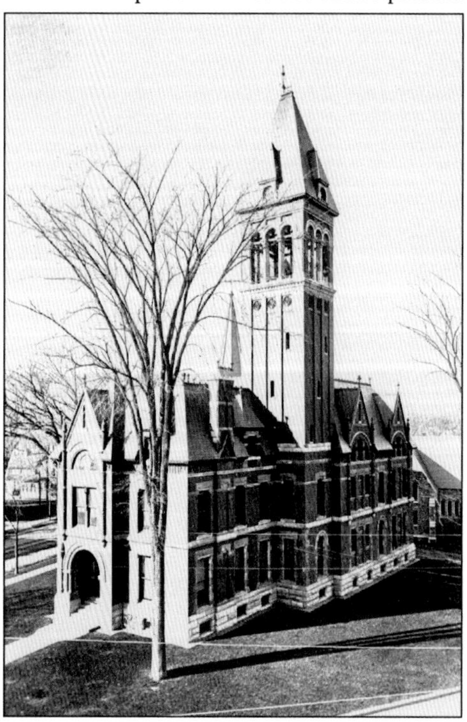

In 1849, Russell Little was involved in an insurance agency. At the time, fire departments had their own insurance companies. Little foresaw the value of uniting the various groups into one organization. By February 1850, a new company was founded. Its prompt payments following the San Francisco earthquake and Great Chicago Fire made it famous. Over the years, many prominent citizens headed the Glens Falls Insurance Company (shown).

On May 30, 1872, a dedication for a monument honoring Civil War heroes from the area who died in the service to their country took place. The 100-ton, 42-foot-tall obelisk was built on property purchased from the Sisson family, one of the first families to settle in the area. It featured a wrought iron fence around a circular plot. A five-foot eagle sits on top a draped American flag.

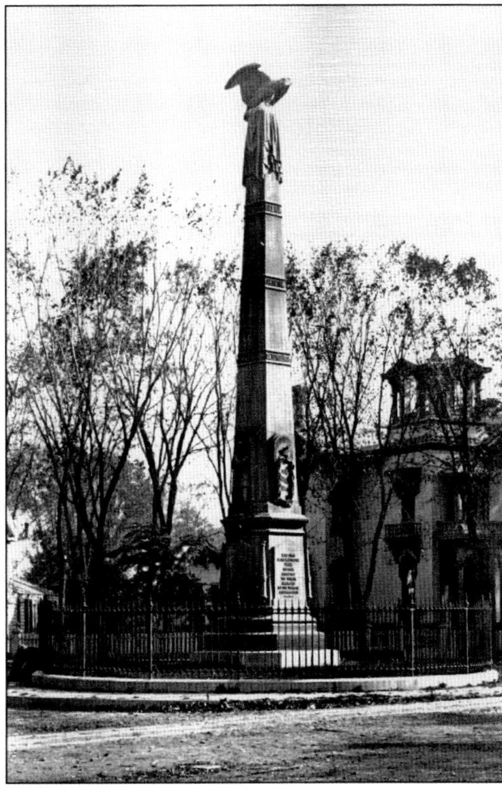

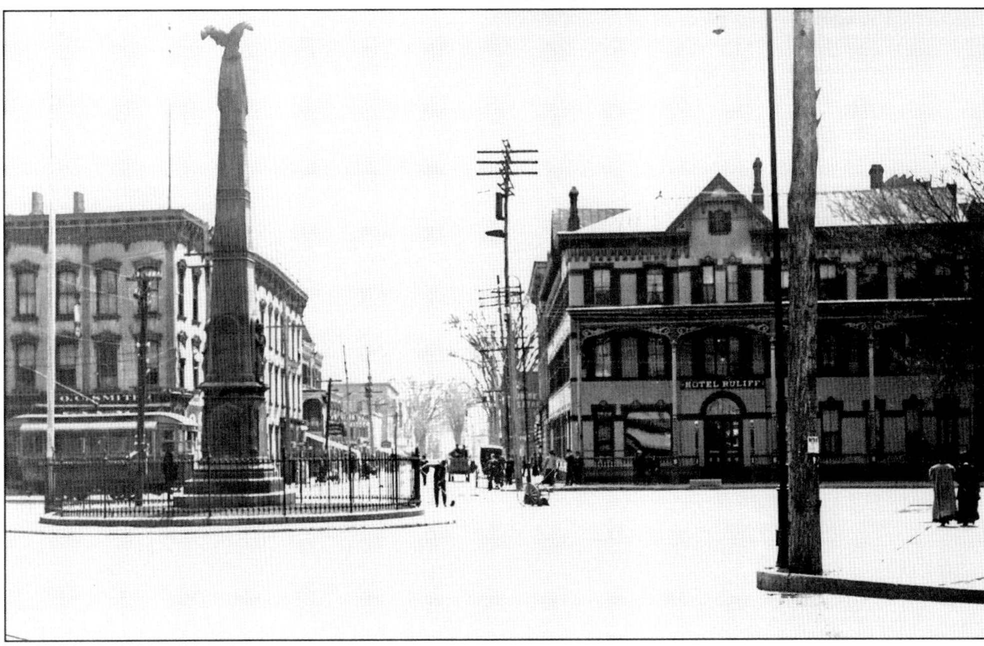

The monument faces west toward South Street. The Hotel Ruliff sits opposite it and was home to the many performers and guests attending events at the Empire Theater behind it on South Street. On the other corner is the Crandall Block, home to groceries, various small shops, and shirt and collar factories on the upper floors.

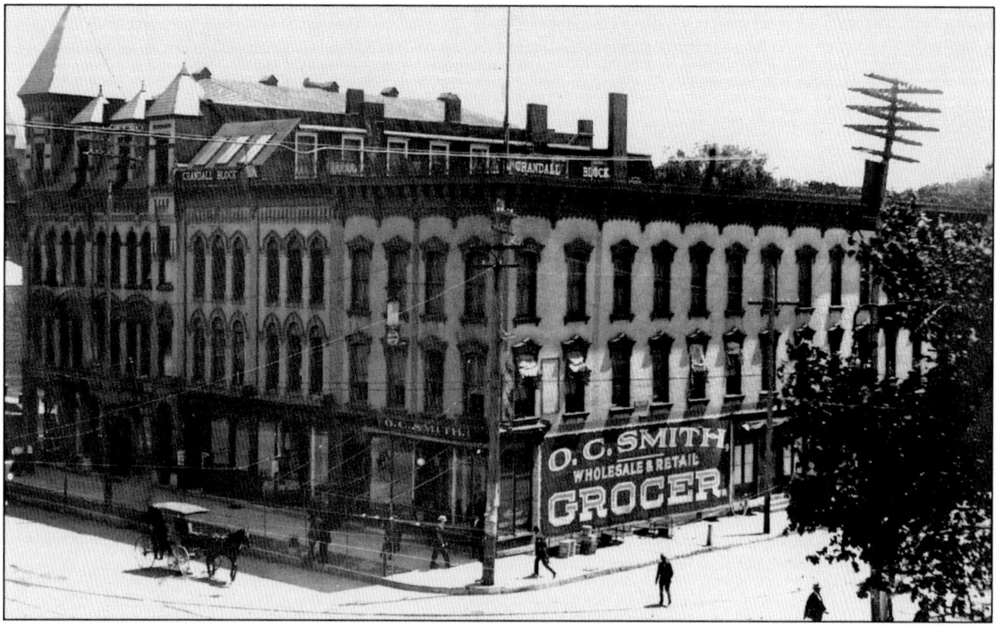

The Crandall Block was built soon after the great fire of 1864 when Glen Street was still unpaved. It was home to O. C. Smith's grocery and Corey's store, while a paper-box factory occupied an upper floor. It was actually four separate buildings with varied forms of architecture. Three of the buildings faced Glen Street while the fourth faced South Street.

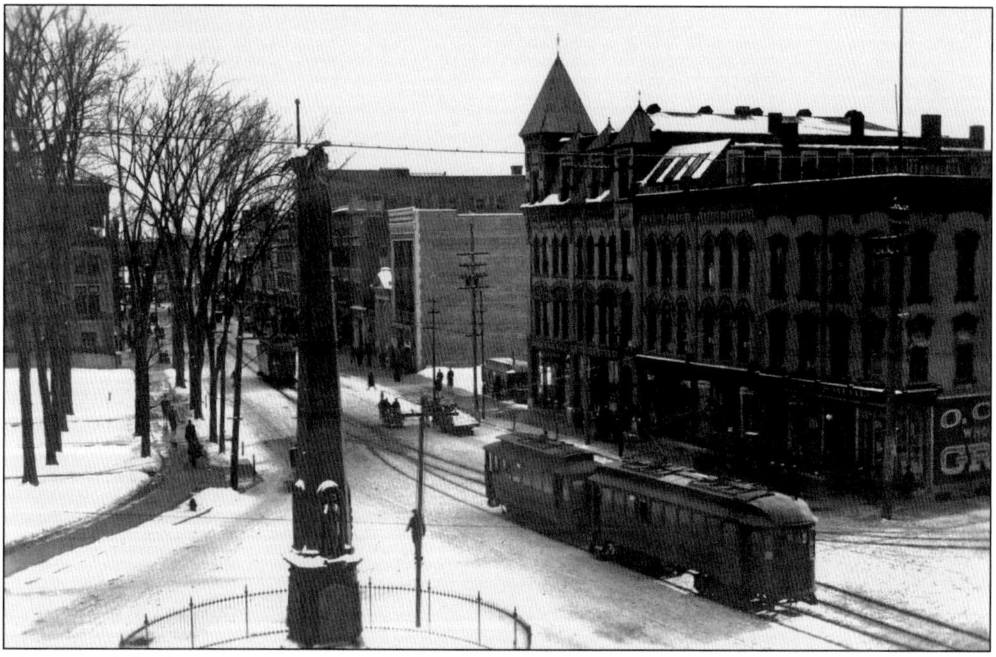

The Crandall Block was located across from City Park and the Civil War monument. The rents obtained from the various businesses in the building went to the Crandall Trust and were used to operate the Crandall Library. In 1963, the building was purchased by the Glens Falls National Bank and was to be demolished. However, a fire broke out in one part of the building and quickly spread, destroying the facility.

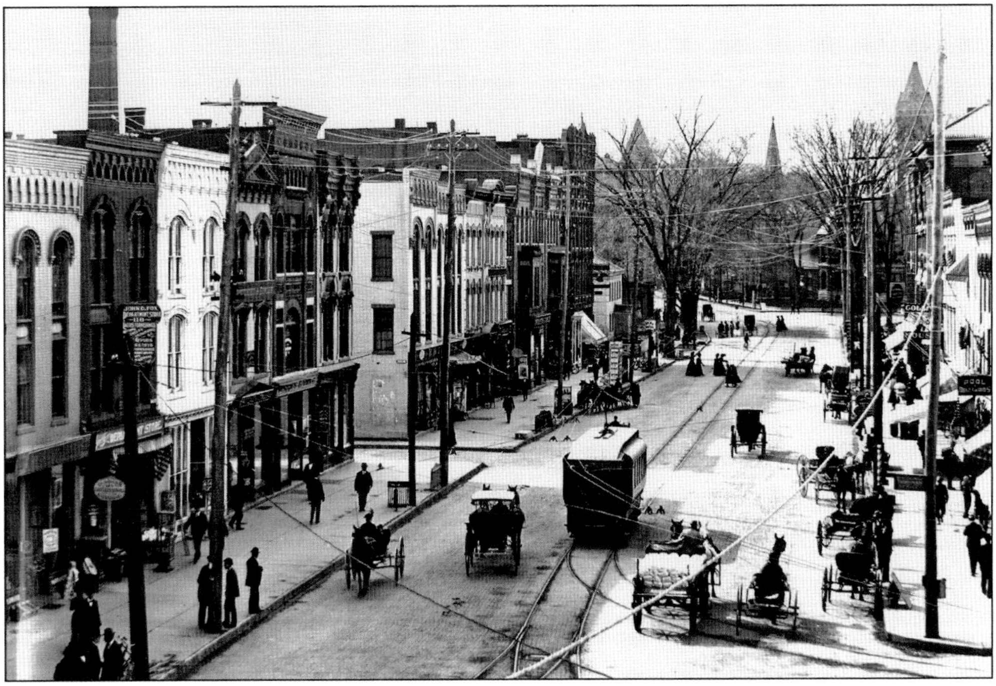

In 1902, Glen Street was a bustling business district featuring mainly small, individually owned shops. Electric trolleys ran on a regular basis, but the main form of personal transportation was horse and wagon. Wires from telephone and electricity zigzagged across the street. Gentlemen wore hats, and ladies wore full-length skirts. The towers from the Crandall Block and Glens Falls Insurance Company are seen in the distance.

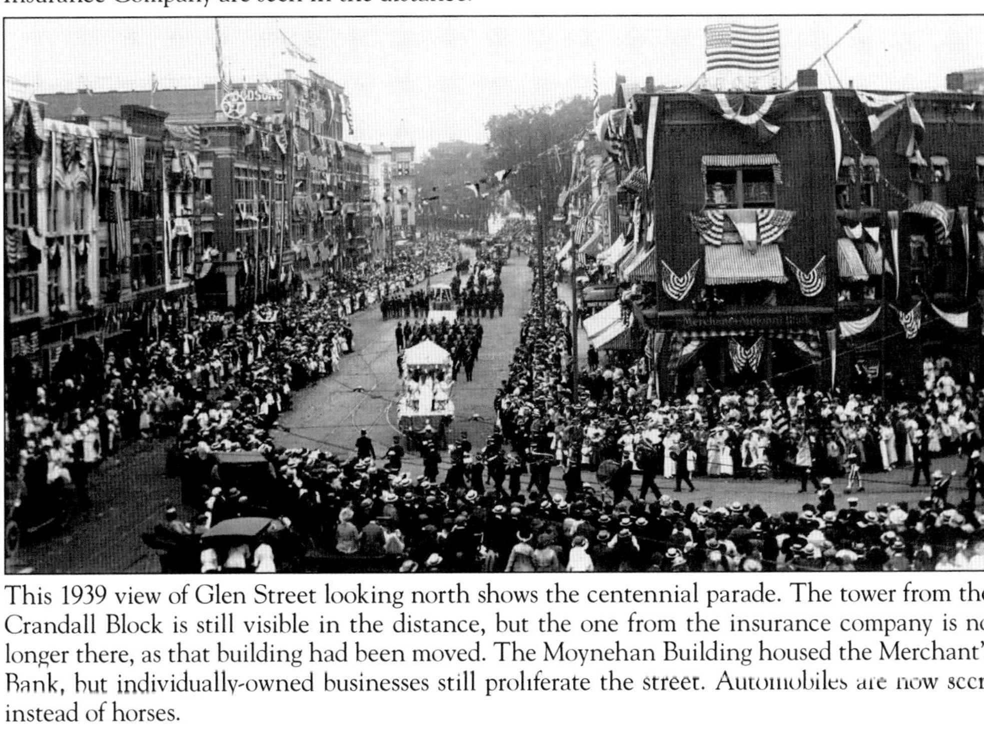

This 1939 view of Glen Street looking north shows the centennial parade. The tower from the Crandall Block is still visible in the distance, but the one from the insurance company is no longer there, as that building had been moved. The Moynehan Building housed the Merchant's Bank, but individually-owned businesses still proliferate the street. Automobiles are now seen instead of horses.

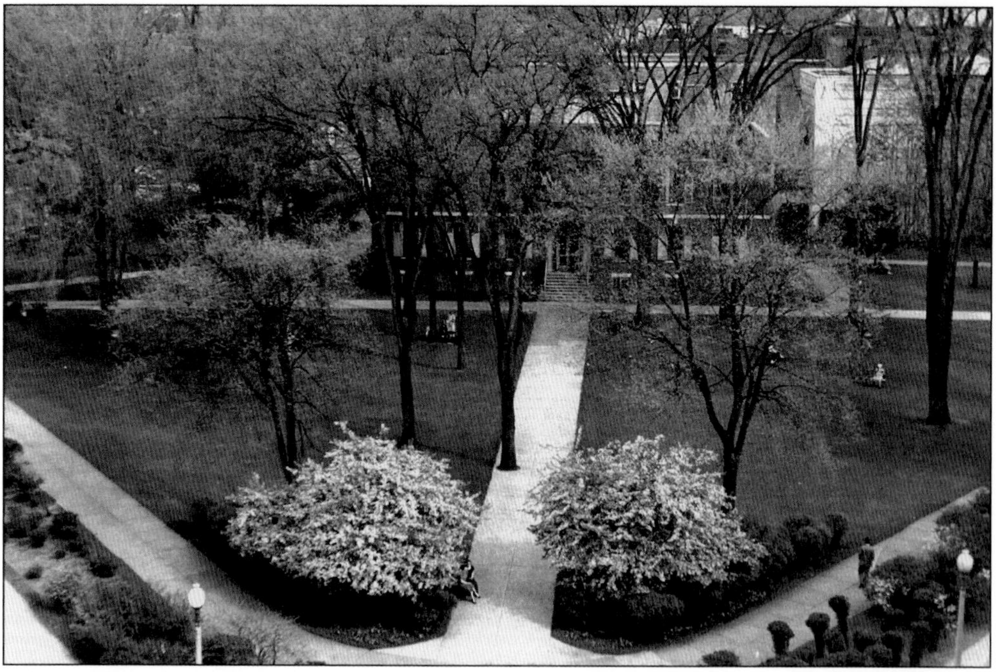

When Henry Crandall set up a trust to maintain the park at the north end of the village, he also included a smaller park in front of the public library. He hoped to call it Crandall Place, but it has evolved into being called City Park. Crandall Library and the City of Glens Falls share its ownership.

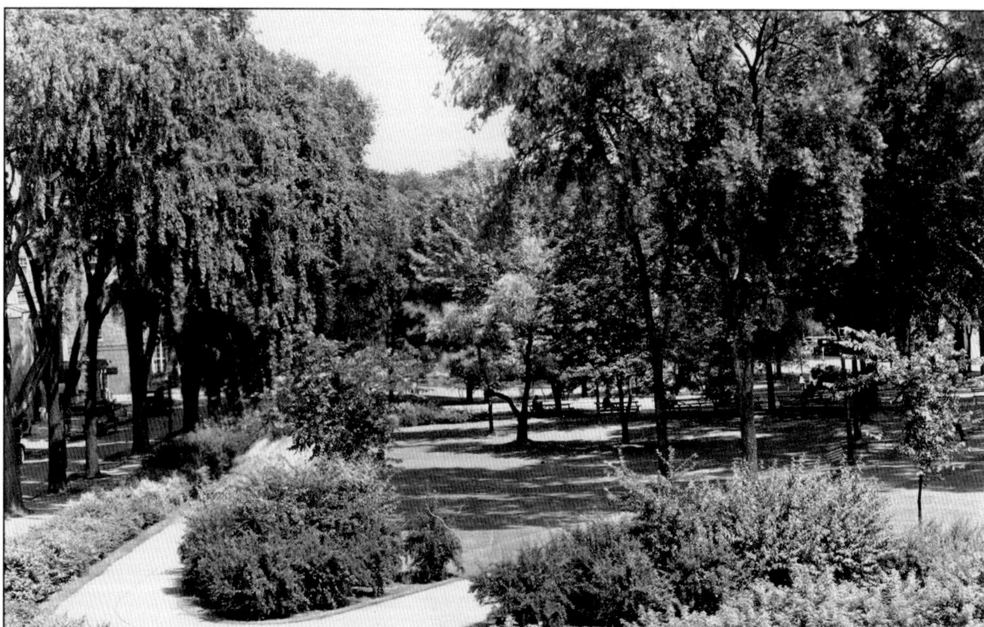

Its stately trees and flowering shrubs make a wonderful park setting in the middle of the commercial part of town. It is home to the annual arts festival, summer concerts, and the Taste of the North Country food extravaganza. Benches provide visitors with a chance to sit and enjoy the shade, eat lunch, and relax in quiet solitude while business goes on as usual all around.

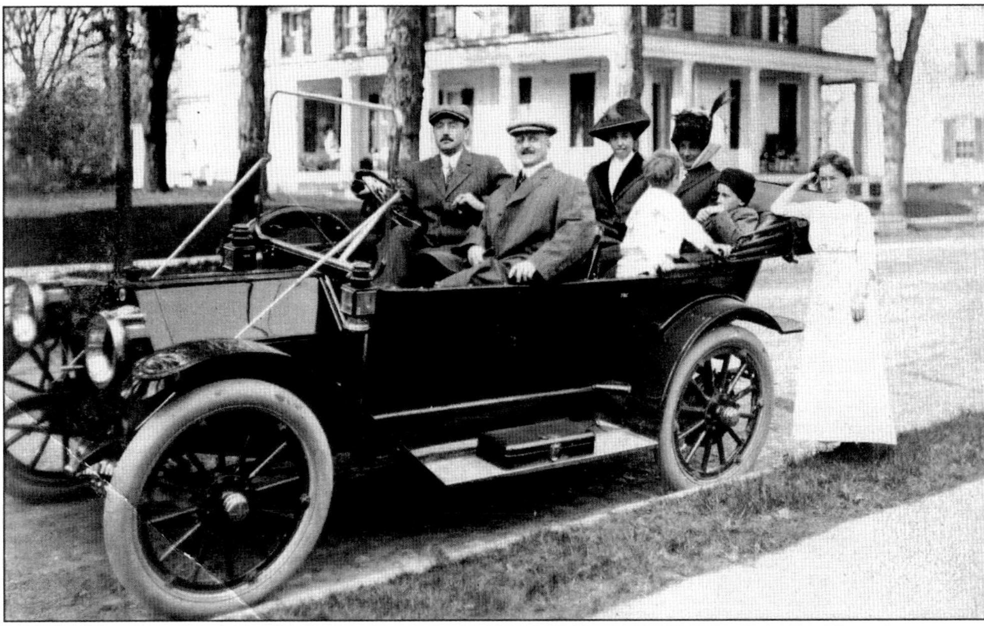

Frederick Chapman, 1875–1957, was born in Glens Falls and attended local schools. He worked 18 years for the post office. In 1901, he started a career with Finch, Pruyn and Company. By 1910, he was treasurer of Jointa Lime, and one year later he opened Braydon and Chapman Music Store. Chapman was an avid sportsman, being interested in bird hunting, golf, and skeet shooting. In 1882, he married Mabel DeLong, the last DeLong to live in the family home on Glen Street. Chapman is shown above driving the family car in the early 1900s. After Mabel died, he married Juliet Goodman in 1942 (right). It was after his death that Juliet gave the DeLong family home to the historical society to be used as a museum. It is now the home of the Chapman Historical Museum.

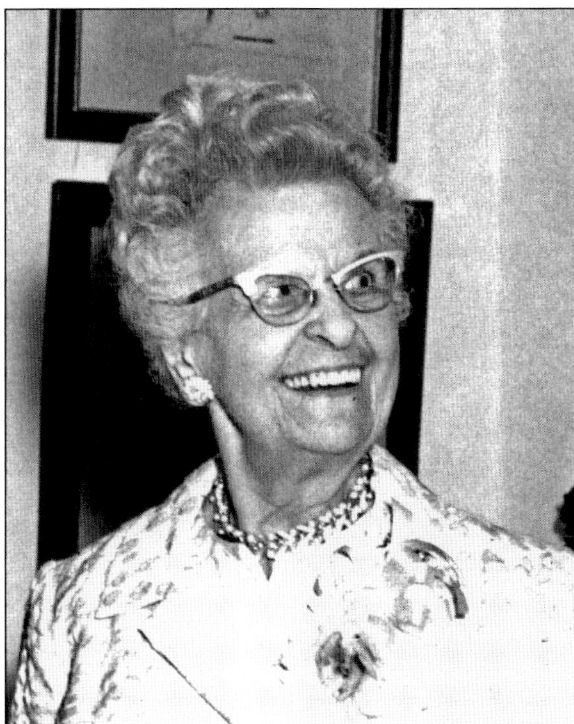

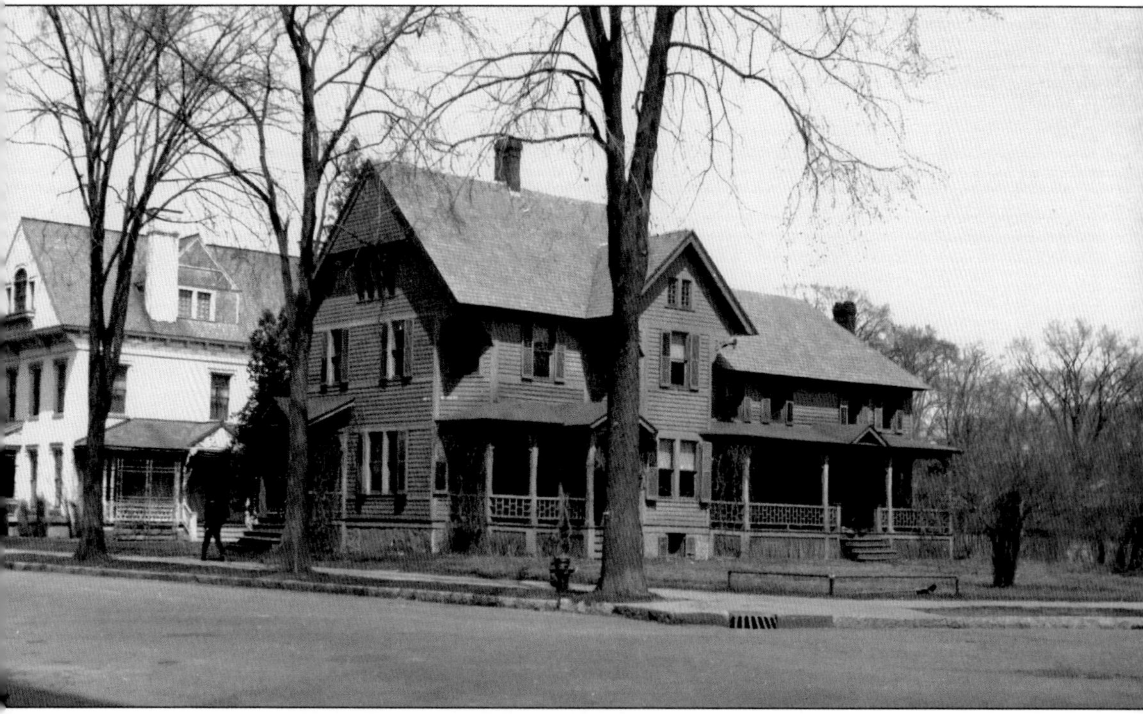

Marion Chitty, 1861–1948, was the fifth child of seven born to the Col. Fred Chitty family. A 1924 photograph shows where the family lived at the corner of Maple and Bay Streets (shown) where the present-day Rogers Building exists. The family eventually moved to the Champlin home on upper Glen Street. Although she was a music teacher, she is remembered as a local historian, basing her research on information from family records, deeds, letters, and newspapers saved by her mother's family. In 1936, she was the first secretary of the Old Glens Falls Club. Later she became program chairperson. The club's purpose was local history. Marion was one of the people instrumental in forming the Glens Falls Historical Society, the forerunner of the Historical Society of Glens Falls and Queensbury at the Chapman Historical Museum. As a member of this organization, she researched Queensbury, Quaker settlements, historic houses, and families in the area. She actively sought a centennial celebration in 1939 for the 100 years as a village.

Addison Colvin, 1858–1939, attended the Glens Falls Academy until he left to work in a store at age 14. He saved money to purchase the equipment to begin a small printing business. By age 21, he began the first daily newspaper, the *Glens Falls Times,* considered the official Republican paper. He was the youngest editor of a daily paper in the United States.

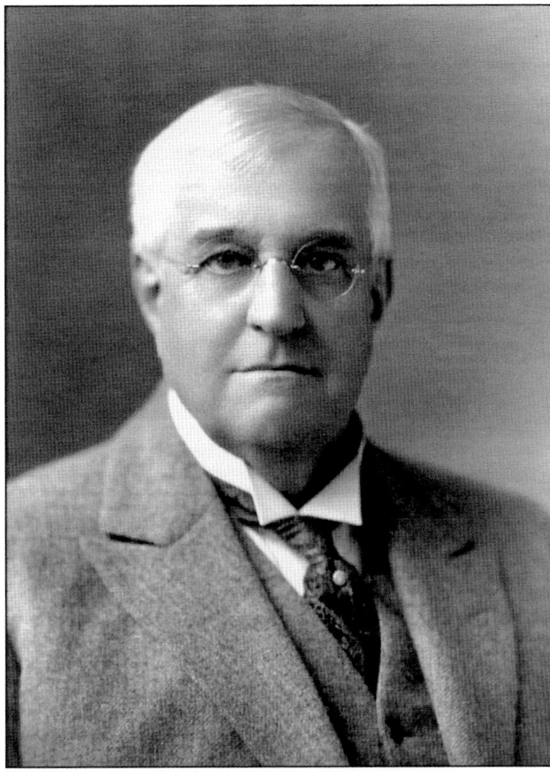

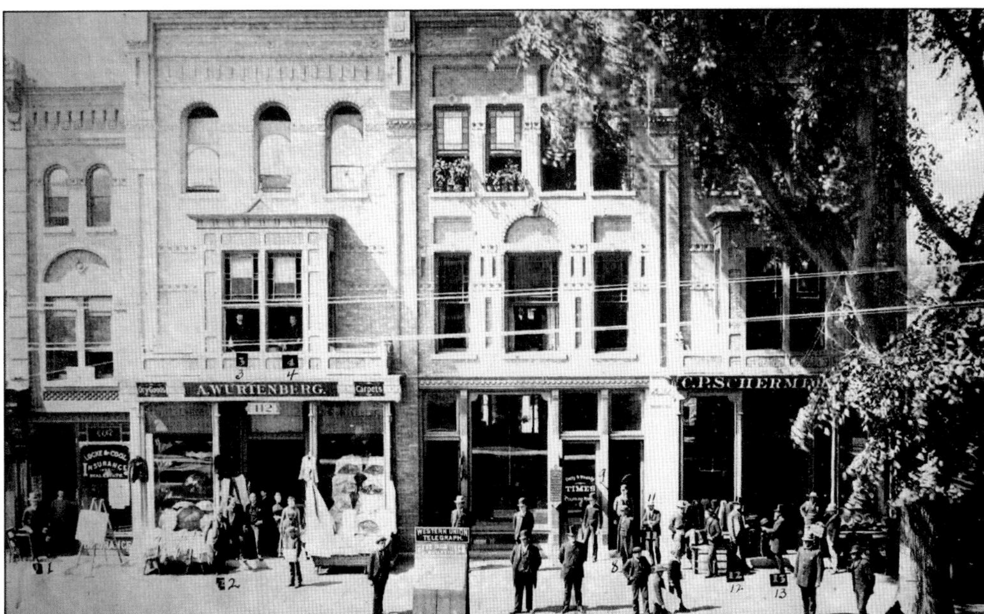

Starting in 1879, Colvin was an officer or director of many businesses in the village. He was involved with the first electric company, promoted the idea of telegraph and telephones, and was president of the Glens Falls Gas and Light Company. The first telephone company was in the Colvin Building, shown here. After the 1902 fire, the building was rebuilt and considered a skyscraper with an elevator that still operates today.

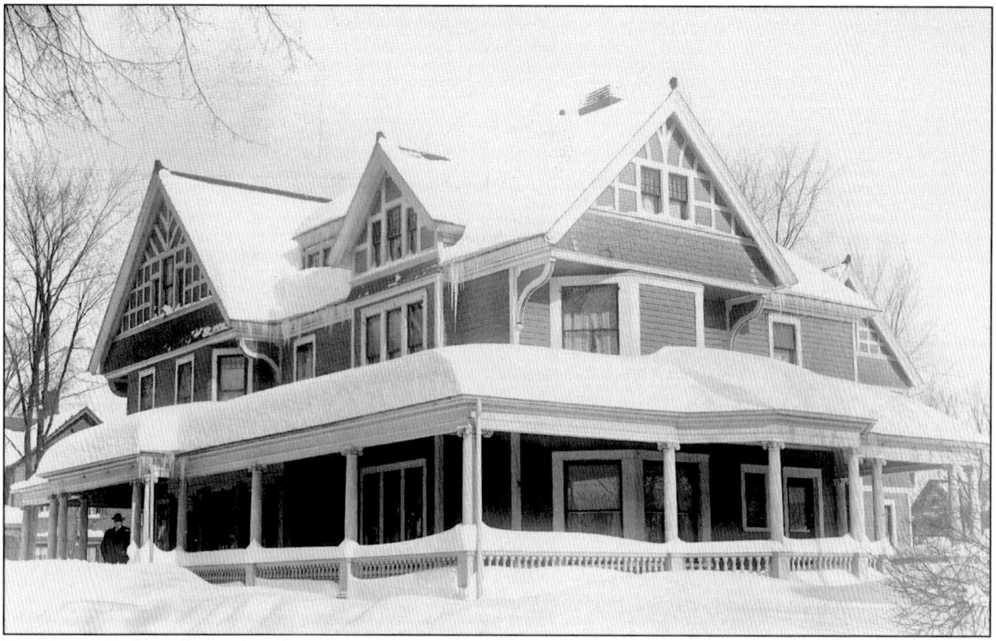

In 1886, Colvin brought the street railway to Glens Falls. It consisted of six cars, drawn by horses, each holding seven passengers and heated with a wood stove in the winter. In 1890, he began the first electric trolley system. He had a button in his home (shown) that could summon the trolley, and he could step out and ride to work.

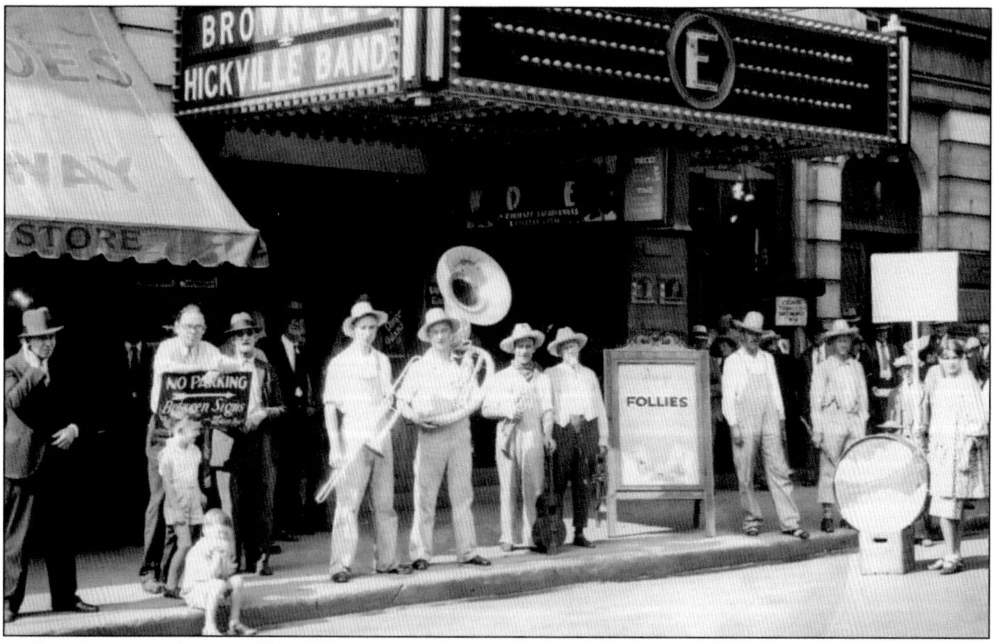

Colvin promoted the building of the neoclassic-style Empire Theater and had a personal box therein. It was the premier theater in the area for many years, and he was the first president and general manager until 1913. It was home to vaudeville, theatrical productions, and musical performances. George Cohan and Al Jolson, along with John, Ethel, and Lionel Barrymore, performed there. This photograph is from 1931.

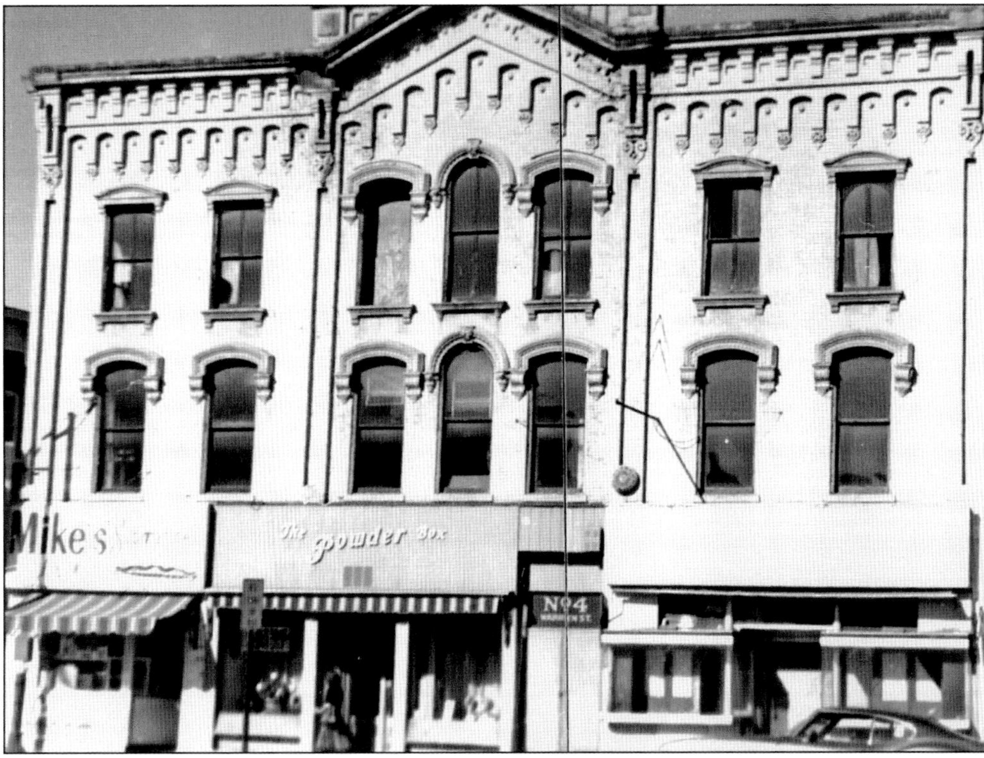

Daniel Howard Cowles, 1810–1891, was born in Hadley, but little is known of his early years. He came to Glens Falls with his employer Henry Rogers of Luzerne. In 1847, he was secretary treasurer of the Plank Road Company and became president of the village in 1859. He was identified with every prominent enterprise in Glens Falls from early banking institutions, the gas company, and the insurance company. Cowles was a lifelong Baptist but participated in many religious movements. Cowles was never married but was closely associated with the Rogers family. His business building at the corner of Warren and Ridge Streets exists today (shown above in the 1960s). His cemetery marker in the Glens Falls Cemetery is a stone tree stump on the Roger's plot (right).

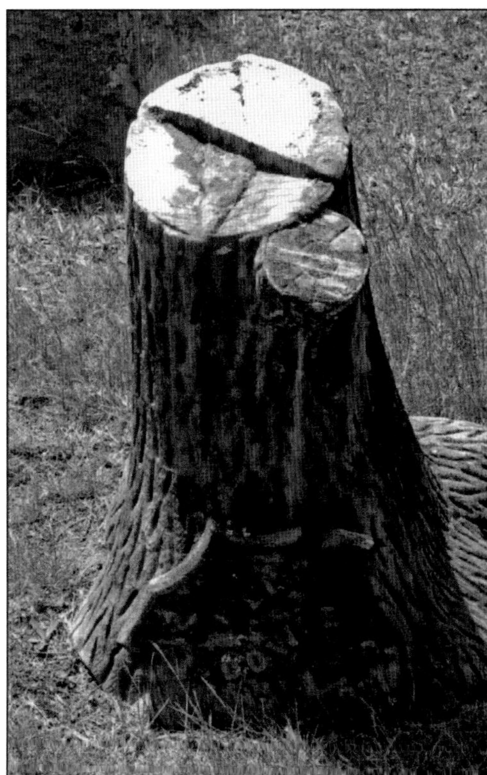

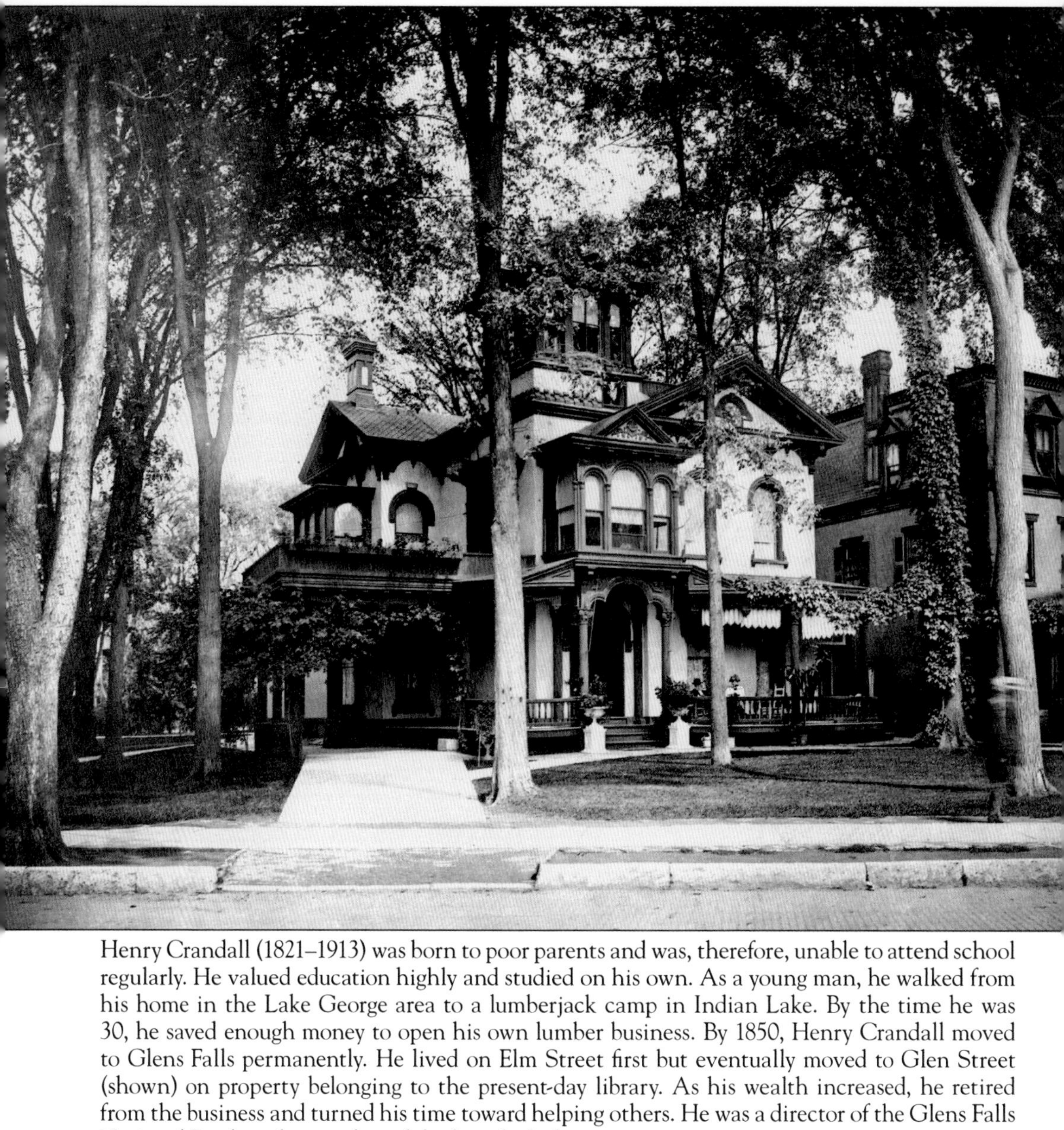

Henry Crandall (1821–1913) was born to poor parents and was, therefore, unable to attend school regularly. He valued education highly and studied on his own. As a young man, he walked from his home in the Lake George area to a lumberjack camp in Indian Lake. By the time he was 30, he saved enough money to open his own lumber business. By 1850, Henry Crandall moved to Glens Falls permanently. He lived on Elm Street first but eventually moved to Glen Street (shown) on property belonging to the present-day library. As his wealth increased, he retired from the business and turned his time toward helping others. He was a director of the Glens Falls National Bank and a member of the board of education.

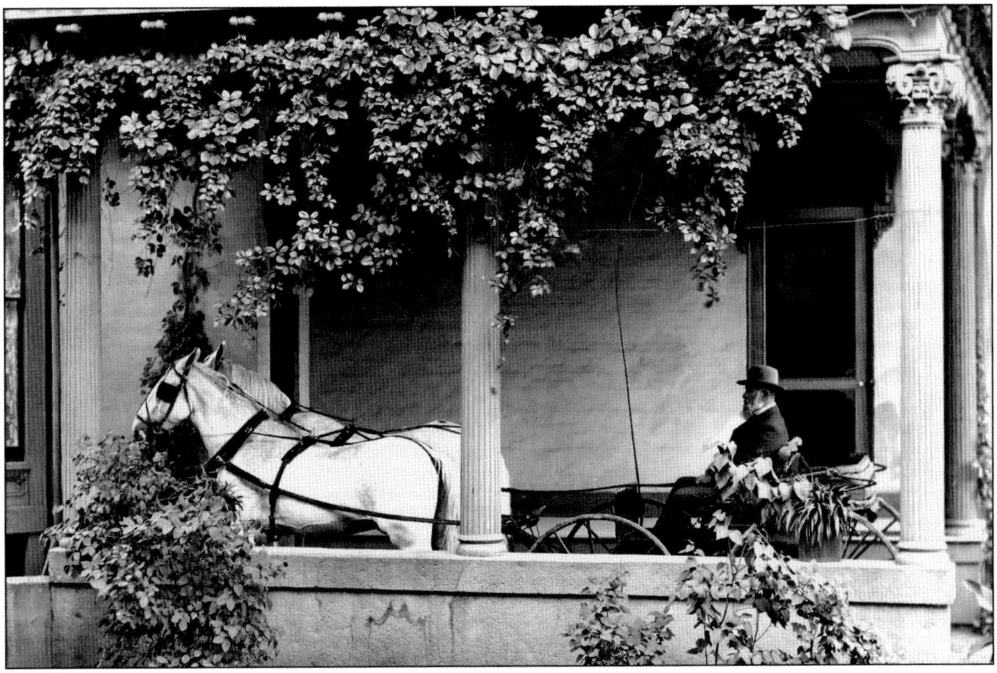

Henry Crandall was often seen daily traveling from his home to the park named in his honor to oversee work being done there. A matched pair of gray-white horses led his wagon, and in their later years, his wife Betsy would accompany him on these sojourns. Local legend has it that the team of horses is buried in the park near the Crandall obelisk.

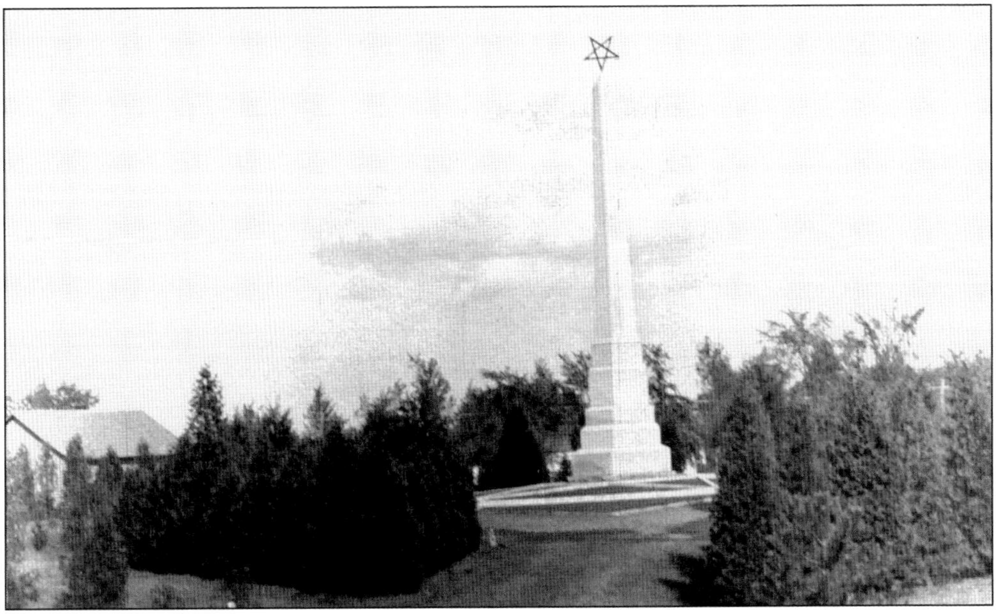

Upon his death, Crandall left his home to become a public library, with the surrounding property turning into a park. Another larger park had been developed on Upper Glen Street. The centerpiece of the setting was the large obelisk that served as a mausoleum for Crandall and his wife. The ponds and surrounding landscape provided a peaceful area for local citizens to relax and enjoy the outdoors.

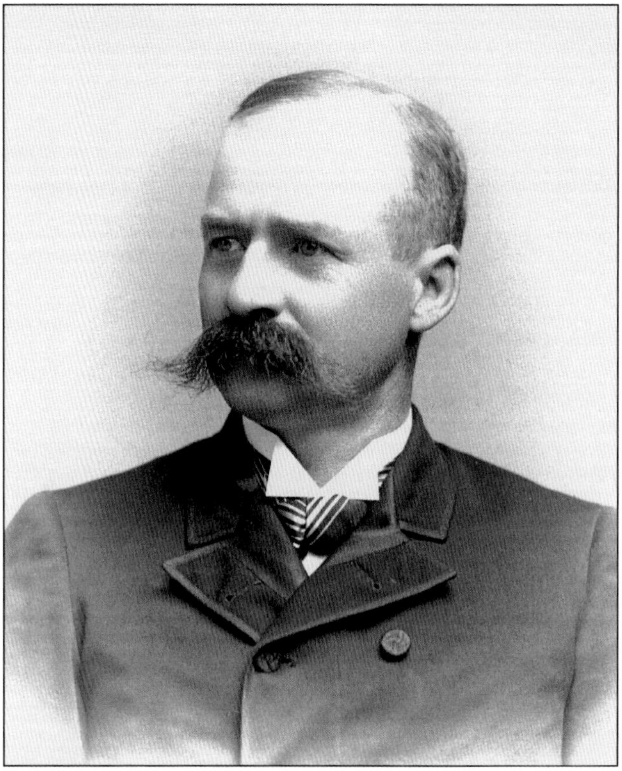

Cutler DeLong, 1846–1928, was born in the town of Day, Saratoga County, 13 years before the family moved to Glens Falls. Descended from French Huguenots, his mother's ancestors fought in the Revolution. He clerked in the First National Bank for eight years, and for five years he worked for the Peck-DeLong Grocers, but he is best known for his 30 years of service as treasurer to the Glens Falls Insurance Company.

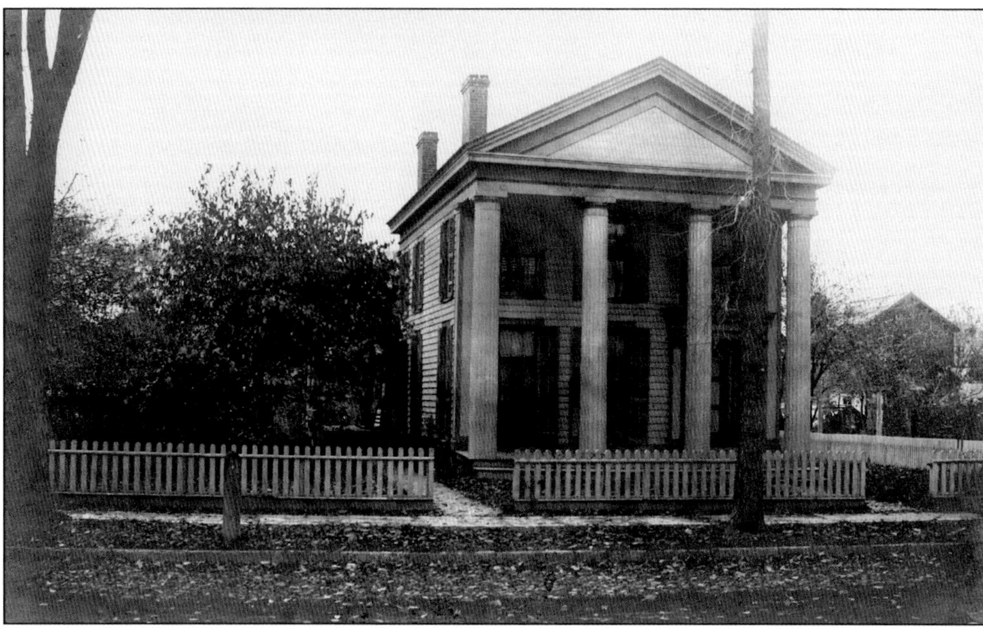

DeLong's home was at 30 Bay Street (shown), where he and his wife Mary Clendon, known as Minnie, raised their four daughters. His daughter Annie was the first librarian in the Crandall Library. When his father died, "Cut," as he was called, took over a family summer home on Lake George. When he died, in his will, he established DeLong Park there, now known as DeLong Usher Park.

Zopher Isaac DeLong, 1815–1901, farmed and ran a general store in the town of Day, Saratoga County, before moving his family to Glens Falls in 1859. Z. I., as he preferred to be called, became partners in a hardware store with Herman Peck. He later served as village board president, town supervisor, and member of the board of health and was active in Queensbury politics.

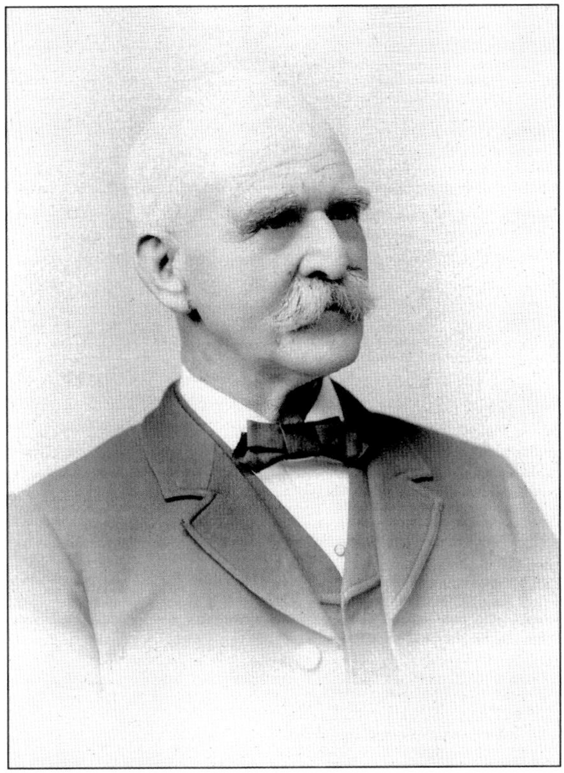

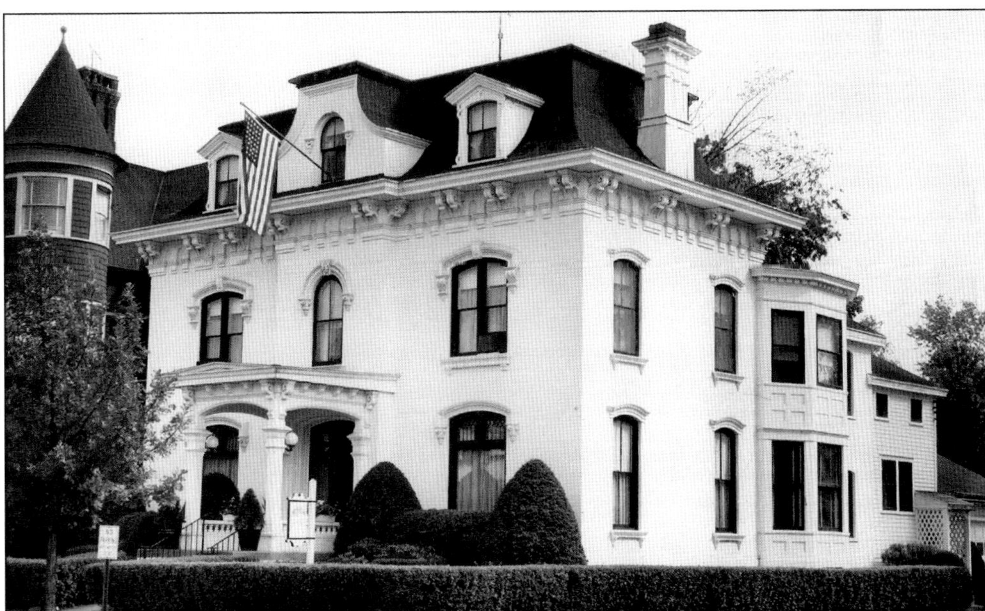

DeLong's Hardware store on Glen Street burned during the 1864 fire. It was rebuilt quickly since he had access to the necessary materials to rebuild the village, thus allowing him to join the emerging upper-middle class. He was able to add on to his small farmhouse and create an Italianate-style Victorian home. It is now the Chapman Historical Museum on Glen Street (shown).

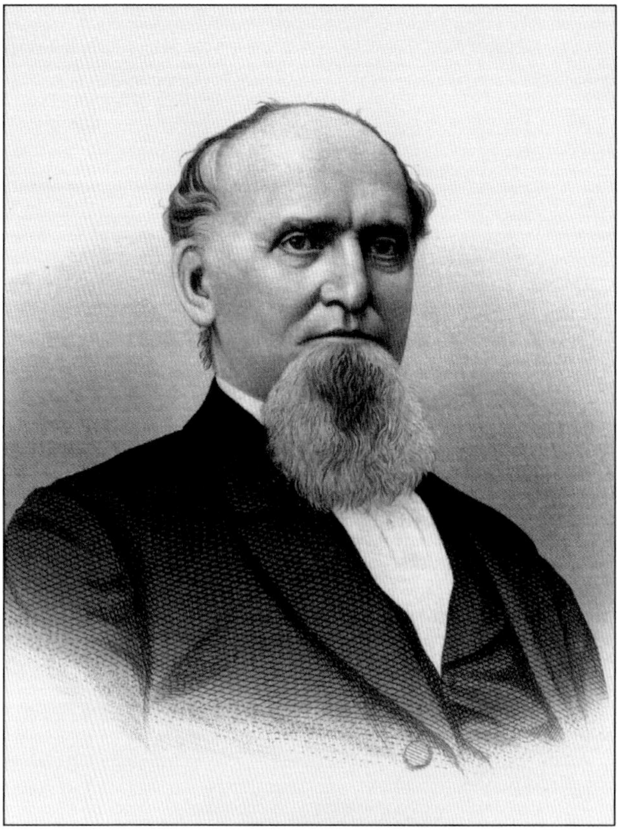

Orange Ferris, 1814–1894, was descended from Quaker and Puritan ancestry. His family was second in importance to the Wings, earliest settlers in the area. He attended the old Quaker school on Ridge Street that his father helped build, later becoming the home of Jerome Lapham. He went on to the University of Vermont.

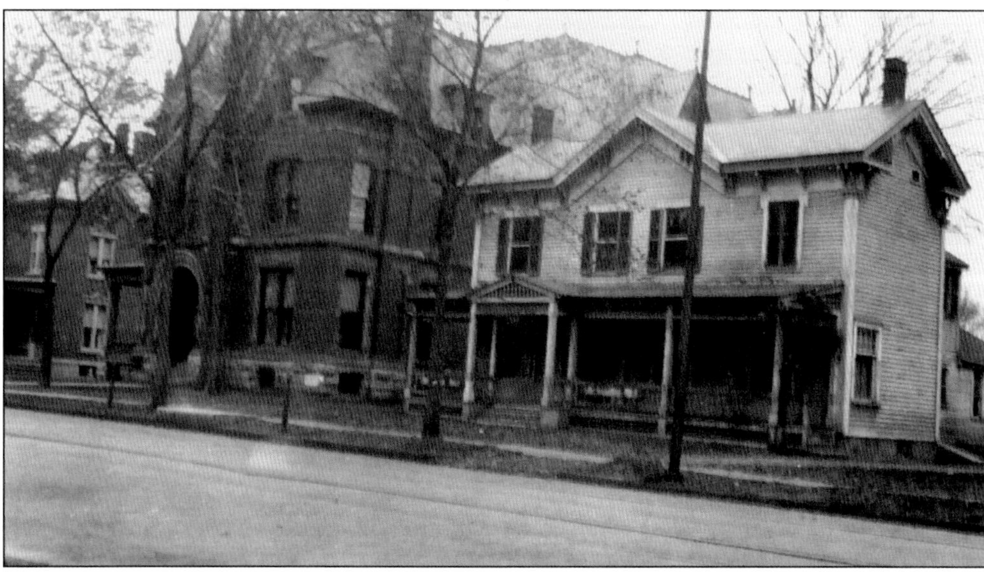

Ferris was first elected to a village office in 1839, living in a home at 206 Glen Street (shown). In 1840, he was admitted to the bar and was appointed surrogate by Gov. William Seward. He went on to be a county judge and reappointed surrogate several times. He was elected a representative to Congress twice, and Pres. Ulysses S. Grant appointed him to a commission to examine claims of loses for loyal southerners.

Jeremiah Finch, 1827–1904, born in Sandy Hill, began work in a general store. In 1863, he joined Samuel Pruyn in forming Finch, Pruyn and Company. He was president of the Glens Falls National Bank for 29 years and served a term as village president. Finch was a leader of the Warren County Democratic Party. A personal friend of Grover Cleveland, he was politically active but never sought public office.

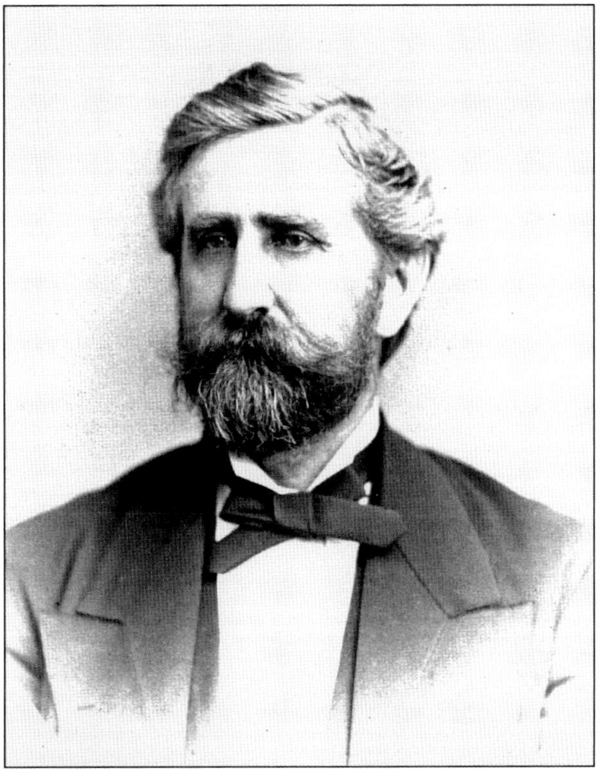

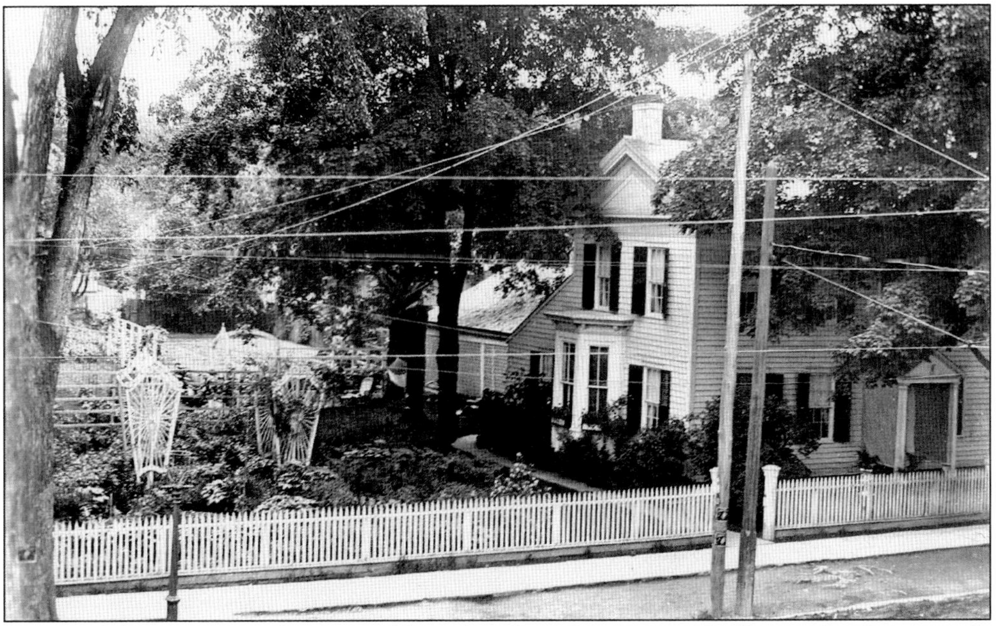

The Finch home was on Glen Street (shown) with gardens surrounded by a picket fence, nearly opposite the First National Bank. He was warden at the Church of the Messiah but also supported the Kingsbury Baptist Church. He and his first wife, Helen, had four children, George, Jeremiah, Helen, and Herbert. Later he married Harriet E. Moore. The Finch Pruyn Company remained family owned for generations.

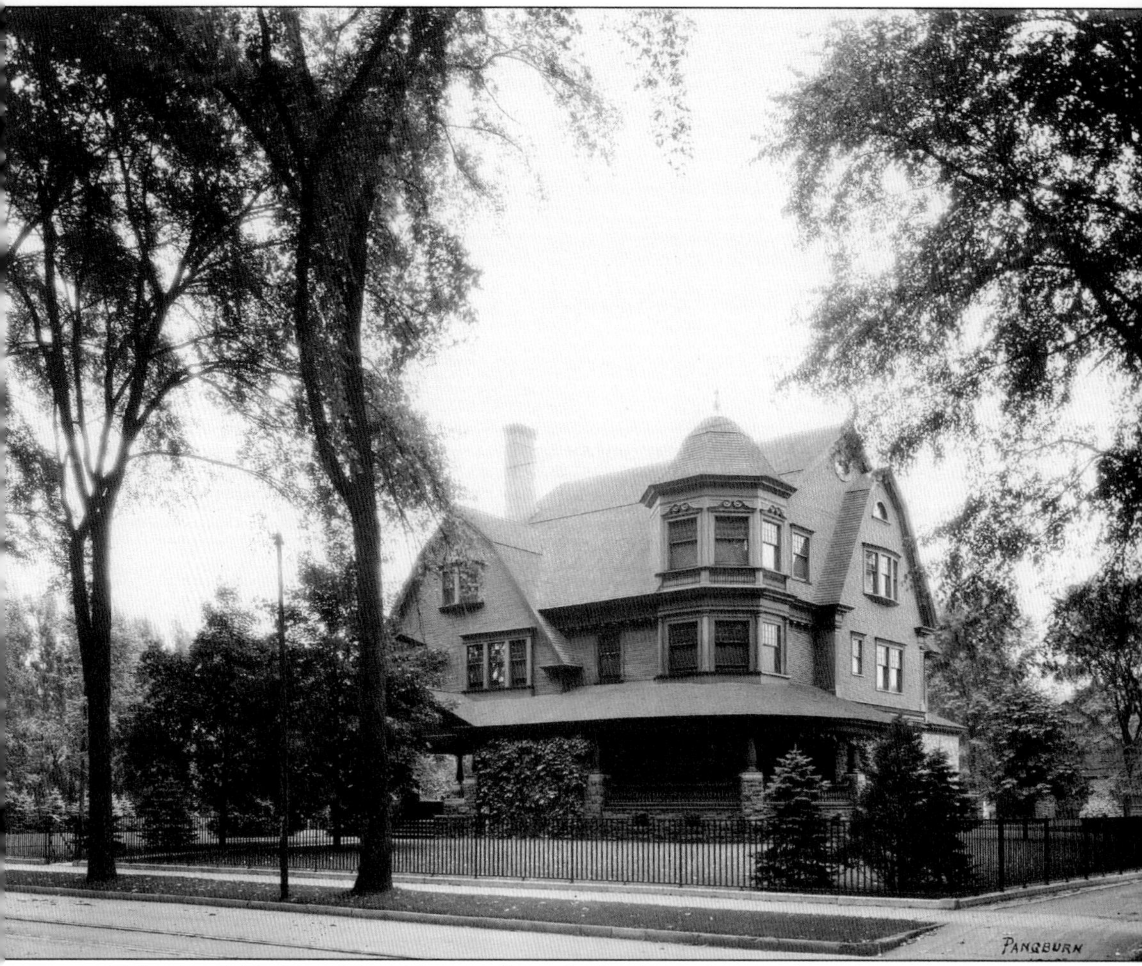

Helen Finch Foulds, 1864–1958, was the only daughter of Jeremiah and Helen Finch. She had three brothers, George, Herbert, and Jeremiah T. She married Thomas Foulds, D.D.S., in 1894, and while on their wedding trip in foreign lands, her father had a huge mansion built for them on Ridge Street (shown). She and her husband had no children. Her behavior was described as dictatorial and terrifying, yet she was secretly benevolent. She received a very large inheritance from her father's estate upon his death. Poor health sent her to the Glens Falls Hospital in 1945, and after surgery she insisted on staying there until her death in 1958. From her fortune she left $4.5 million to the Metropolitan Museum of Art in New York City and only $500,000 divided between church, relatives, and other Glens Falls interests, much to the chagrin of the locals.

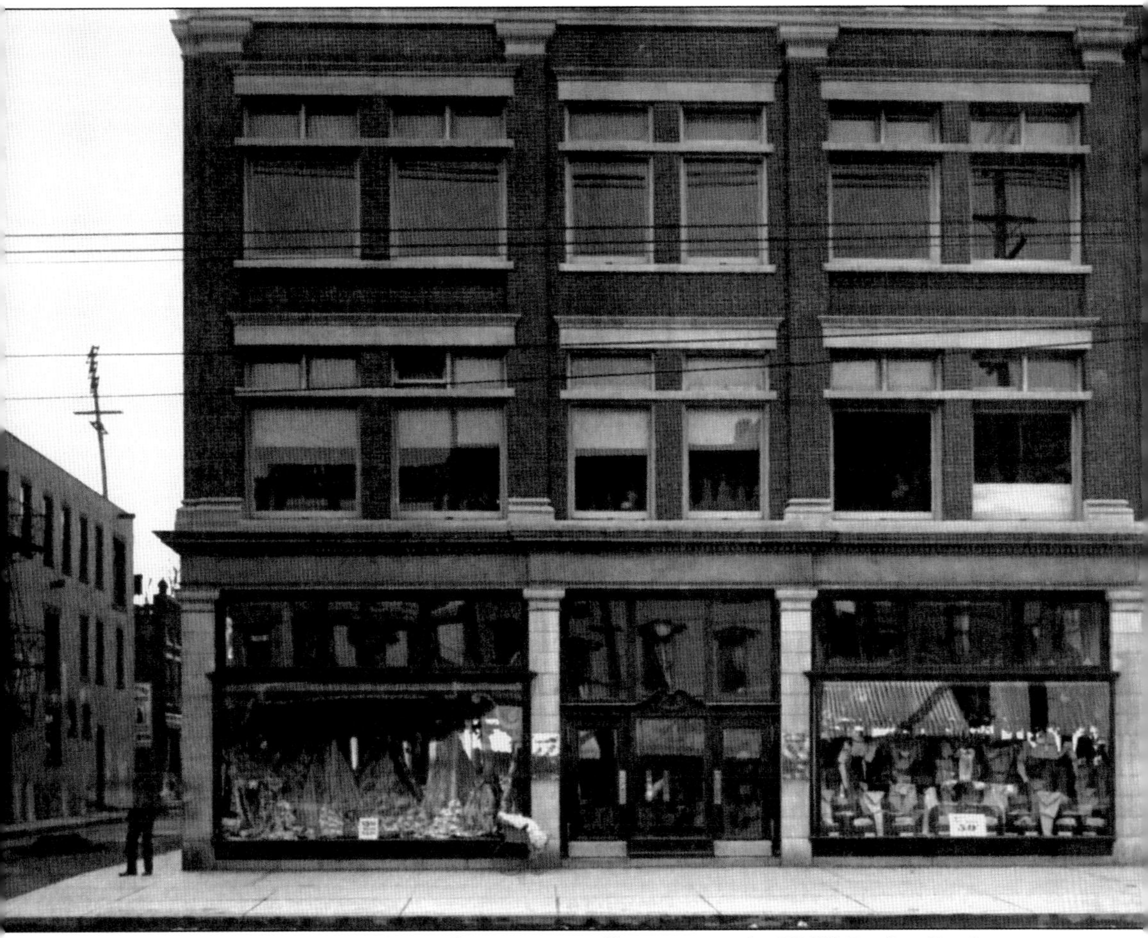

Byron Baker Fowler, 1845–1936, began his career as office manager for W. W. Rockwell, who ran a store at the corner of Glen and Exchange Streets. In 1869, "B. B.," as he was known, and his brother Joseph, bought the business. After Joseph left to work for Jointa Lime, B. B. ran it alone until 1900. He was the first to introduce a ready-to-wear line of women's clothing. When the store burned in 1902, it was promptly rebuilt (building shown). He introduced a horse-drawn delivery service and soon replaced it with an auto truck. His store was one of the first to be lit by gas lamps and have an elevator. He was well known for keeping a bushel of lollipops on a counter for kids to enjoy. In addition to his business, he served as a director and vice president of the First National Bank and later president of the Glens Falls Savings and Loan. He died at the age of 90, one month after retiring.

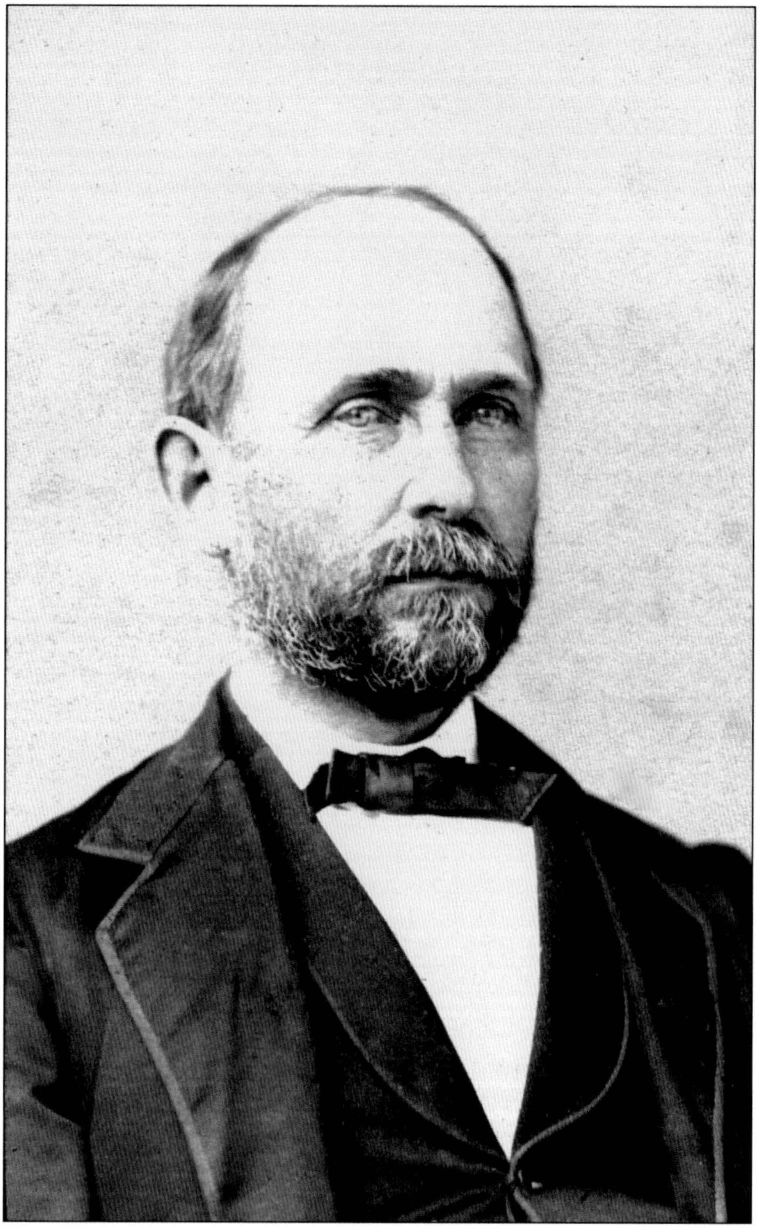

Austin Wells Holden, M.D., 1819–1891, was born in Washington County, and in 1836, at the age of 17, he came to Glens Falls. He studied law for one year, stopping to earn money as a cabinetmaker. He taught school in the area and was even superintendent for the Common School District for two years. Holden was a leader in state and national homeopathic medical groups and was chief of staff of a hospital in New York City. He was the editor of the *Glens Falls Times* and the first from Warren County to enlist for Union duty in the Civil War. Holden was elected to the state assembly as a Democrat from Warren County in 1874. He collected historical materials, and they became the core of the Holden Collection at the Crandall Public Library. Abraham Wing III loaned Holden all his personal papers, and while in his possession, the Wing home burned, so all the documents on the Wing family were preserved for history. Holden wrote *The History of the Town of Queensbury*, for which he is best remembered.

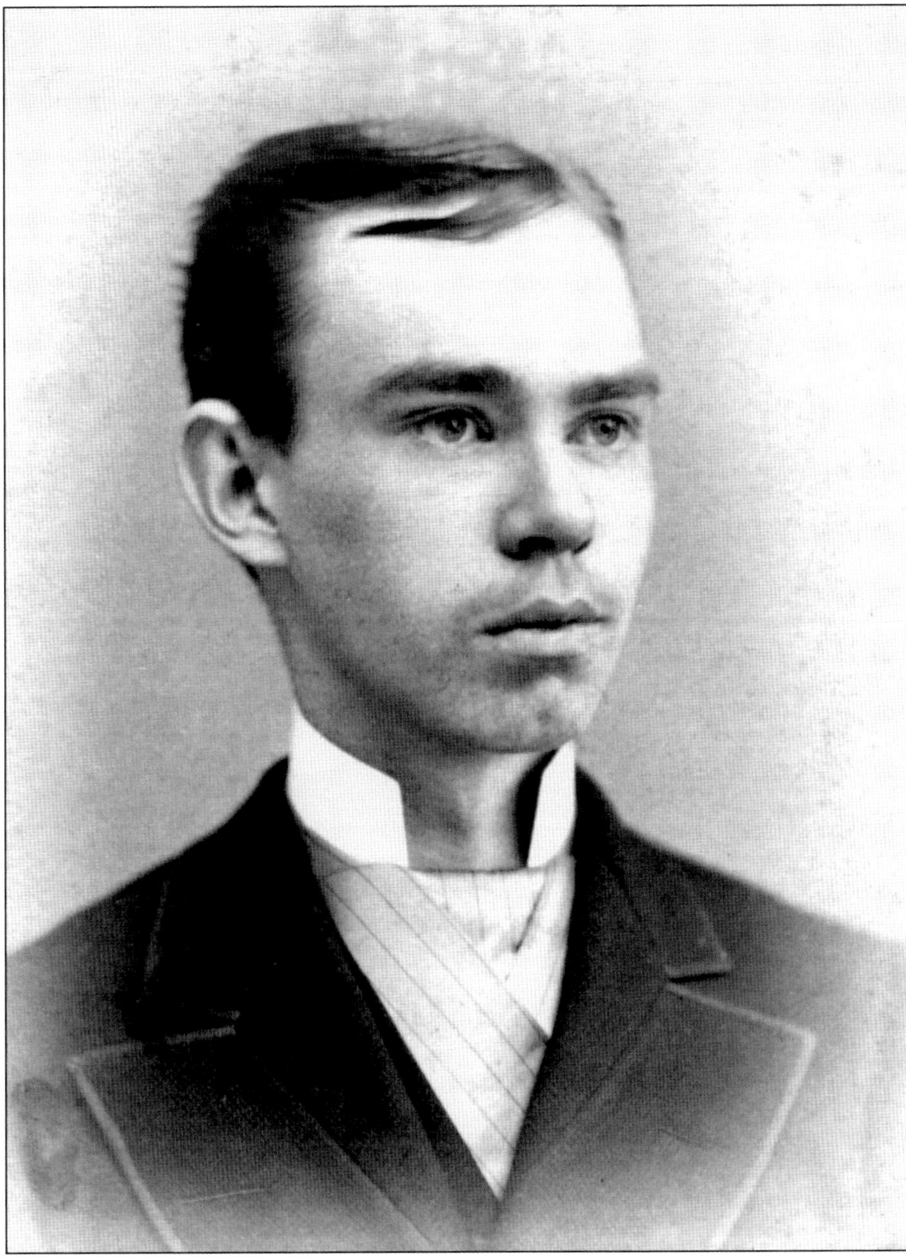

James Holden, 1861–1918, the son of Dr. Austin and Elizabeth Holden, was born and raised in Glens Falls. After graduating from Williams College in 1885, he went into the newspaper business. By 1891, Holden was editor and publisher of the *Glens Falls Times*. He joined the Jerome Lapham Hose Company, and four years later he was elected foreman. Holden was active in many organizations, including board member of the following: Crandall Library, Home of the Aged Women, Glens Falls Trust Company, and the board of education. He was an original stockholder of the Empire Theater and manager for many years. After marriage to Mary Belle, daughter of Charles and Isabelle Everest, they lived for many years at 27 Elm Street. He was Glens Falls village trustee, helping to write the city charter. Holden is best remembered for being the New York state historian appointed during Gov. John Alden Dix's administration.

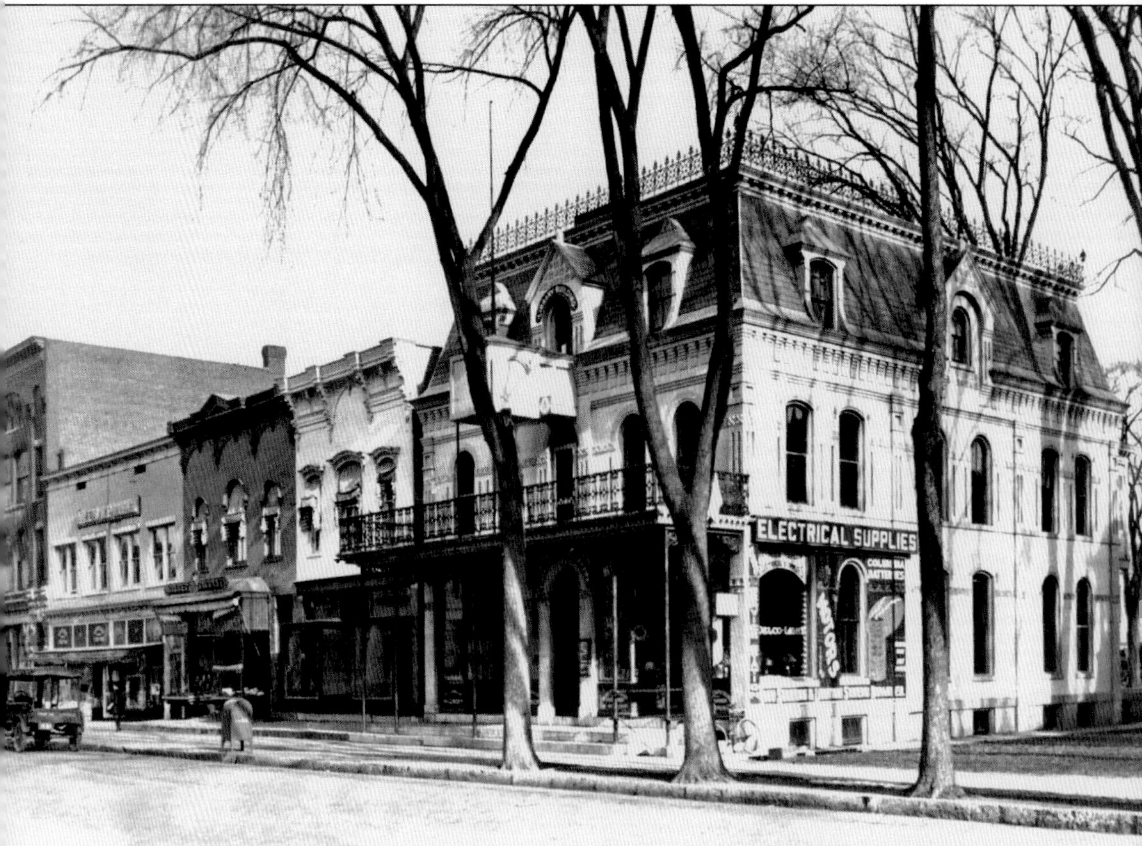

Louis Juvet, 1838–1930, was born in Switzerland, where he learned the art of watchmaking. He opened a watchmaker and jewelry shop on Bay Street, shown here, but he also manufactured school globes at a plant in Canajoharie. He completed his first time globe in 1867, a combination of clock and globe that was used to determine the time at any location on earth as well as the earth's relative position to the sun. His time globe was exhibited at the Philadelphia Centennial Exposition in 1876. Juvet received the Medal of Merit for his accomplishment. This was shortly after he became a naturalized citizen of the United States of America. Juvet was also involved with the Saratoga, Mount McGregor and Lake George Railroad Company. The reproduction model of his time globe dated April 3, 1877, is in the archives at the Chapman Historical Museum.

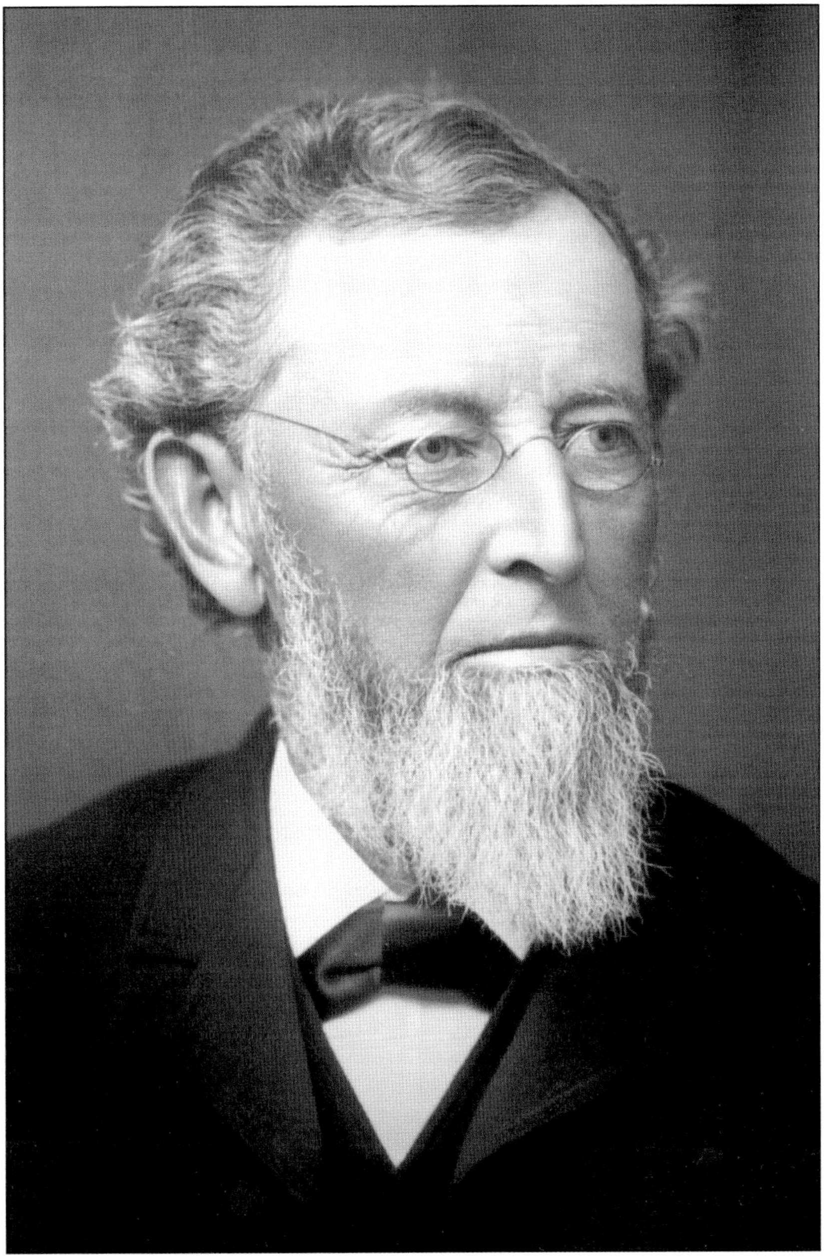

Jerome Lapham, 1828–1898, was born in the area, his family moving to the village in 1832. He spent one term in the Glens Falls Academy and then went to the Common School on West Street. In his early life, he was a farmer, canal driver, boat hand, teamster, and at the age of 20, a store clerk. By 1850, Lapham was active in the lumber business. He moved to New York City but returned to Glens Falls to join with James Morgan in a business partnership. The business ended in 1857, and Lapham went into lumbering and canal transportation. Lapham was a member of the board of directors of the Glens Falls Railroad Company, the First National Bank, the Glens Falls Insurance Company, and president of the village. In 1865, he was a member of the New York State Assembly, served four years as a supervisor of the town of Queensbury, and served as trustee of the Glens Falls Academy.

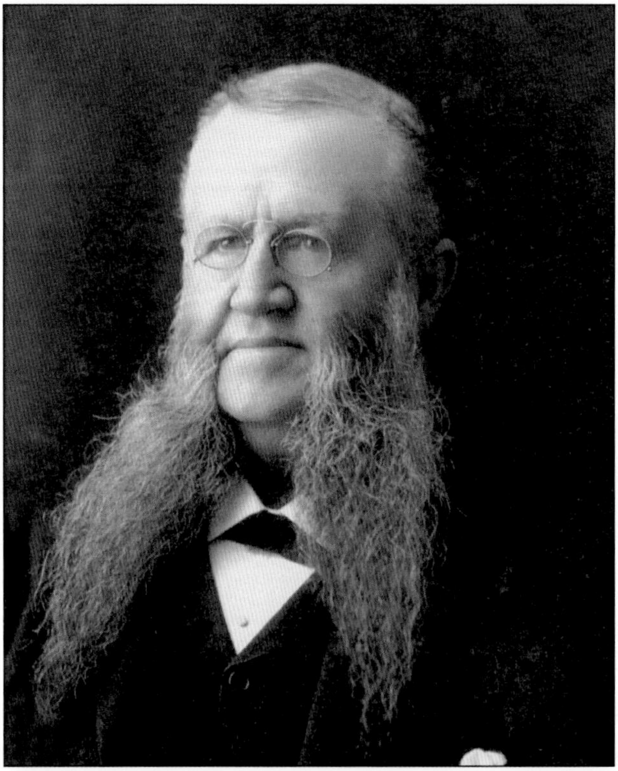

George Little, M.D., 1836–1911, graduated from Albany Medical College in 1858. He was Warren County coroner, but practiced medicine in Fort Edward and Glens Falls for 53 years. His office contained over 2,000 orchids, plus additional plants. In his waiting room was a collection of songbirds and pheasants. There was also a monkey that was allowed to be loose until it bit someone, and then it had to be caged.

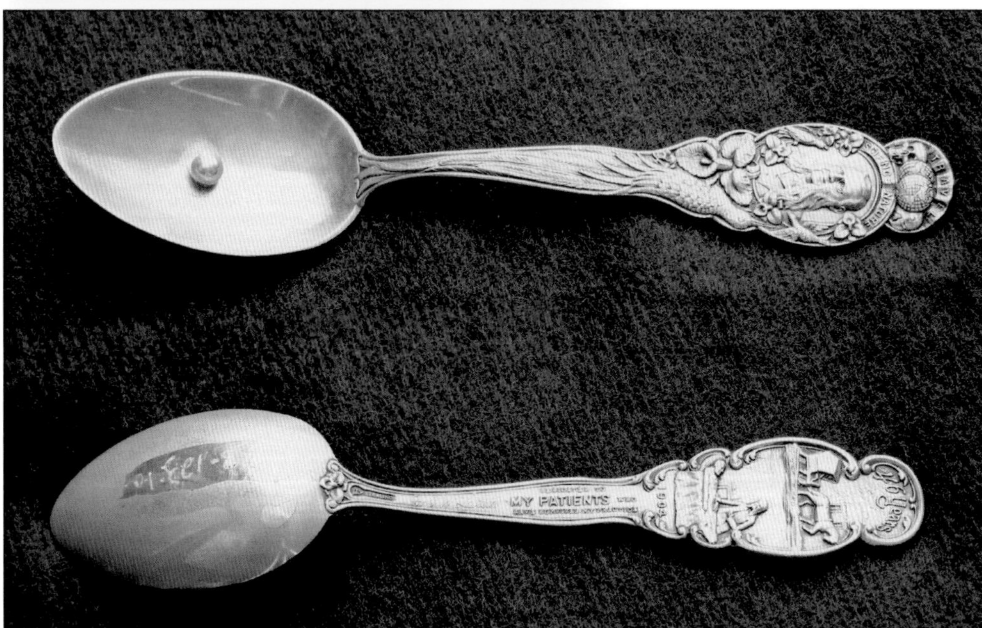

Dr. Little, nearing his retirement, commissioned Tiffany and Company to design a sterling silver spoon for his patients. Engraved with a pheasant, orchids, and medical symbols, it said, "To those patients who survived my practice, best wishes, George W. Little." In the bowl of the spoon was a tiny silver pill. One of the spoons is on display at the Chapman Historical Museum.

Russell Little, 1808–1891, was educated in Massachusetts and entered the ministry in 1828. He was a minister for 12 years in the Troy Methodist Conference. He is best known as the founder and president of the Dividend Mutual Insurance Company in 1849. It was later to become the Glens Falls Insurance Company in 1864.

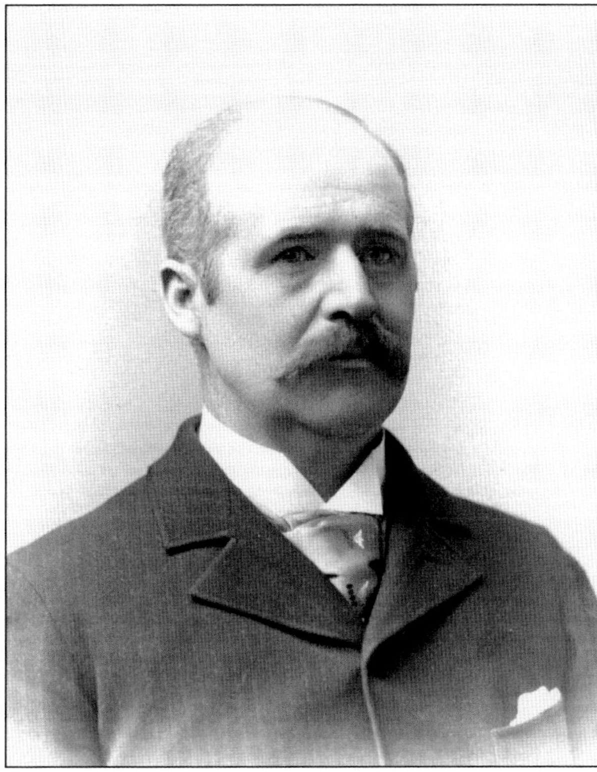

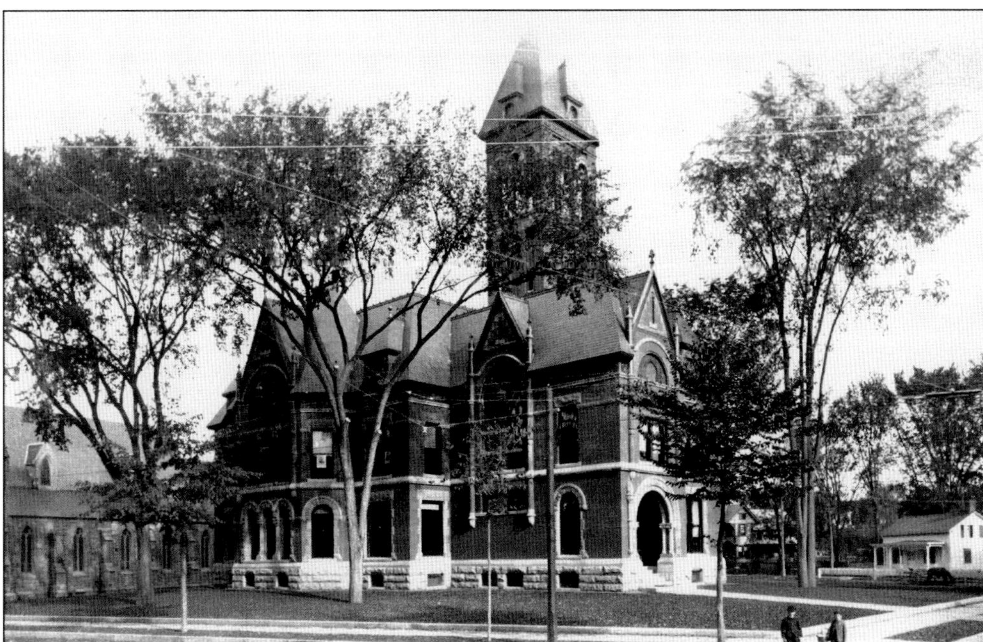

Little was a delegate to the convention where Abraham Lincoln was nominated for president. At the time, he was a New York state senator. He was a kind and generous person but always an astute businessman. He never actually retired, dying six months after the insurance building at the comer of Glen and Bay Streets was completed (shown).

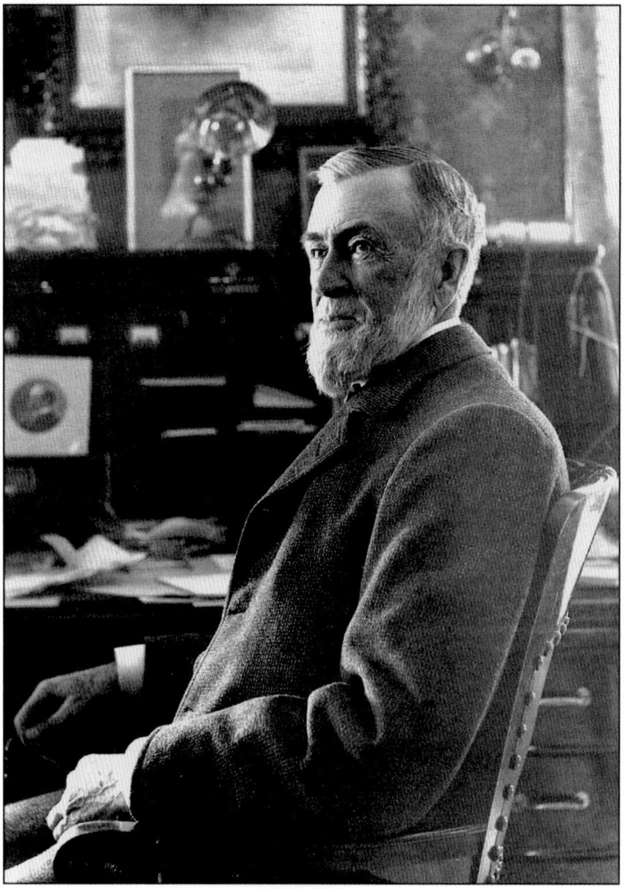

William McEchron, 1831–1906, was a tow boy on the Champlain Canal and a baggage handler for the Fort Edward Railroad. He married in 1858, and in 1863, the couple moved to Glens Falls. He became a partner with James Morgan in the limestone and lumber industry. Upon the death of Morgan, McEchron became the head of the company. He was chief of a local fire department, on the board of education, and served as president of the YMCA. He was also director of the Glens Falls Insurance Company and the First National Bank. His main accomplishment was establishing the village water supply system, still in use today. McEchron built a mansion on Ridge Street in 1891 (below). Upon his death the property was transferred to the city to be used as a health center and office for several service organizations.

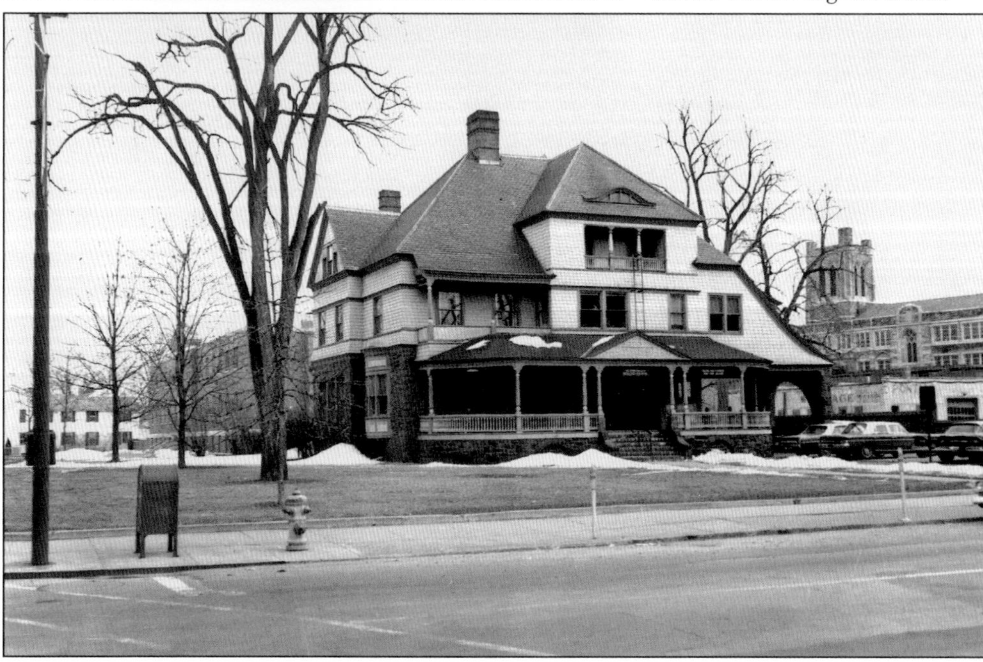

Patrick Moynehan, 1849–1920, came to North Creek from Ireland at age eight after having had some schooling. At the age of 15, he worked in a tannery, and a year later began work cutting logs. Moynehan moved up to foreman, then superintendent, and finally the owner of many lumber industries. Moynehan was considered a man of wealth and influence.

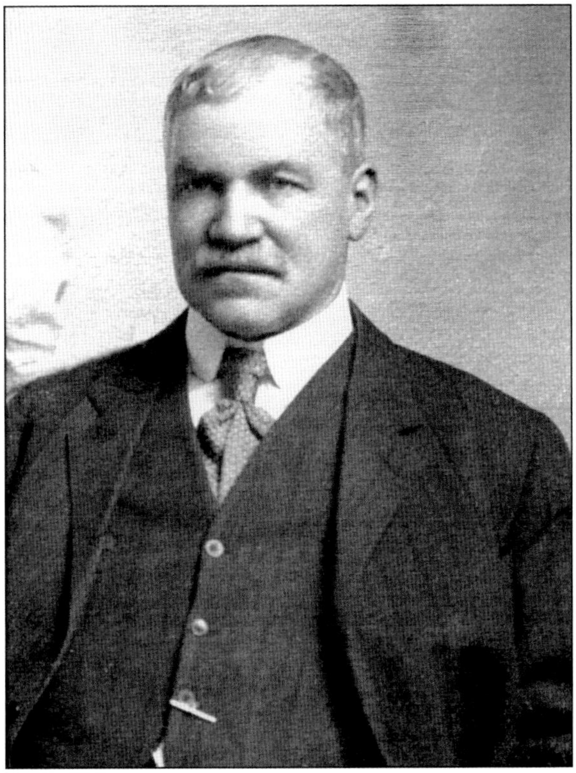

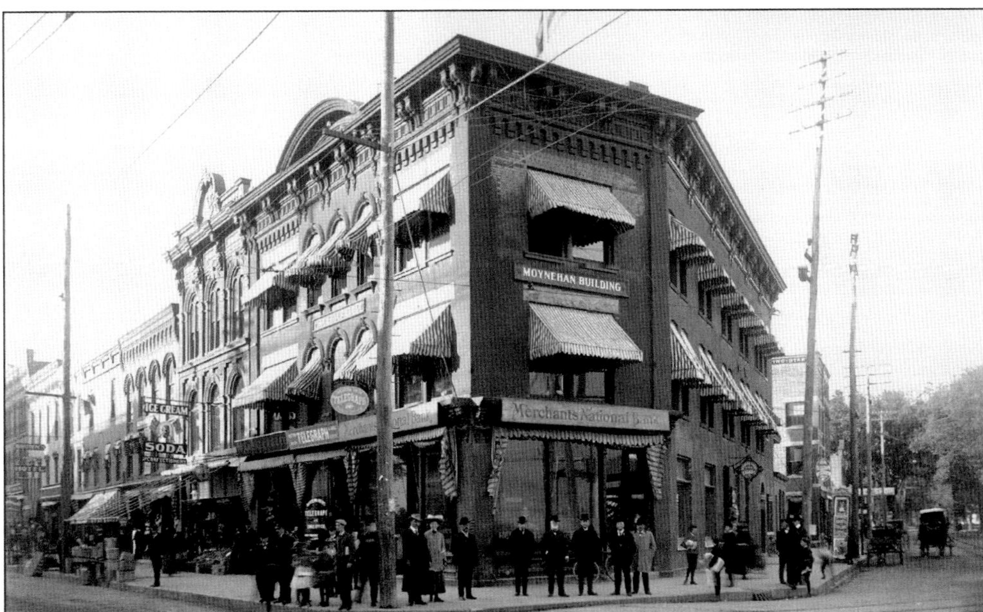

It was said Moynehan was one of the largest individual real estate owners in the city. He was president of the Glens Falls Post Publishing Company and a director of the First National Bank. He maintained many businesses in North Creek, Raquette Lake, and Pierce Field. He owned a steamboat and a hotel and was a political leader. Moynehan went on to own a business block at Ridge and Glen Streets (shown).

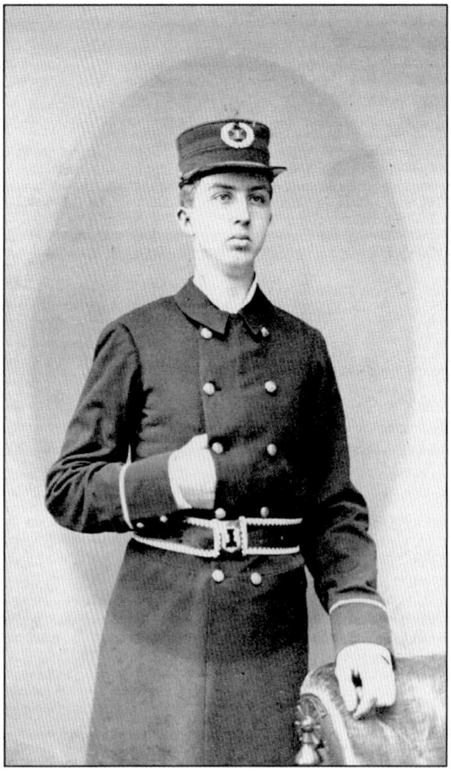

Ephraim Potter, 1855–1925, was educated in local schools, while learning carpentry from his father, a millwright. Shown at left, at an early age he was a member of the Finch and Cunningham Hose Company. From age 30 until his death, he devoted his life to architecture. He designed many major industrial, commercial, and residential buildings in the area. Potter designed the Native Textiles complex on Warren Street in 1893, for which he received an architectural design award. He also designed the Fowler and Englander buildings on Glen Street (below) and the Glen Street building of the Glens Falls High School. The *New York Times* proclaimed him one of the wealthiest men in northern New York. Potter was hit and killed by a rural free delivery truck while riding his bicycle in Glens Falls.

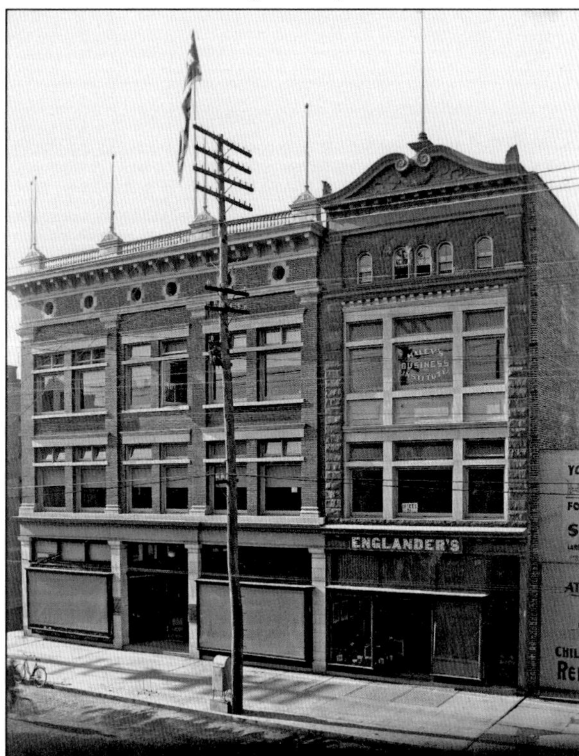

Three

THE EAST

The section of Glens Falls referred to as the East End brings to mind factories, transportation hubs, and the homes of the Irish and Italian immigrants in the area. This part of town supported St. Mary's, the Irish Italian Catholic church. Small grocery stores and family-run restaurants and other service businesses existed at street intersections. Many of the working-class families did not own cars, so they relied on early trolleys, buses, or simply walking. Therefore the neighborhood store, bar, or beauty shop was an important part of the community. The residents in the East End have always been extremely independent, as evidenced by their refusal to join the Union School District. They continue to maintain their own elementary school as a Common School District to this day. Because of the number of large industries in this end of town, school taxes are kept low. This chapter will concentrate on the businesses, including the armory, Glens Falls Academy, Imperial Wall Paper Company, Joseph's Fruit Market, Noble Grocery, the opera house, the Peyser Factory, Portland Cement, the railroad, St. Mary's Church, and the Troy Shirt Maker's Guild. The many historic figures connected with the East End include Eugene Ashley, Thomas Burnham, Billy Joe Clark, Charles and Keyes Cool, Douglas Crockwell, John Alden Dix, James Ferguson, Thomas Henning, Charles Evan Hughes, Charlotte Hyde, Edward Joubert, William McDonald, J. Ernest Miller, Alonzo Morgan, James Ordway, Robert Patterson, Buell Streeter, Lemon Thomson, James White, Abraham Wing, and Harriet and Halsey Wing.

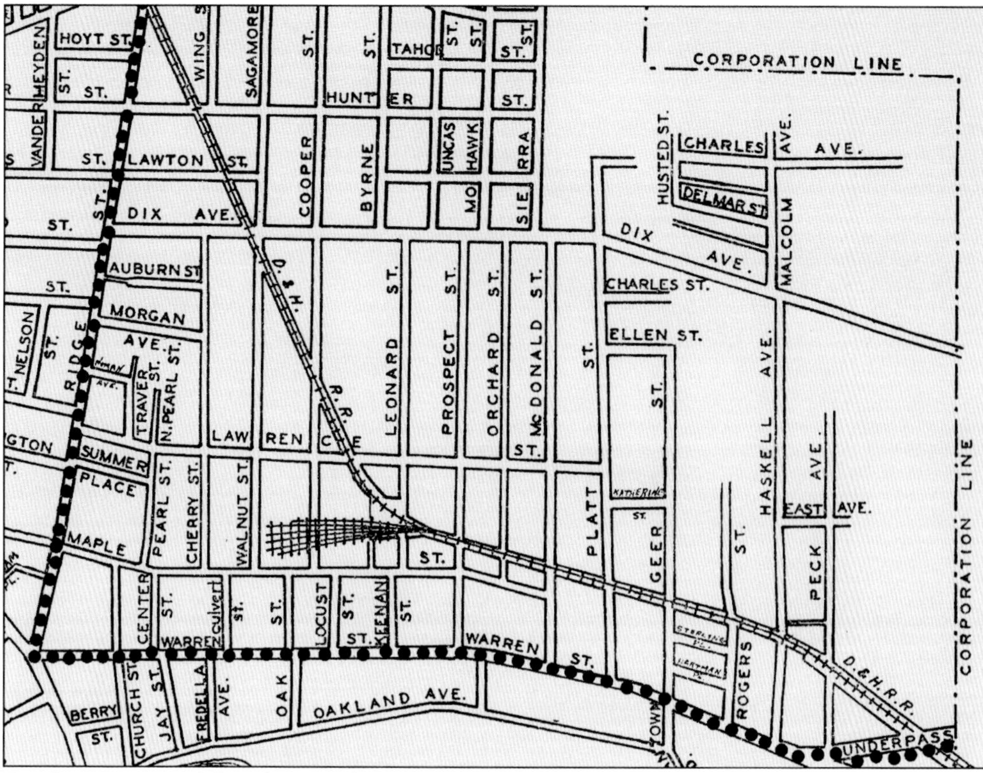

For the purposes of this chapter, the East End will refer to an L-shaped area of town starting at the intersection of Ridge and Warren Streets, going north on the east side of Ridge Street to the city limits, and Warren Street from Glen Street going east to the Queensbury town line.

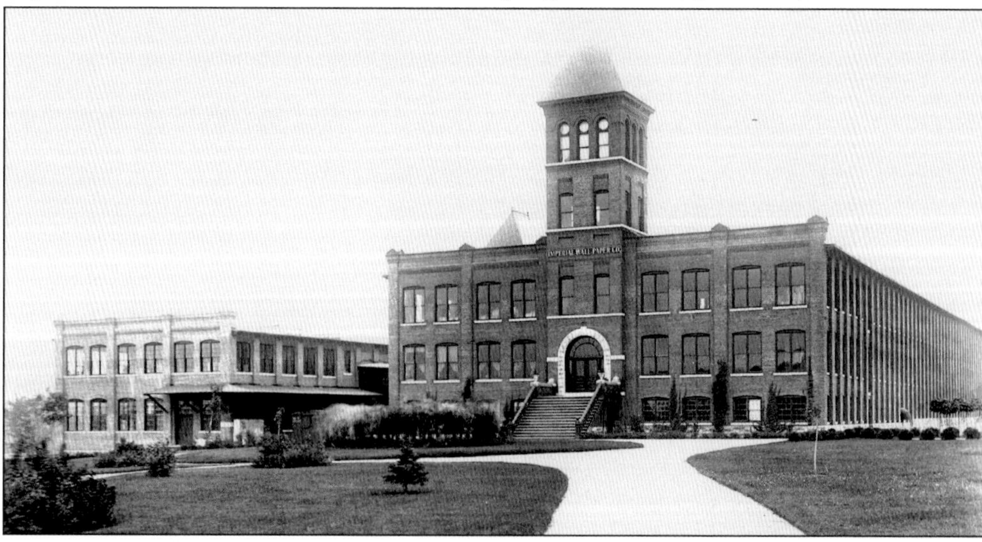

George Tait headed Imperial Wall Paper Company when it made and sold wallpaper from "stock paper." The colored dyes were purchased from various sources. Beginning in 1907, chemist Karl McBride began manufacturing pigments within the company. Various divisions of the company were developed to create Imperial Paper and Color Corporation. It soon became Hercules Pigment and then Ciba-Geigy. It closed in 1987, and the buildings were leveled.

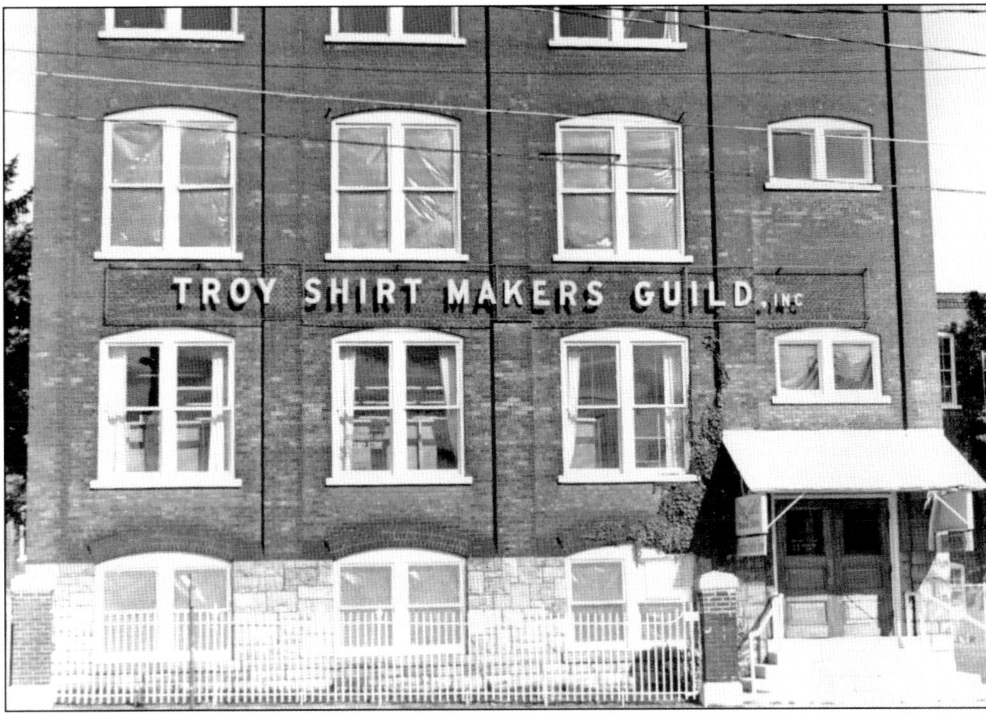

The McMullen-Leavens Company began as a shirt factory but was known worldwide for its production of women's dresses that came into demand after World War II when women suddenly joined the workforce. In 1949, the Troy Shirt Maker Guild was formed and the production of quality men's shirts became the focus again. In 1996, the company closed for good due to competition from less-expensive imported goods.

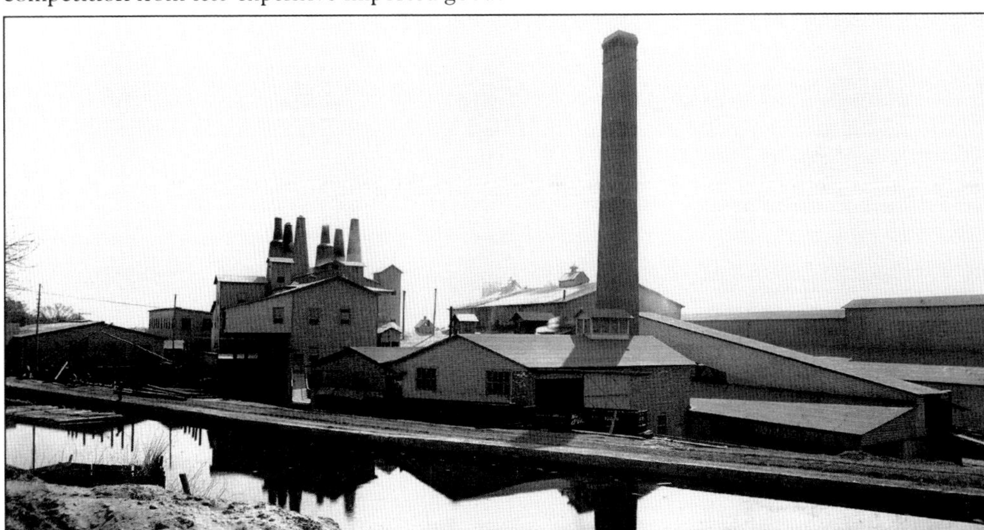

The Glens Falls Portland Cement Company began in 1893 as a small industry producing 100 barrels a day, and over time production grew to 5,000 barrels. Much less was produced during the Depression, but defense contracts during World War II again increased demands. Kilns and grinding machines were part of the cement-making process. Modernization improvements over the years, along with corporate name changes, have created a $15 million industry.

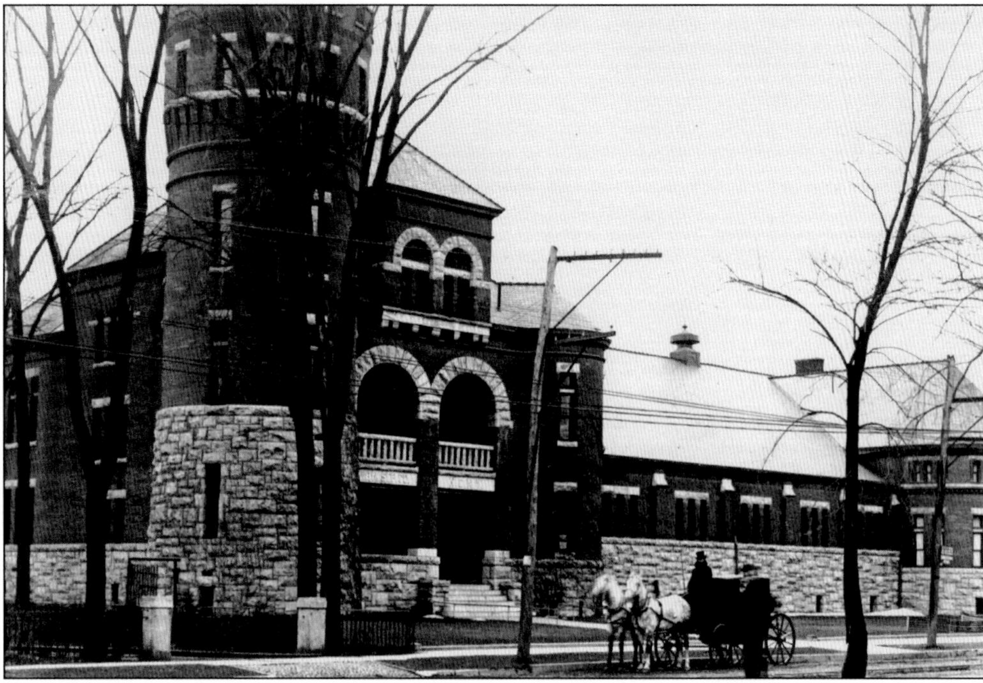

In 1895, the armory was built to house the New York National Guard. At that time Warren Street was not paved and horses were still a major way of travel, although the trolley system was in place. Today the 646th Medical Company, Company K of the National Guard, and 105th Infantry units are headquartered there.

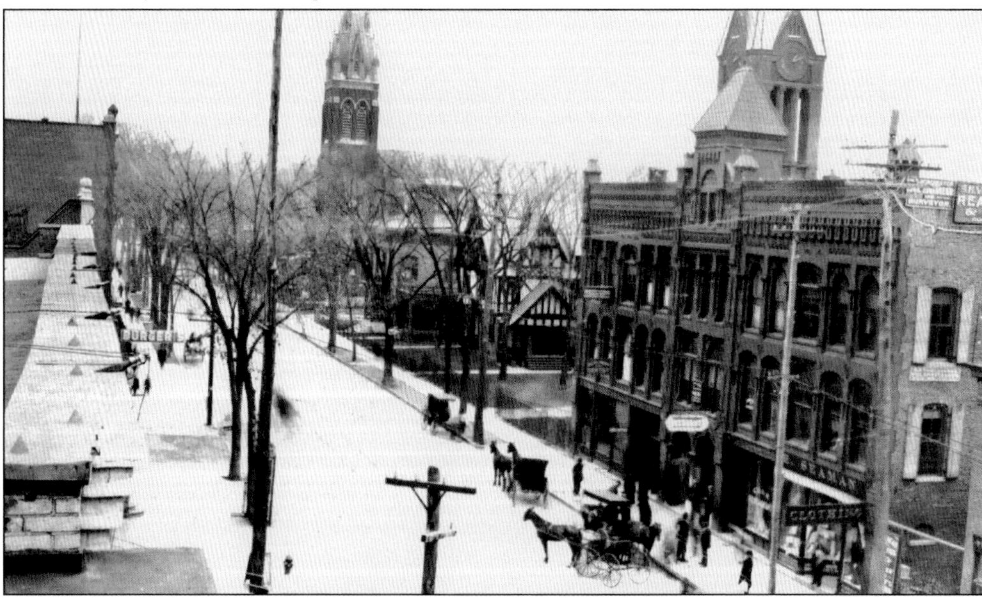

The Glens Falls Opera House (shown on right) opened its doors in 1871 on Warren Street in the first block from Glen Street. It was able to seat 1,600 people, including space for concerts, plays, lectures, and bicycle racing. Prior to the opening of the armory, the military used the facility for its drills. The building was destroyed in a fire in 1884 and was rebuilt, eventually becoming the Rialto Theater.

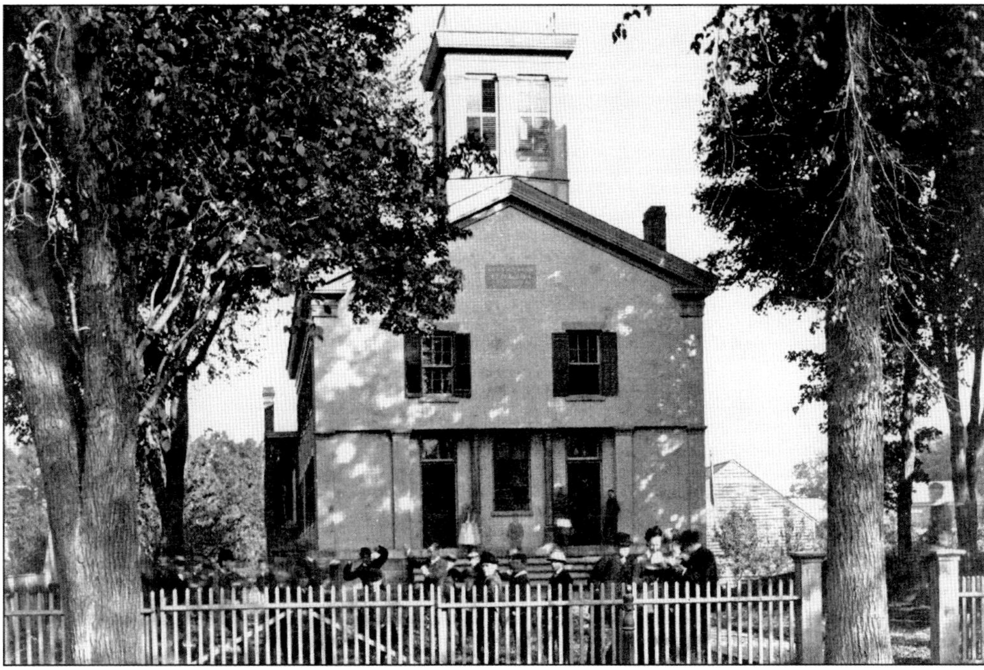

The Glens Falls Academy, 1814–1937, was established as a private school to accommodate the demands of the wealthy families of the village. The Warren Street building (shown) was built in 1841. It was designed as a college preparatory school for the area. The year was divided into three 15-week sessions. The building suffered fire damage in 1912, and the school moved to a new building on Chester Street.

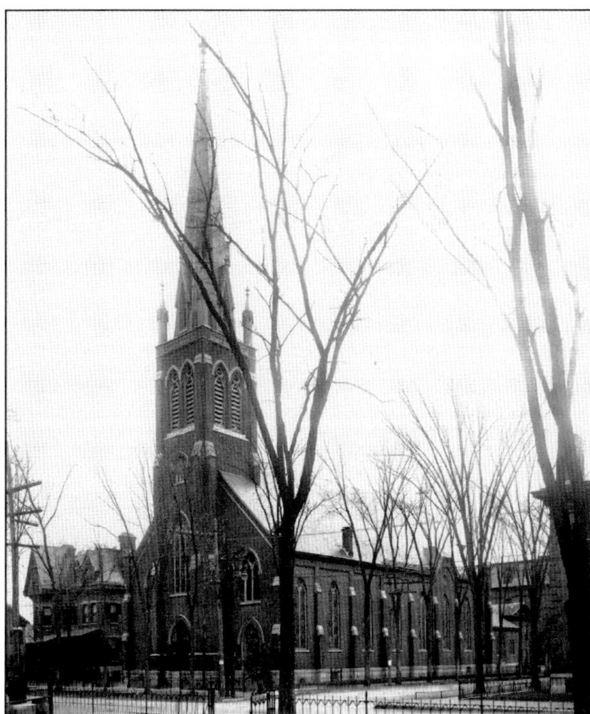

St. Mary's Church's first building started as a Methodist church in 1829. Located on Church Street, it was sold to the Roman Catholic parish in 1849. It served the Irish and Italian immigrants who settled in the east end of the village. Eventually the number of parishioners outgrew the building, and in 1869, a new building opened on the corner of Church and Warren Streets (shown).

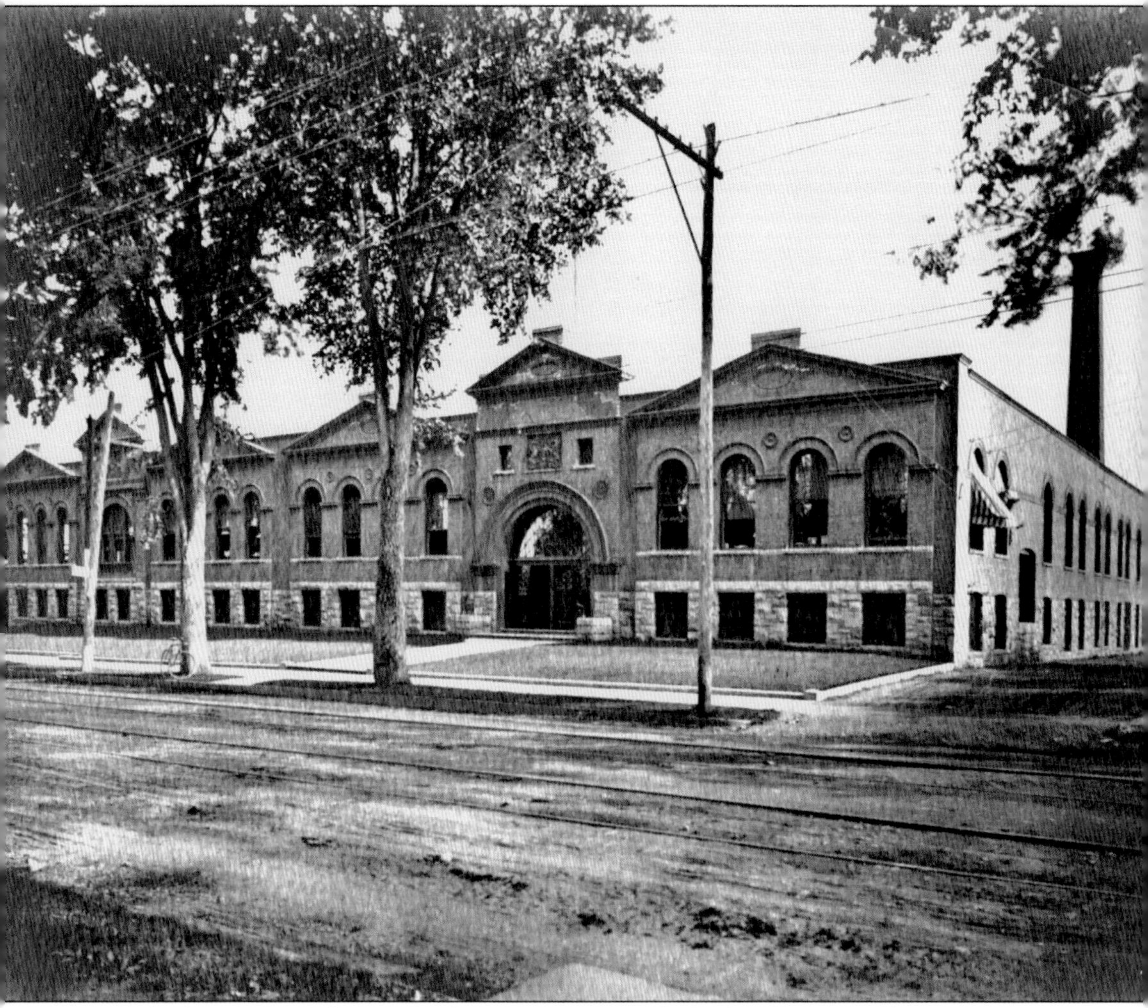

In the later part of the 1800s, the Peyser Factory, shown here, originated on Warren Street in Glens Falls. It manufactured collars and cuffs for men's shirts. The facility was turned into the production of fine Raschel lace in 1916. This delicate fabric is named after the machine that was used to make this particular kind of lace. The company was then owned and run by the Binch family members and was renamed H. and F. Binch Company. The plant was able to dye and finish the material produced there. Later it became Native Laces and Textiles that produced intimate apparel, home furnishings, active wear, and some swimwear. It sold directly to well-known companies such as Playtex, Maidenform, Vanity Fair, and Catalina. There were no direct sales to the public. Products were generally made from polyester and nylon tricot. By 1983, sales overall were around $58 million and production amounted to over 275,000 pounds of fabric and lace a week.

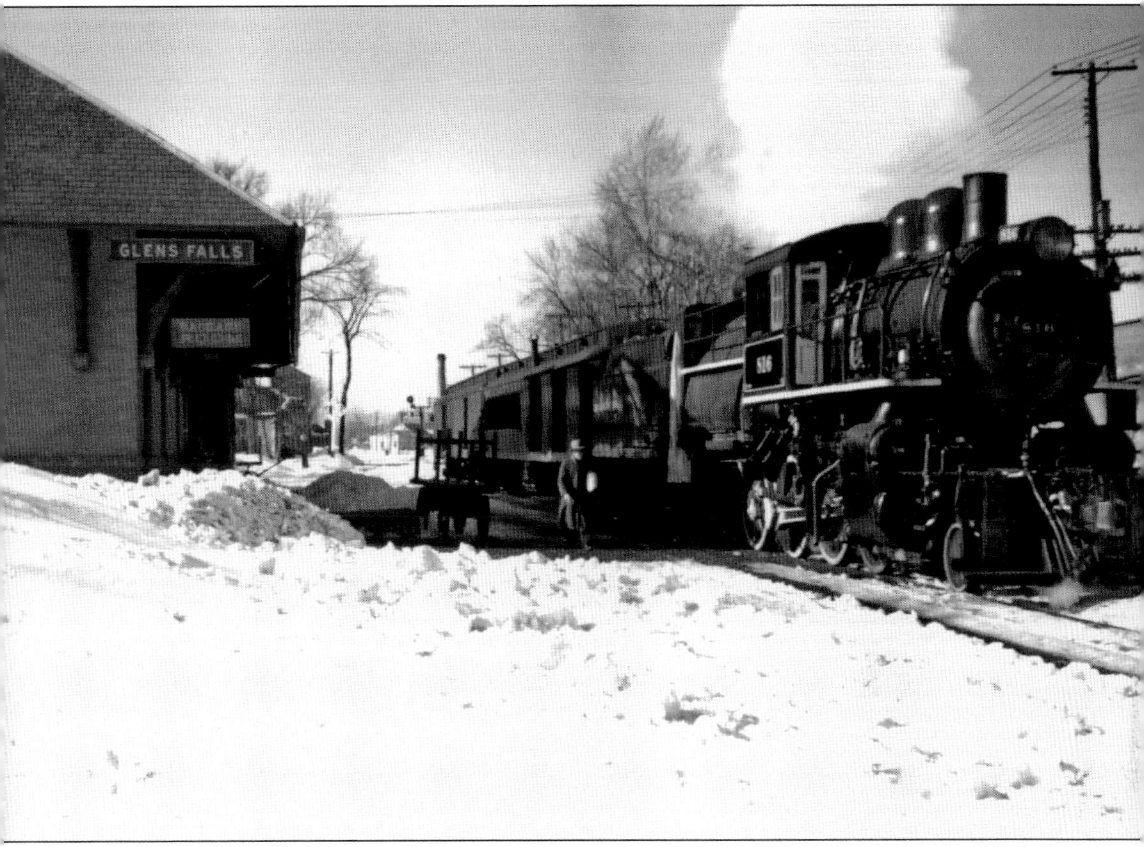

When the railroad spur came to Glens Falls in 1869, the passenger station was on the north side of Maple Street opposite Oak Street. It was later moved down the street opposite Locust Street, but a second building was built on the corner of Lawrence and Cooper Streets where the Post Star newspaper now stands. The spur allowed businesses that needed transportation to develop in this section of town. Round-trips between Fort Edward and Glens Falls ran regularly, connecting to Albany and New York City to the south and Montreal to the north. This replaced the slower travel of barges on the canal system. Supplies of coal and food were brought into the city while factory goods, paper, and limestone were shipped out. Train service, with its spur to Lake George, brought tourists to the area. Seen here, a train leaves Glens Falls on January 10, 1958.

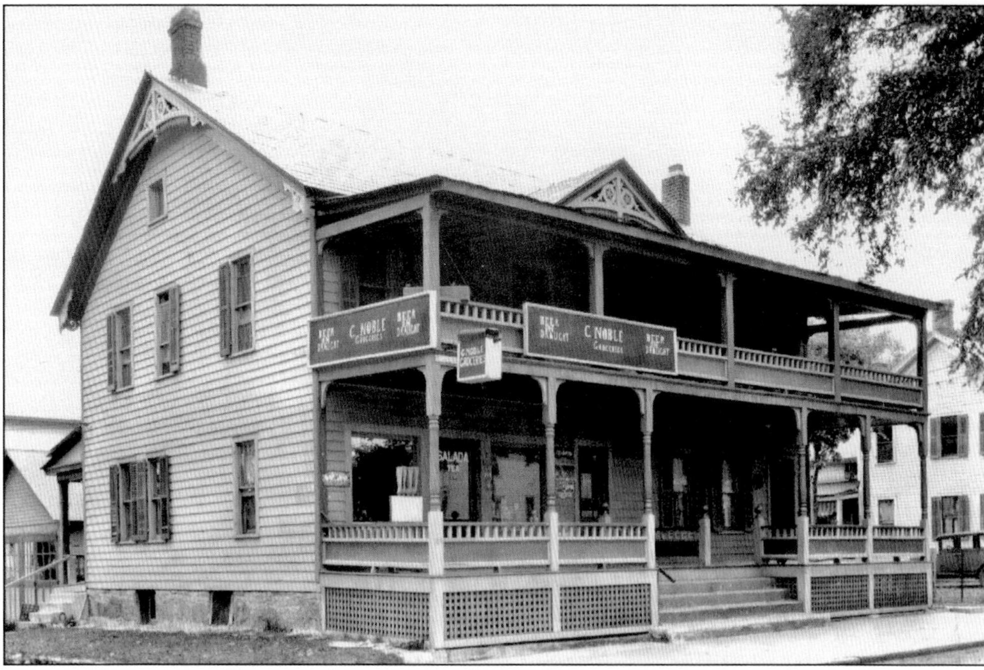

In 1913, Carmine Noble arrived in Glens Falls as a laborer. In 1933, he and his wife Micheline Funicello owned the Noble Grocery Store on Lawrence Street, later operating it as a restaurant. Members of the family lived in the area into this century. Prior to World War II, and in the years following, small groceries and specialty shops existed in all neighborhoods where people could simply walk to the corner or down the block to shop. One such business was Joseph's Fruit Market on Warren Street. In time, the family business evolved into an excellent full-service restaurant and catering business. (Above, courtesy of the Noble-DeMarino family; below, courtesy of the Joseph family.)

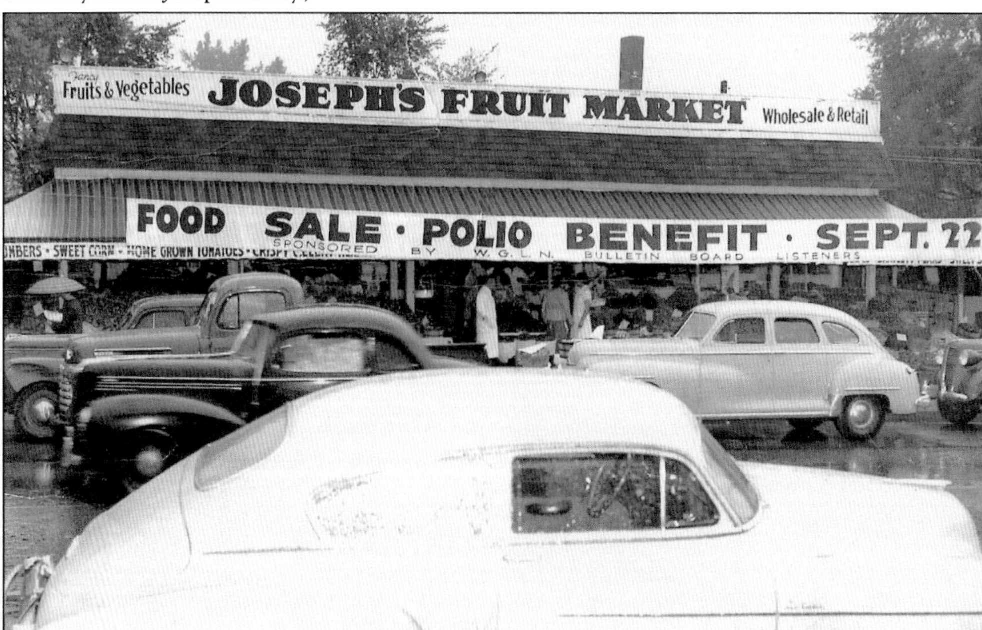

Eugene Ashley, 1863–1917, was born in Fort Ann but moved to Glens Falls around 1873. He became a lawyer known as an "idea person," with endless energy and ambition. He bought a failing paper/flax mill and discovered how to purify the water to reuse it for the pulp process, making him wealthy. Ashley began construction of a dam on the Hudson River to control water flow to the Finch Pruyn Mill. The work was completed with simple equipment and horses (below). Money ran out, but the project was completed in 1903, thanks to the financial support of William Spiers, for whom the dam was named. It was hydroelectric power, beginning an age of reliable, affordable electricity. However, Ashley lost over $16 million in the banker's panic of 1907. He moved to South Carolina and Georgia and through perseverance returned a millionaire.

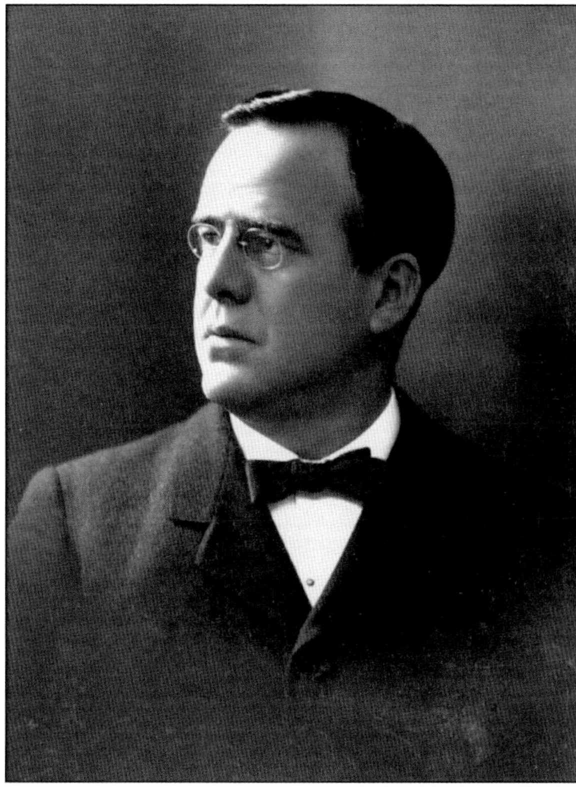

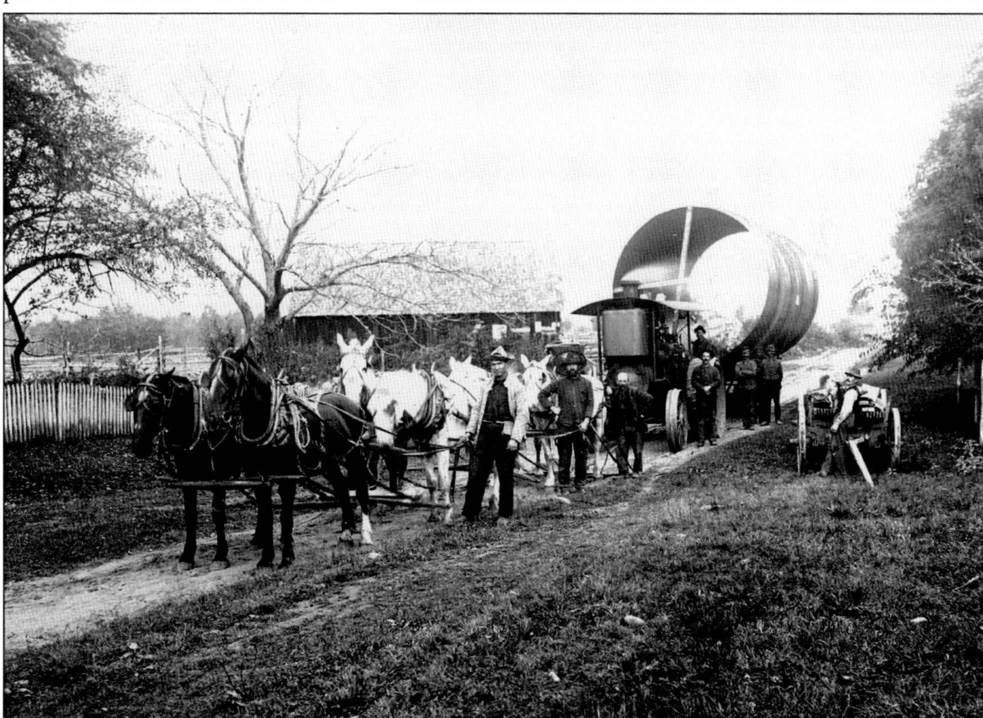

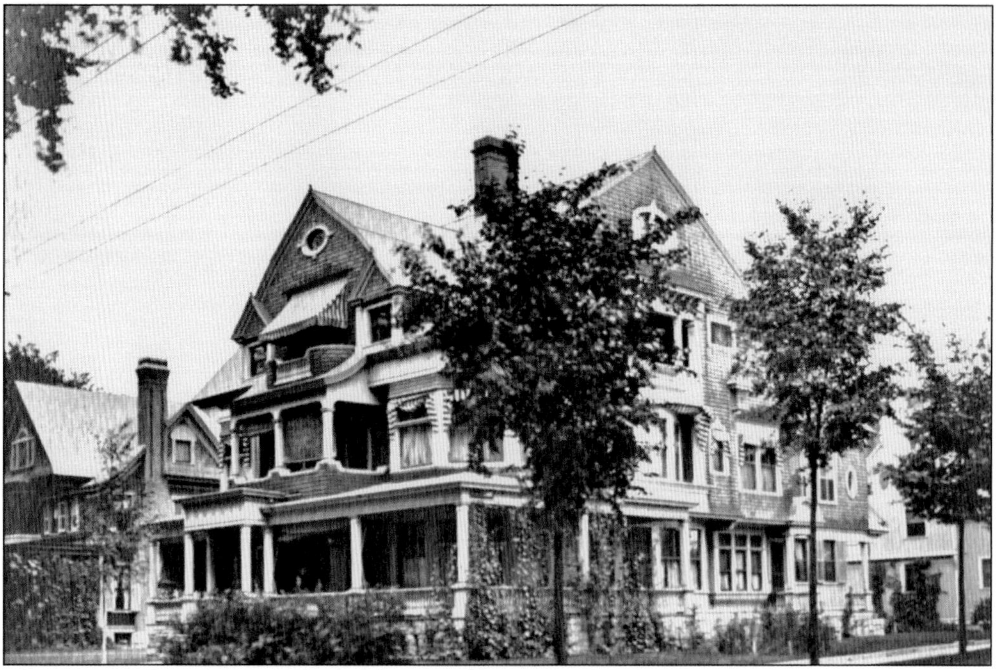

Thomas Burnham, 1808–1898, was born in Moreau but lived in many different places. He was in the canal boat business on the Champlain Canal and a tycoon in the iron industry in Ohio. When he came to Glens Falls he apparently had a lumber business where he obtained materials to build his house at 149 Ridge Street (above). Ephram Potter, renowned local architect, drew up plans for the unique two-and-a-half-story Queen Anne–style home. This was Potter's most complex residential commission, with many projecting and recessed porches. There were 20 different types of windows, including bays, ovals, stained glass, and leaded rectangles, as seen below. In his will, Burnham left the home and his wealth to his wife Sarah as long as she remained a widow.

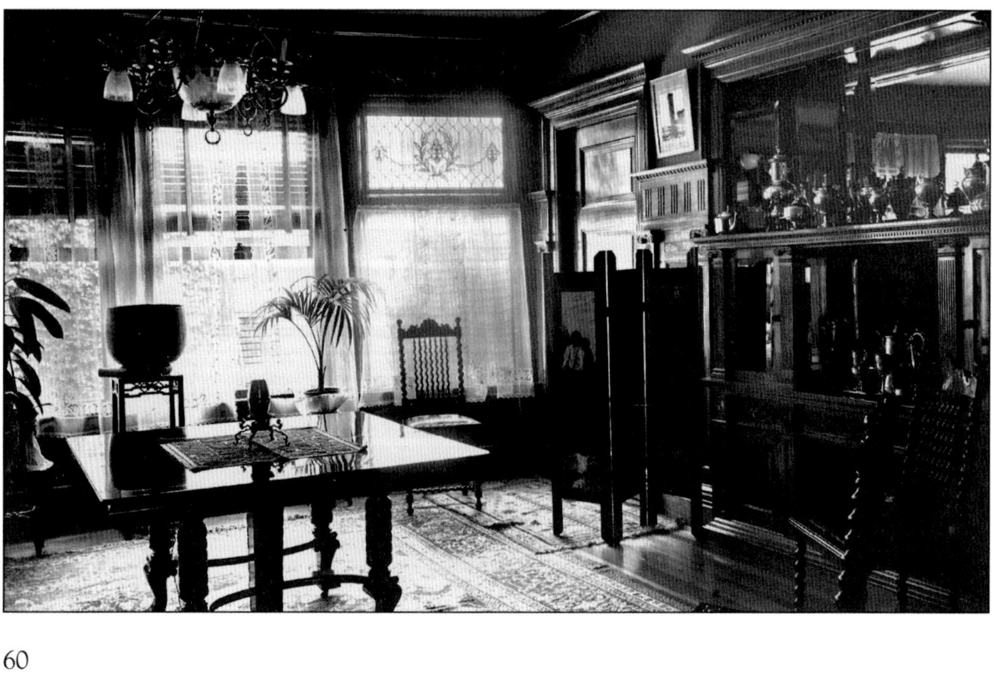

Billy Joe Clark, M.D., 1778–1866, was born in Northampton, Massachusetts, but was raised in Pownal, Vermont. His early life found him farming, clerking in a store, and tending bar in his father's business. Rum fustian, a favorite drink of the lumbermen at the time, included mixing one gallon of rum, one pint of gin, one quart of beer, a bottle of sherry, one dozen egg yolks, some sugar, and nutmeg.

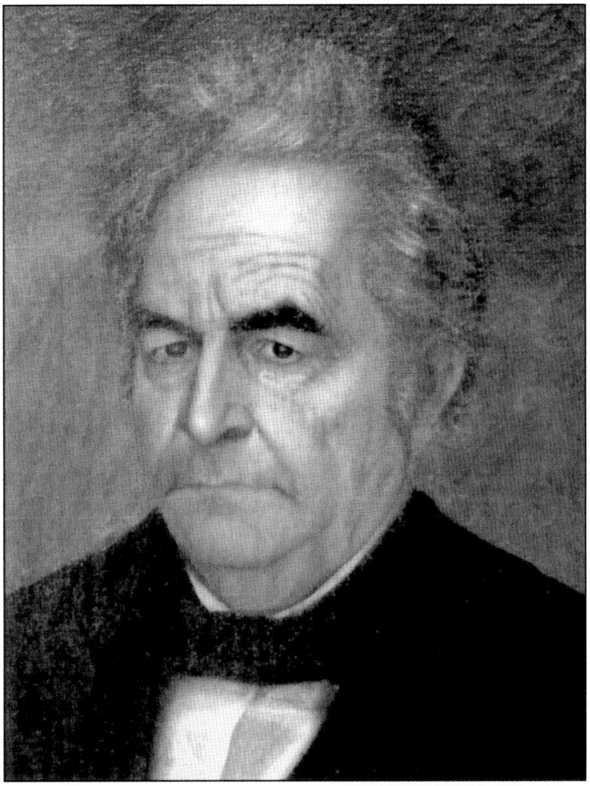

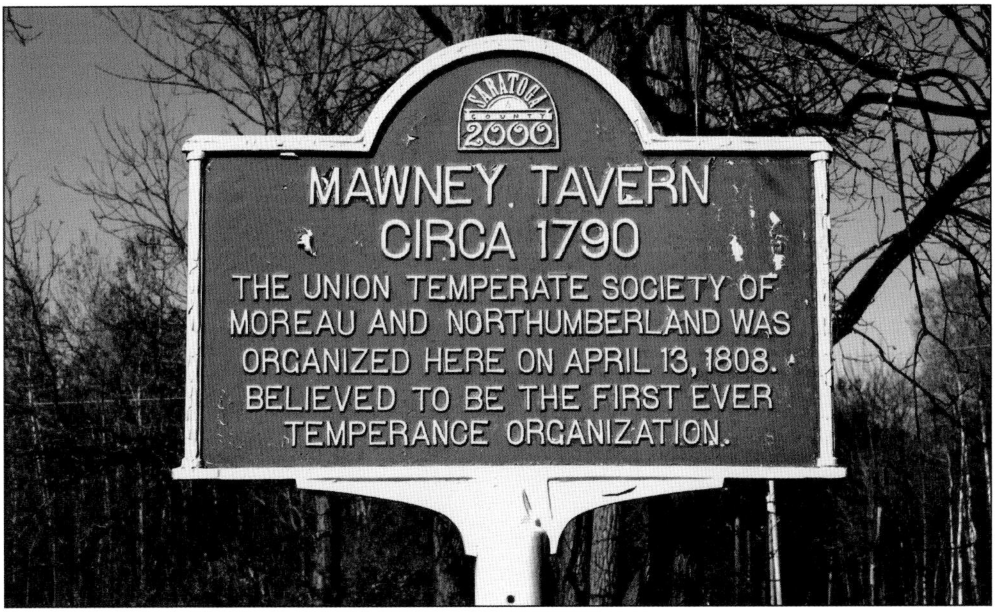

Dr. Clark established his medical practice in the town of Moreau. Dr. Clark observed that women and children were drinking hard cider, beer, and wine. In 1808, he organized the first temperance society in the United States. In 1820, he served as representative to the state assembly. In 1833, he moved to Glens Falls, opening a drugstore with Dr. Bethuel Peck. Upon his retirement, he returned to his Moreau farm.

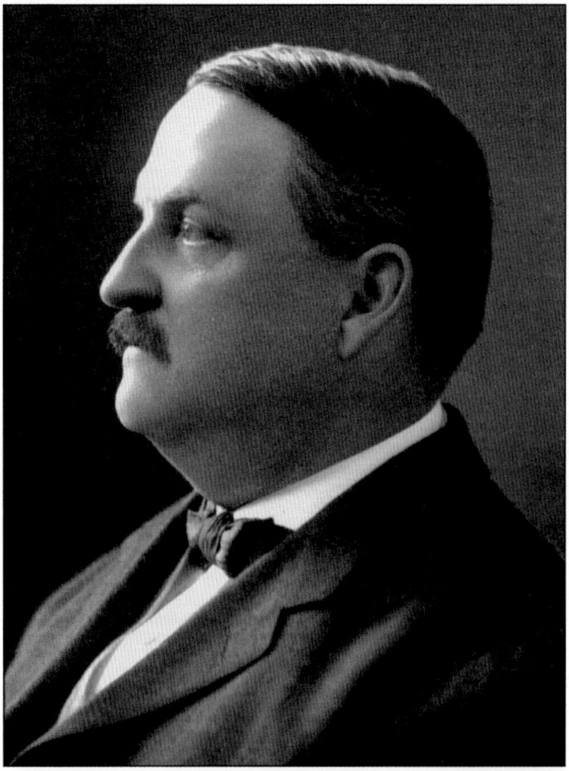

Charles Cool, 1858–1932, began the Cool Insuring Company in 1879 where he remained most of his life. As village president, he served on the committee to draft the city charter that left much power in the hands of the mayor. He won the election for mayor of the new "city" in 1908, when both Democratic and Republican parties endorsed him.

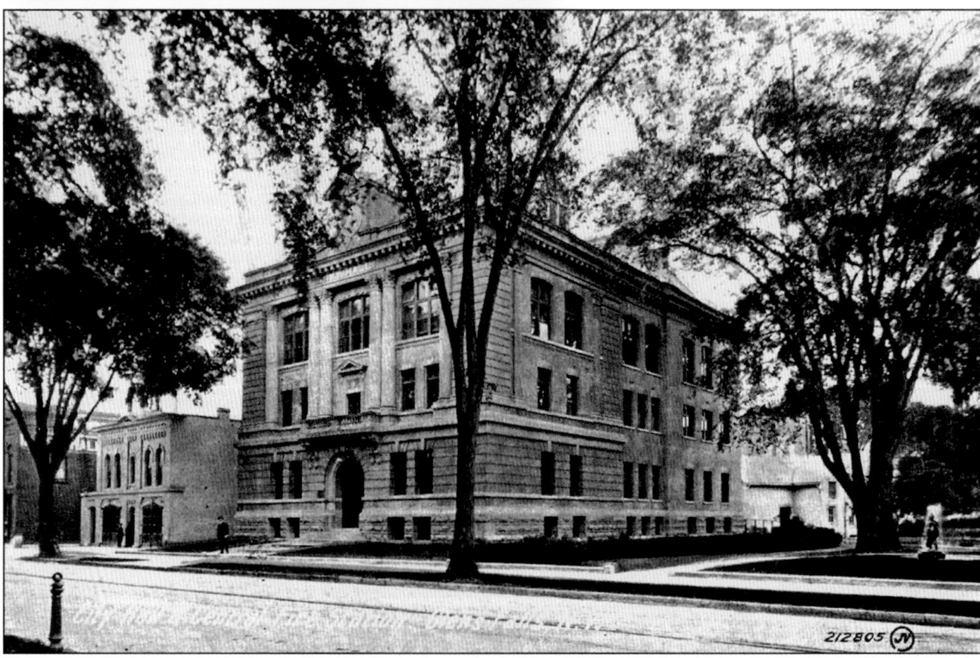

As the first mayor, he administered from the city hall (shown) as the village was incorporated in that year. During his last year in office, he set up the first recreation department. This allowed for the development of sports fields in Crandall Park, Haviland's Cove, and East Field. This legacy lives on today. Cool died at home in 1932 at the age of 74.

Keyes Cool, 1795–1889, was born in Vergennes, Vermont. He arrived in Glens Falls in 1828 and soon involved himself in the lumber business. He was also the first to ship limestone from the area on the newly-constructed Feeder Canal. New York City was developing and needed raw material from the area. He specialized in construction of buildings and making cabinets.

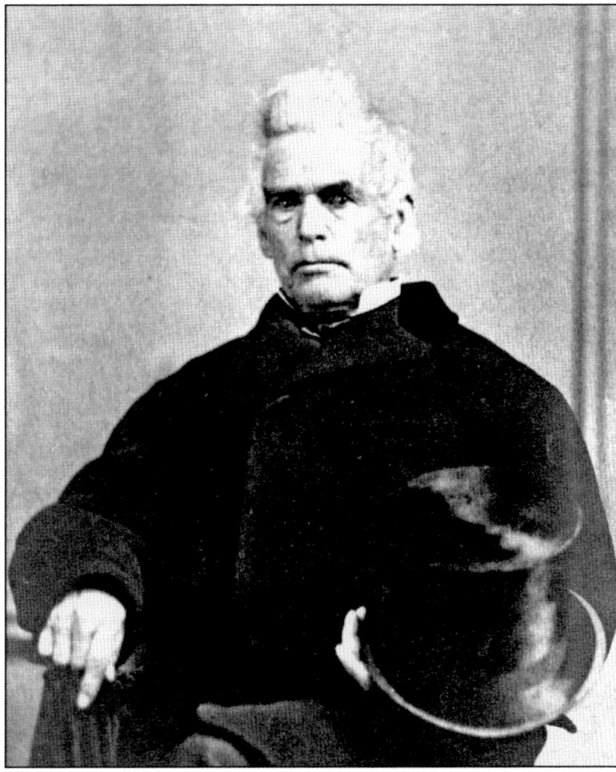

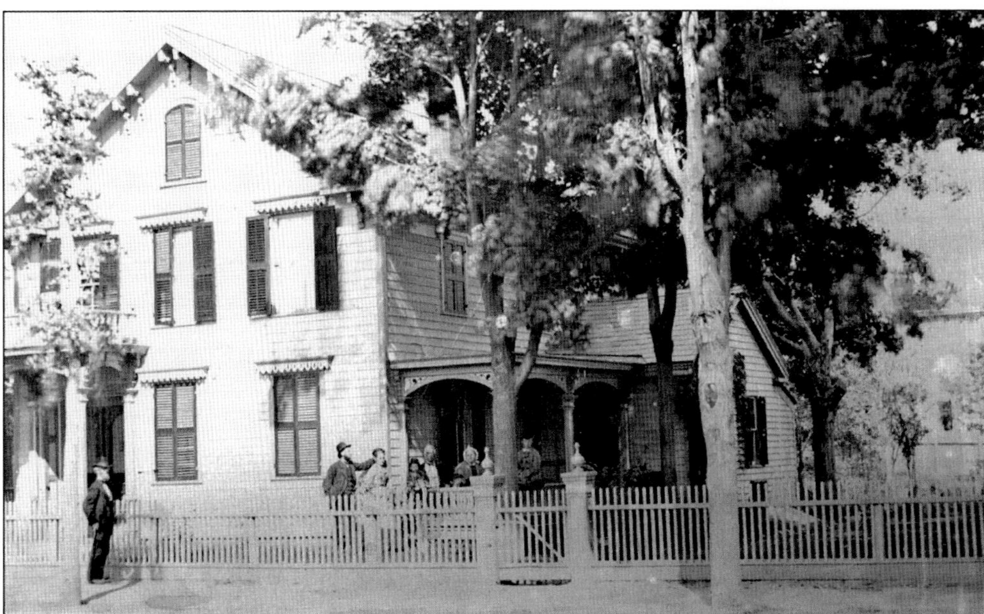

The Cool homestead was built at 50 Warren Street in 1830, shown here. There were two other homes on the property built for his son Joseph and grandson Charles. Six generations of the family lived in these houses. Keyes built the first Methodist church in Glens Falls on Church Street for a total of $1,500. It was known as the Old Stone Church, which remained there from 1829 until 1847.

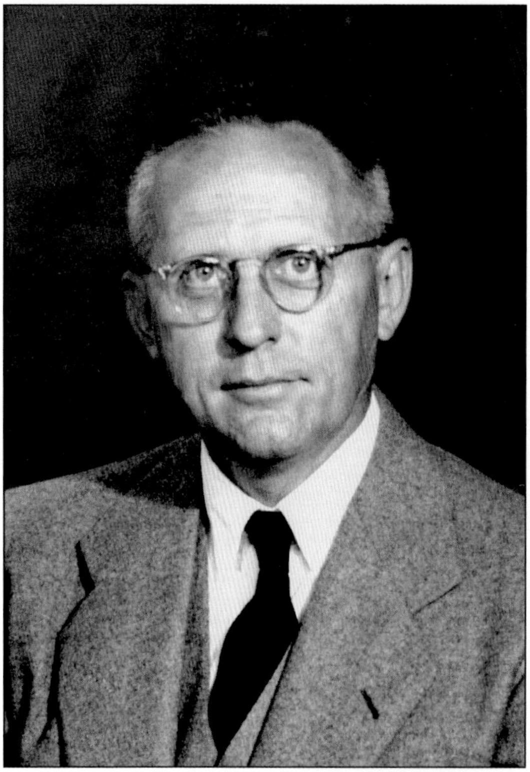

Douglas Crockwell, 1904–1968, was born in Ohio and attended art schools in the Midwest. He arrived in Glens Falls in 1933, the year his first *Saturday Evening Post* cover was accepted. After his marriage to Margaret Braman, they settled on 160 acres on East Sanford Street, part of which is now the Glens Falls Swim and Tennis Club. Crockwell's community involvements included chamber of commerce director; member of the Civil Service Committee, board of education, and city planning board; and director of the Hyde Collection. Known for his magazine advertisements (sample shown below), wartime posters, and *Saturday Evening Post* covers using local models, he also experimented with animated motion pictures. One, *The Glens Falls Sequence,* won at the 1955 Illinois Film Festival. Because his style was similar to his contemporary Norman Rockwell, he signed his artwork "Douglas" in deference to Rockwell.

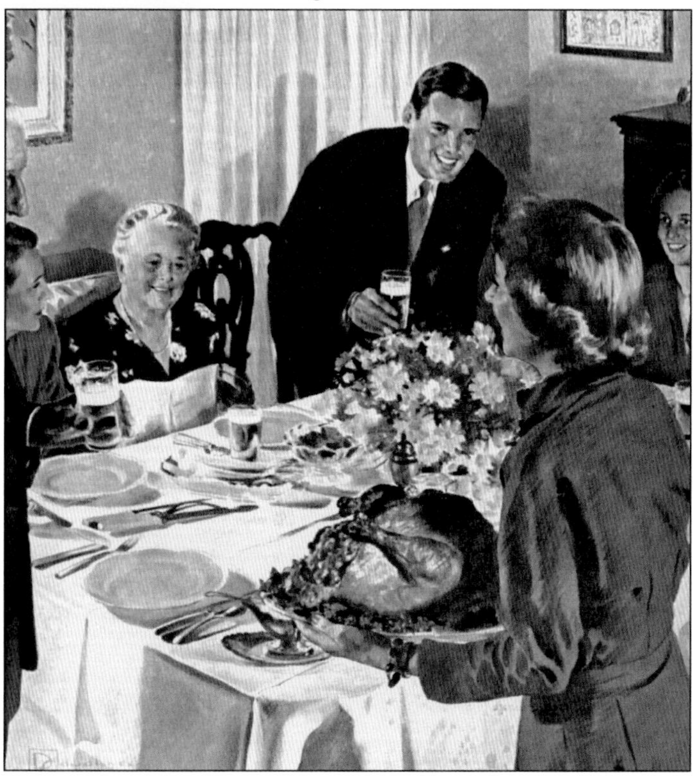

John Alden Dix, 1860–1928, was born at home on Ridge Street in Glens Falls (shown below in 1997). He attended school in Glens Falls and continued on to Cornell University, excelling in sports and its social life but not graduating. He was director of the Glens Falls Trust but resigned to run for governor in 1906. Dix owned extensive Adirondack timberlands with Dr. Lemon Thomson and as a staunch conservationist advocated a new tree planted for every one cut. He was known for his business acumen rather than his political knowledge. However, he was Democratic Party chairman for Washington County and New York State. In 1889, he married Thomson's daughter Gertrude and resided in Thomson, New York. Dix was elected 41st governor of New York State for the 1911–1912 term. He later lost his fortune, home, and business. He went on to become a minor clerk in the state offices in Albany.

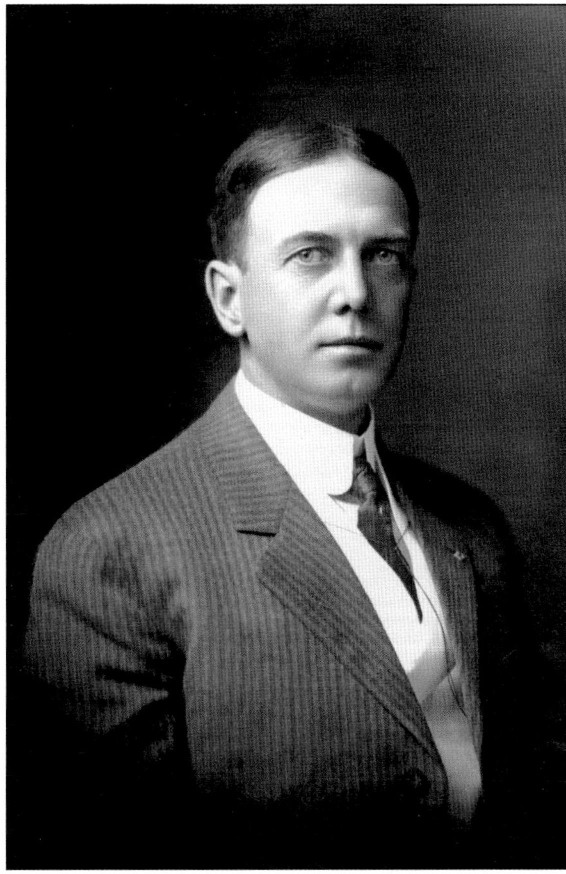

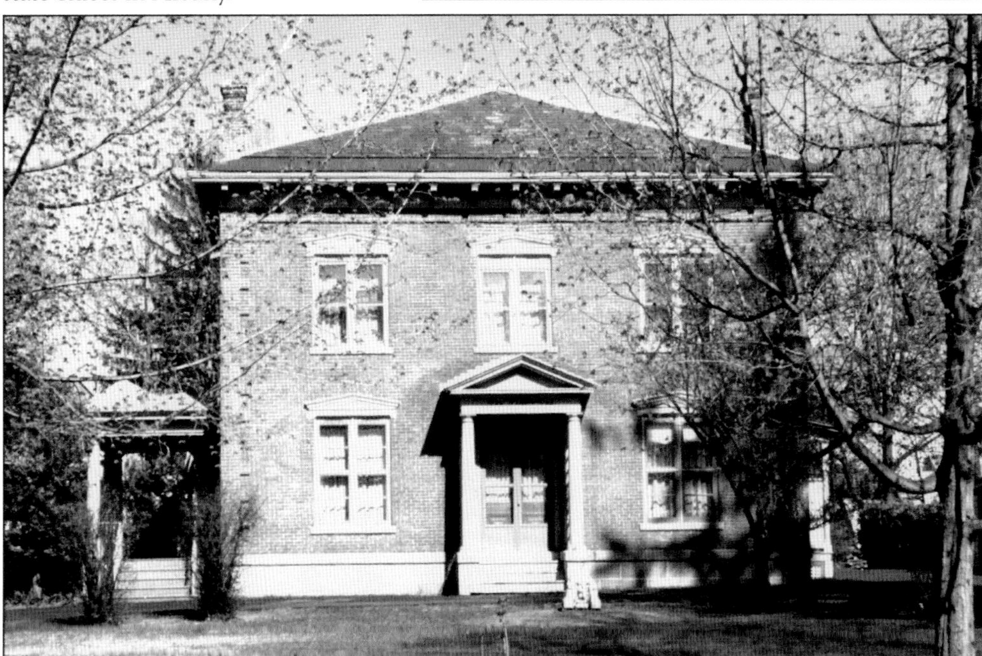

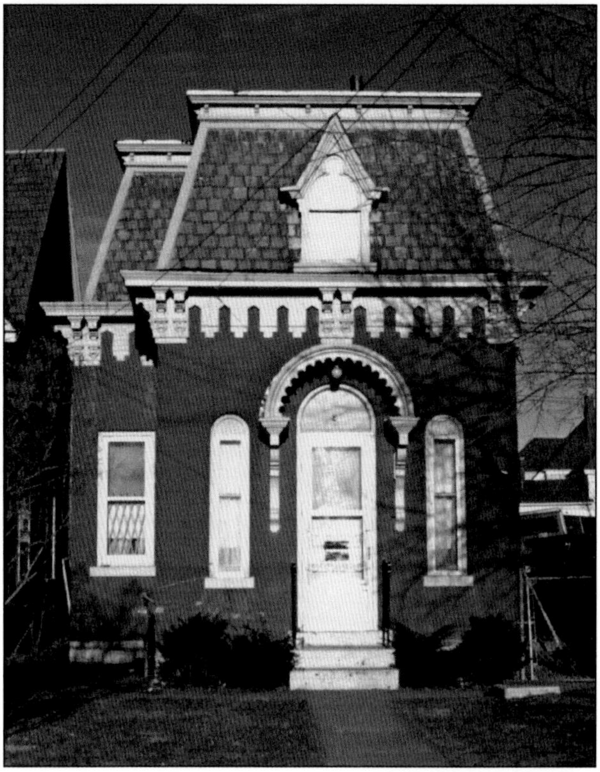

James Ferguson, M.D., 1818–1892, graduated from the Academy of Medicine in Castleton, Vermont, in 1841 and moved to Glens Falls 10 years later. He lived on Warren Street and had his office in a miniature-sized Victorian building, seen at left, around the corner at 1 Culvert Street. In 1877, Ferguson bought Prospect Mountain in Lake George, and for a time he referred to it as Mount Ferguson. He constructed a carriage road to the summit where he erected a hotel. However, in 1880, it was destroyed in a forest fire, and when it was rebuilt, it was sold to William Peck. Dr. Ferguson is buried in the Glens Falls Cemetery, and his monument, seen below, is a statue of him standing on a large boulder.

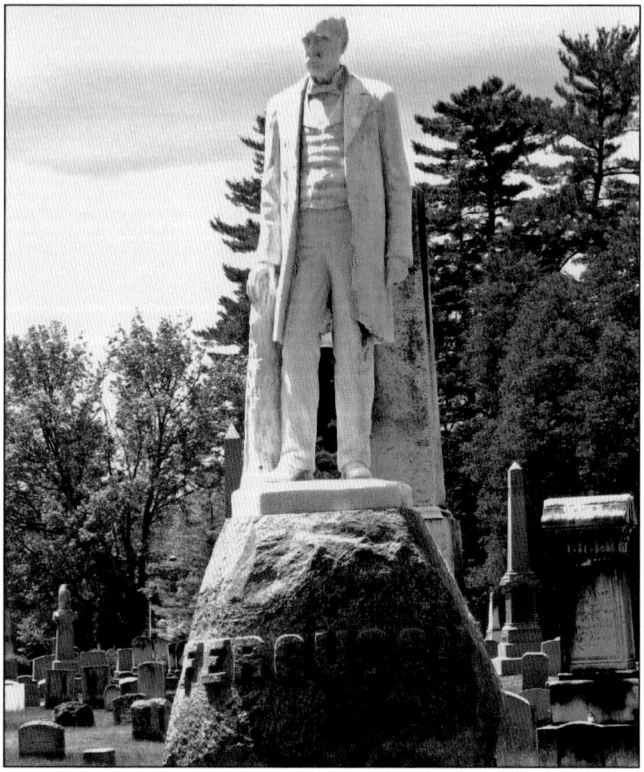

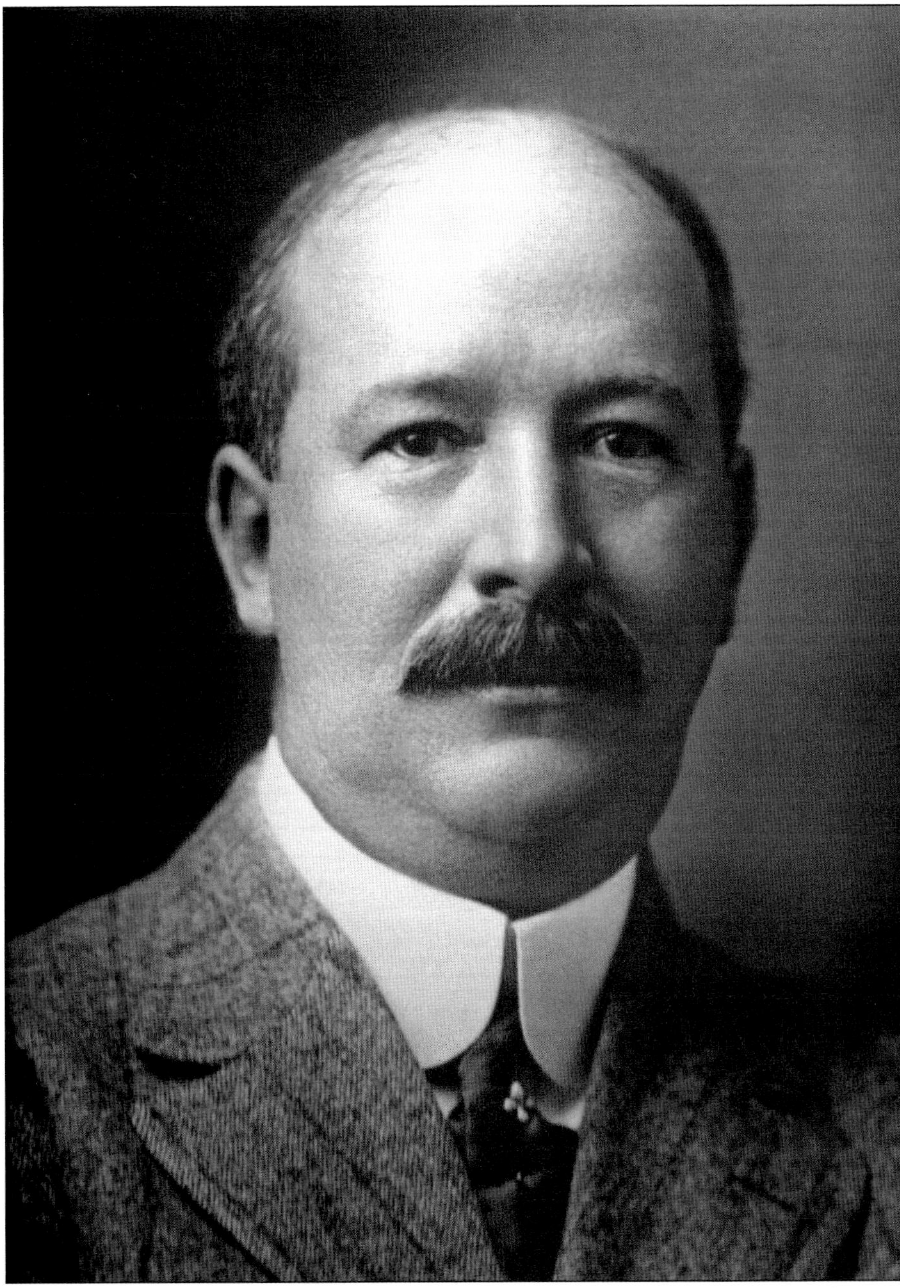

Thomas Henning, M.D., 1863–1949, was born in North Argyle to Rev. William and Jane Irwin Henning but went to live with his uncle in Ireland at the age of 16. Most of his education was acquired there, graduating from Queens College in Galway and Royal College of Physicians and Surgeons in London in 1890. Henning was registered as a practicing physician in Warren County from 1891 until 1928. He was on the consulting staff of the Glens Falls Hospital but also had an office at 67 Ridge Street. Henning was associated with Dr. James Ferguson, whose practice he eventually took over. He was a member of the Warren County Medical Society starting in 1900. He married his first wife, Emma Roberson, in 1896, and his second wife, Ethlyn Goodman, in 1922. Dr. Henning is buried in the Glens Falls Cemetery on Bay Street.

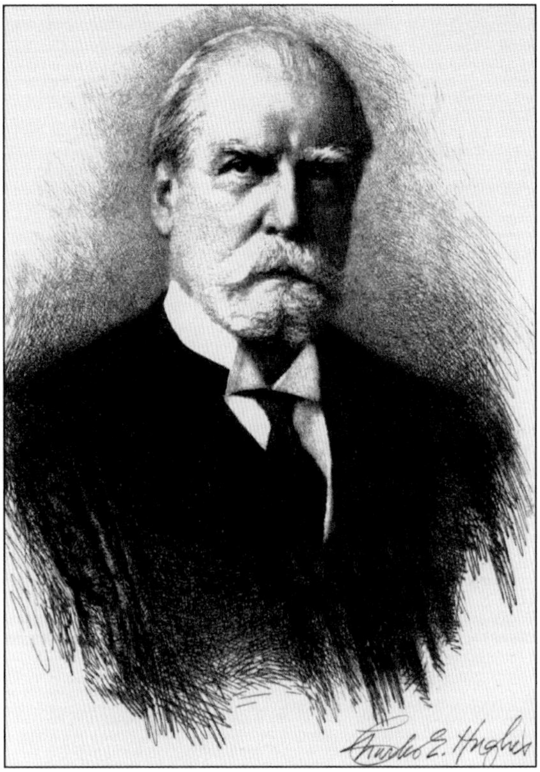

Charles Evan Hughes, 1862–1948, was born to Rev. David Charles and Mary Connelly Hughes, pastor of the First Baptist Church on Maple Street. Charles, a very bright child, was reading at age 3 and by age 6, set up an educational plan of study, finishing high school by age 11. He attended Madison College (now Colgate University) and then Brown University. He had a celebrated law practice in New York City.

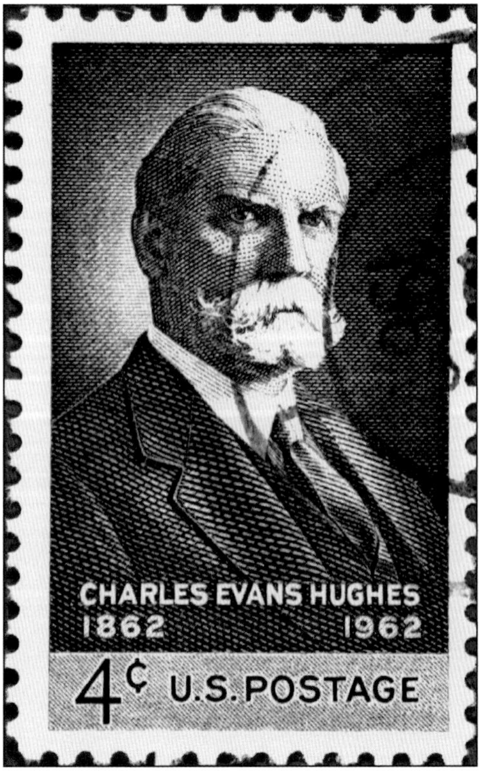

Hughes turned down the opportunity to run for mayor of New York City, instead running for governor of the state. As governor in 1908, he signed the charter for Glens Falls to become a city. He was careful to protect the interests of farmers and the labor population. In 1962, he was honored with a stamp for the 100th anniversary of his birth, shown here.

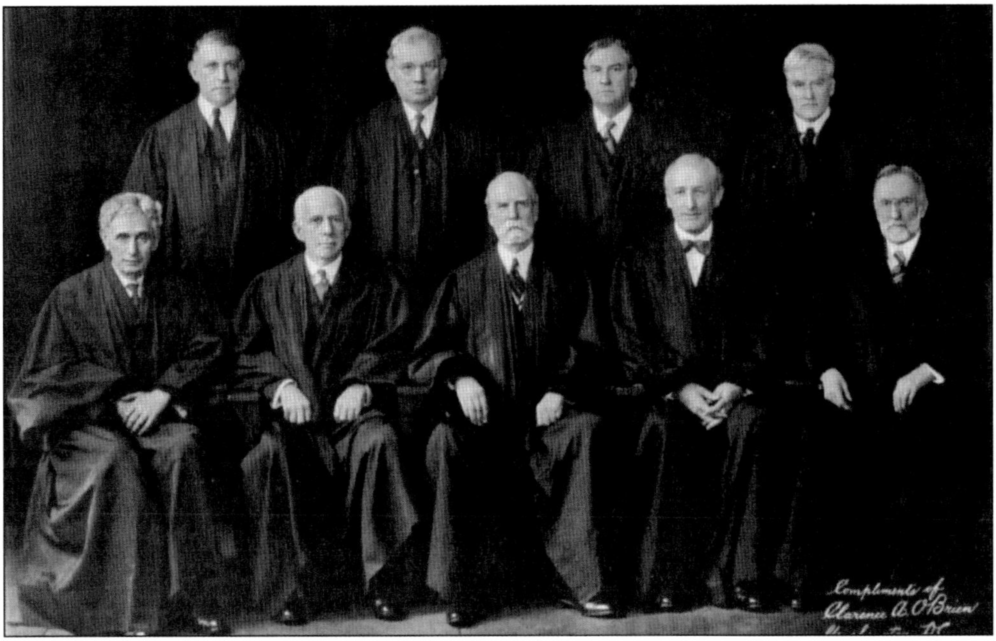

Hughes argued that racetrack betting was illegal, thus affecting racing in Saratoga. He signed legislation putting many racetracks out of business, also making "oral betting" illegal. Saratoga saw no racing in 1911 and 1912. After two terms, he was appointed associate justice of the U.S. Supreme Court, resigning in 1916 to run for president of the United States but losing at the electoral level. Hughes served as secretary of state in the Harding and Coolidge administrations. In 1930, Pres. Herbert Hoover named him chief justice where he served from 1930 to 1941 as a strict interpreter of the Constitution. He regulated the railroad industry so it provided inexpensive, nondiscriminatory service, thus beginning the Public Service Commission. Hughes returned to the area for two years to be near his ailing daughter until her death. His childhood home has been moved to 16 Center Street (below).

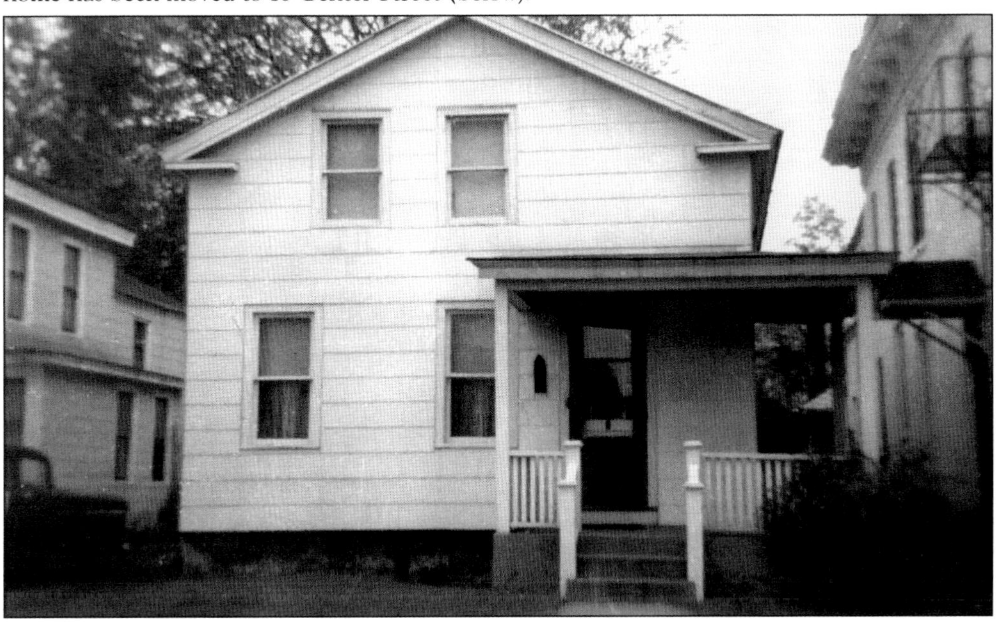

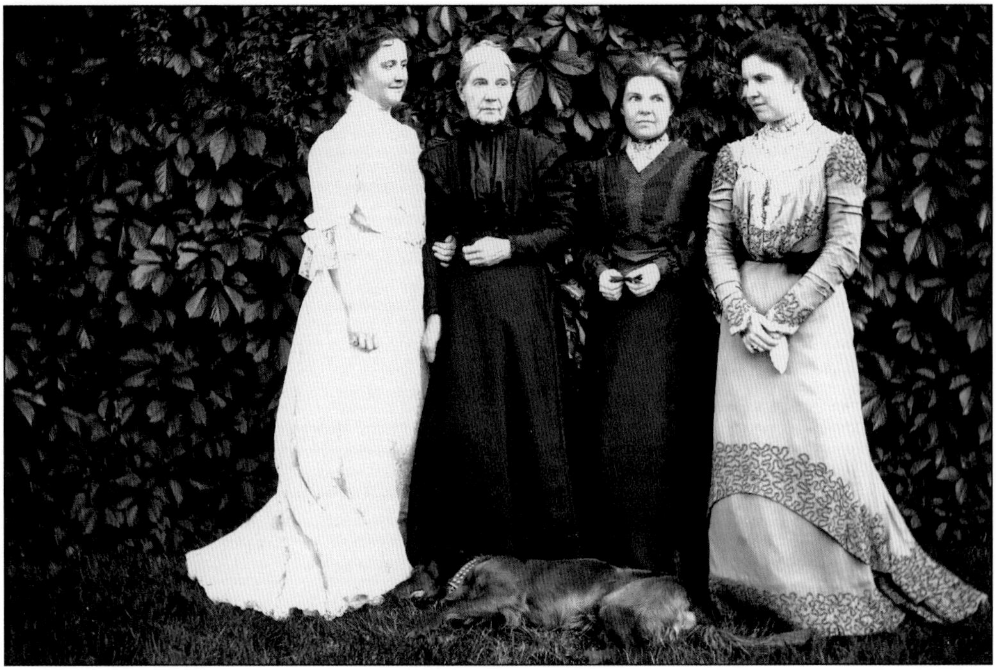

Charlotte Pruyn Hyde, 1867–1963, daughter of Samuel Pruyn, attended schools in the area but finished her education in Boston, where she developed a keen interest in books, art, and cultural activities. In the photograph she is shown second from the right with her sisters and mother. She married Louis Hyde in 1901 after a long courtship. Their home reflected the love of European and especially Italian renaissance. Windowless walls allowed for the display of their art and antique collections, and a large indoor courtyard reflected a Florentine villa. Louis has a place in Glens Falls history through his publishing of the book *History of Glens Falls, New York and Its Settlement.* After Louis's death, Charlotte allowed the public to visit various areas of the home, and upon her death, it was turned into a first-class, world-famous museum, seen below.

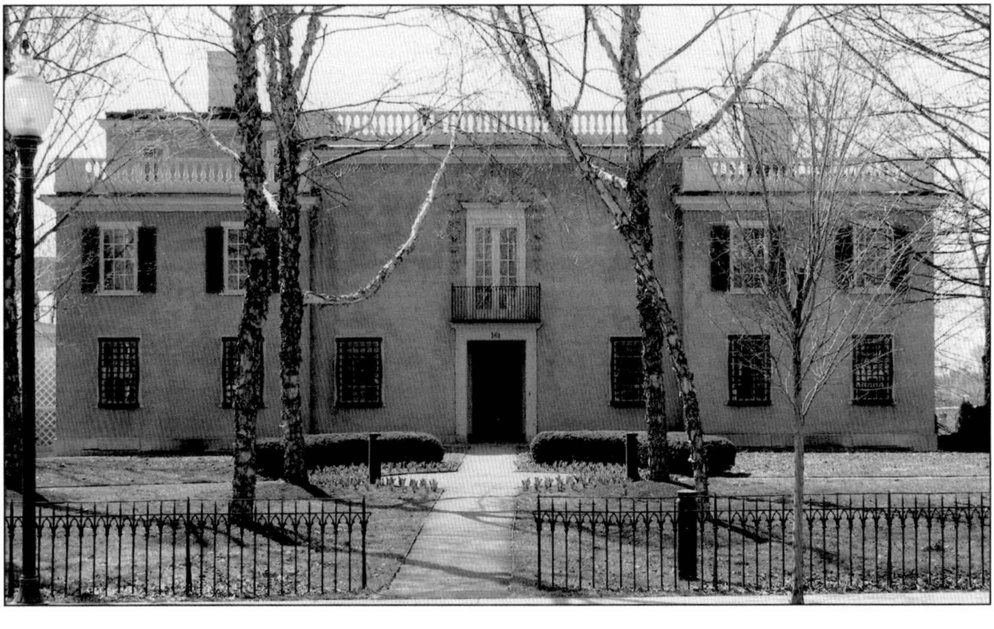

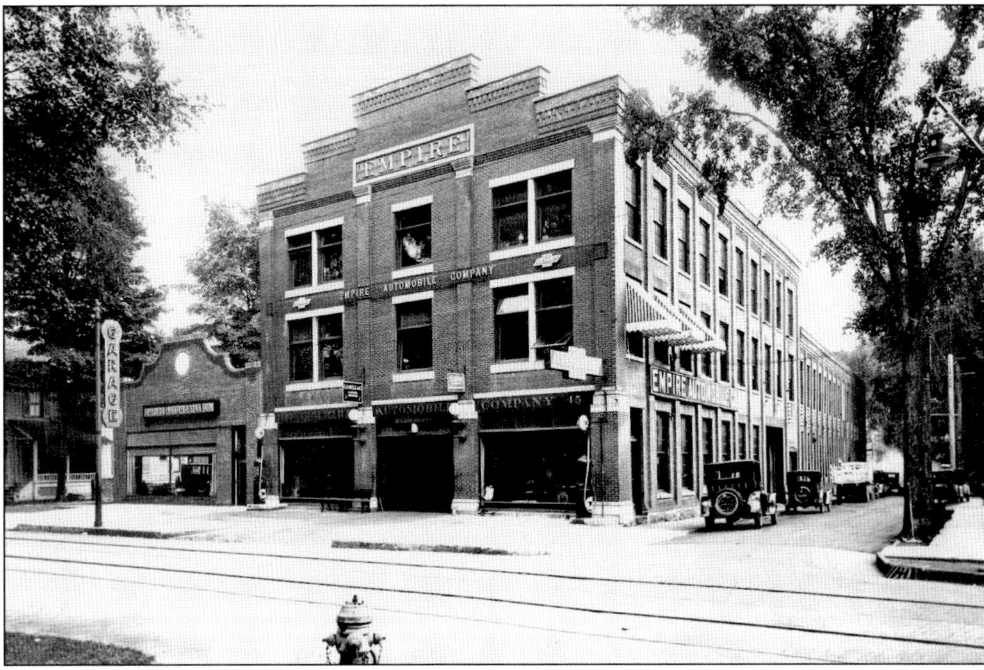

Edward Joubert, who died in 1890, was a skilled carriage maker, but little is known of his early life. With $50 in borrowed money, Edward Joubert and J. Hyler White formed a company, Joubert and White, that was to attain international acclaim. The uniqueness of his wagons was the suspension system that made for a more comfortable ride. His building is shown at a later date when it had become Empire Automobile.

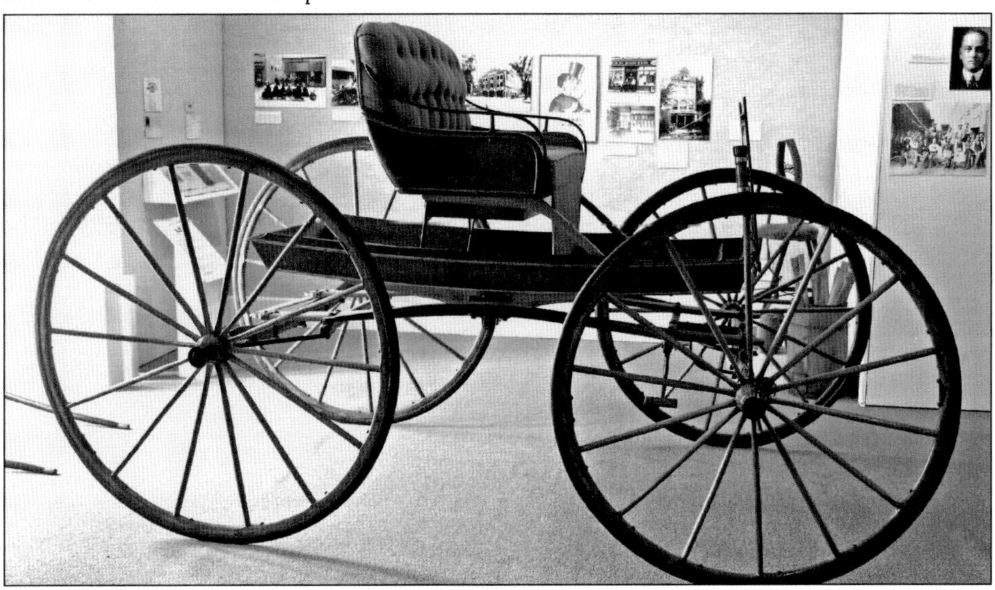

Joubert's wagons varied from simple buckboards to stately carriages, purchased by families with names such as Astor, Vanderbilt, Morgan, Rockefeller, Trask, Carnegie, and Tiffany, as well as Lord Aberdeen of Canada and Lord Brassey of England. Wagons were also sold in Italy, France, and Scotland. An example of a Joubert and White Wagon can be seen at the Chapman Historical Museum in Glens Falls (shown). Joubert died in 1890, leaving the business to his partner.

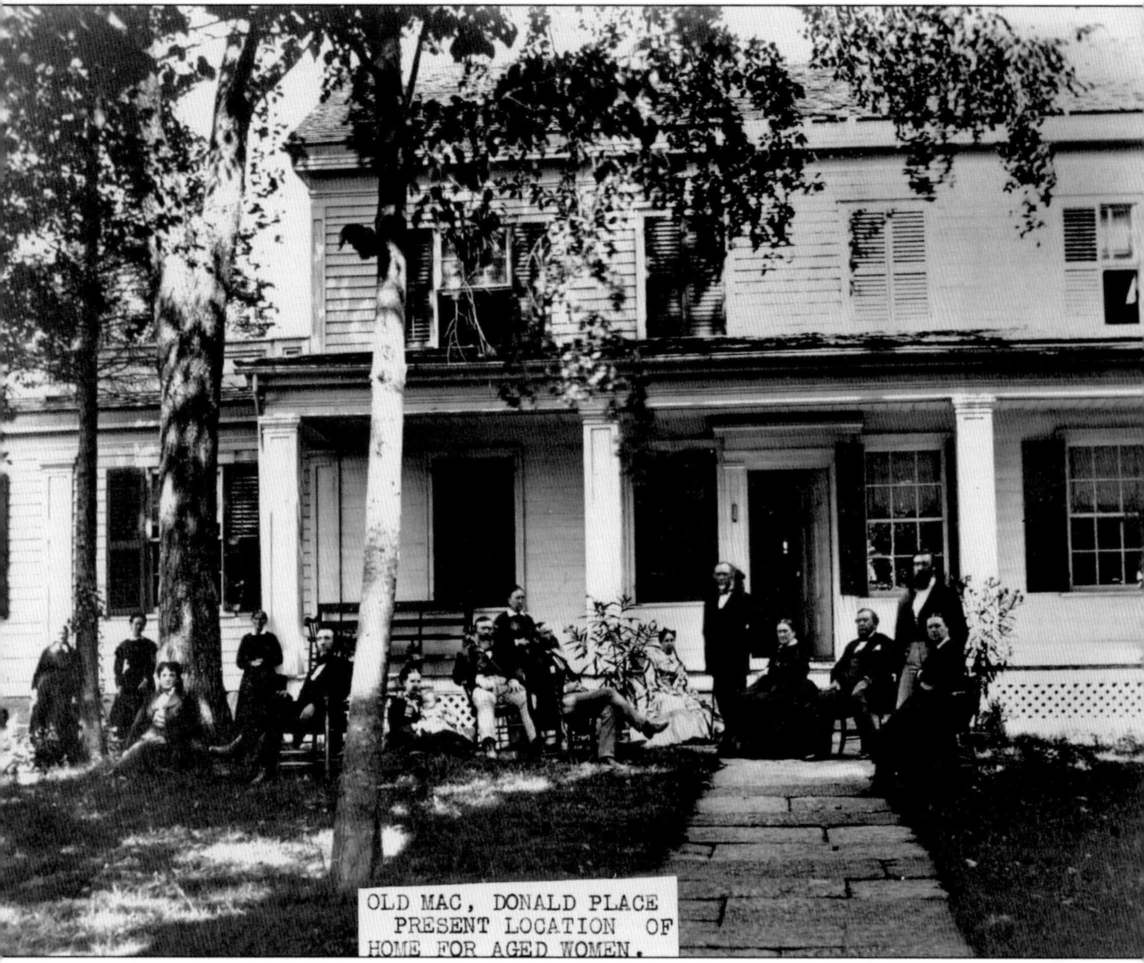

William McDonald, 1784–1870, was born in Connecticut but moved to the "Ridge" in Queensbury at the age of eight. He was sent back to Connecticut in order to get a good education. When he returned to the area, he became an accountant for his uncle David Sandford. From 1808 through 1820, McDonald ran a business in Waterford, returning again to run a mercantile on the Ridge Road. During this time he began his family that included 11 children; however, 3 died very young. In 1823, he bought the farm owned by Abraham Wing on Warren Street, turning it into an elegant mansion for its time (shown with family). In 1821, he was elected to the New York State Assembly and was reelected three more times. McDonald was active in the Church of the Messiah and served as a village trustee. He was able to secure the funding necessary for the survey and construction of the Feeder Canal. The opening of the canal introduced greater prosperity to Glens Falls and made it part of the "Great American Canal Era."

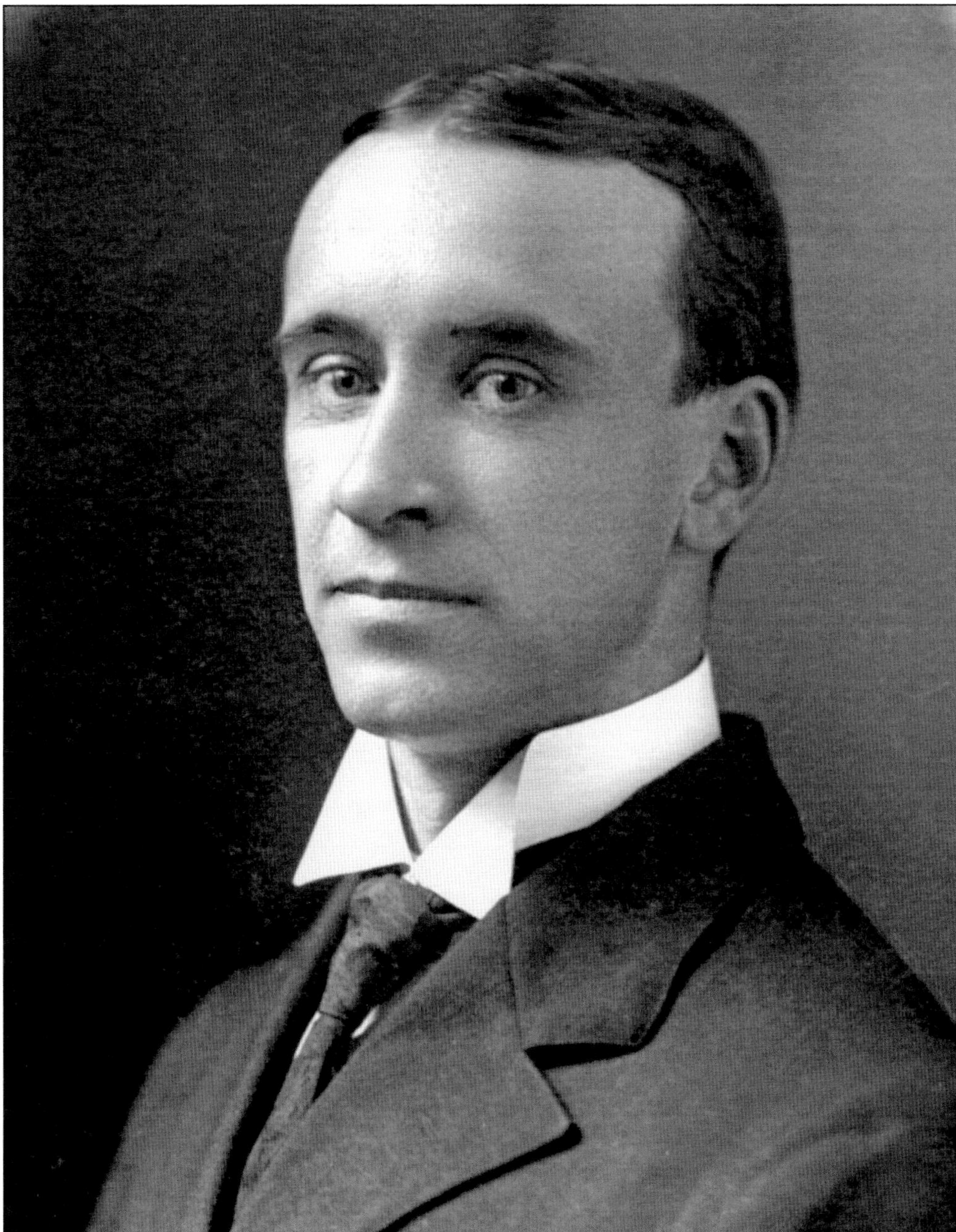

J. Ernest Miller, 1875–1968, was born of Irish immigrant parents on Miller Hill in Queensbury. He attended a one-room school on Miller Hill and then the Glens Falls Academy. Miller, along with his brother Frank and sister H. Louise, ran the Miller Brother's Garage at 12–14 Maple Street beginning in 1902. They sold Edison and Victor talking machines and bicycles. They expanded to become the first Buick dealership in the area and ran it for 39 years. It was the third-oldest dealership in the country. They also owned the first roller-skating rink in northern New York. He retired from the agency but returned to work nine years later as a salesman for the Cortright Buick dealership. Miller was, at one point, the oldest active member of the YMCA. Present-day Aviation Road was once called Miller Hill Road after the family.

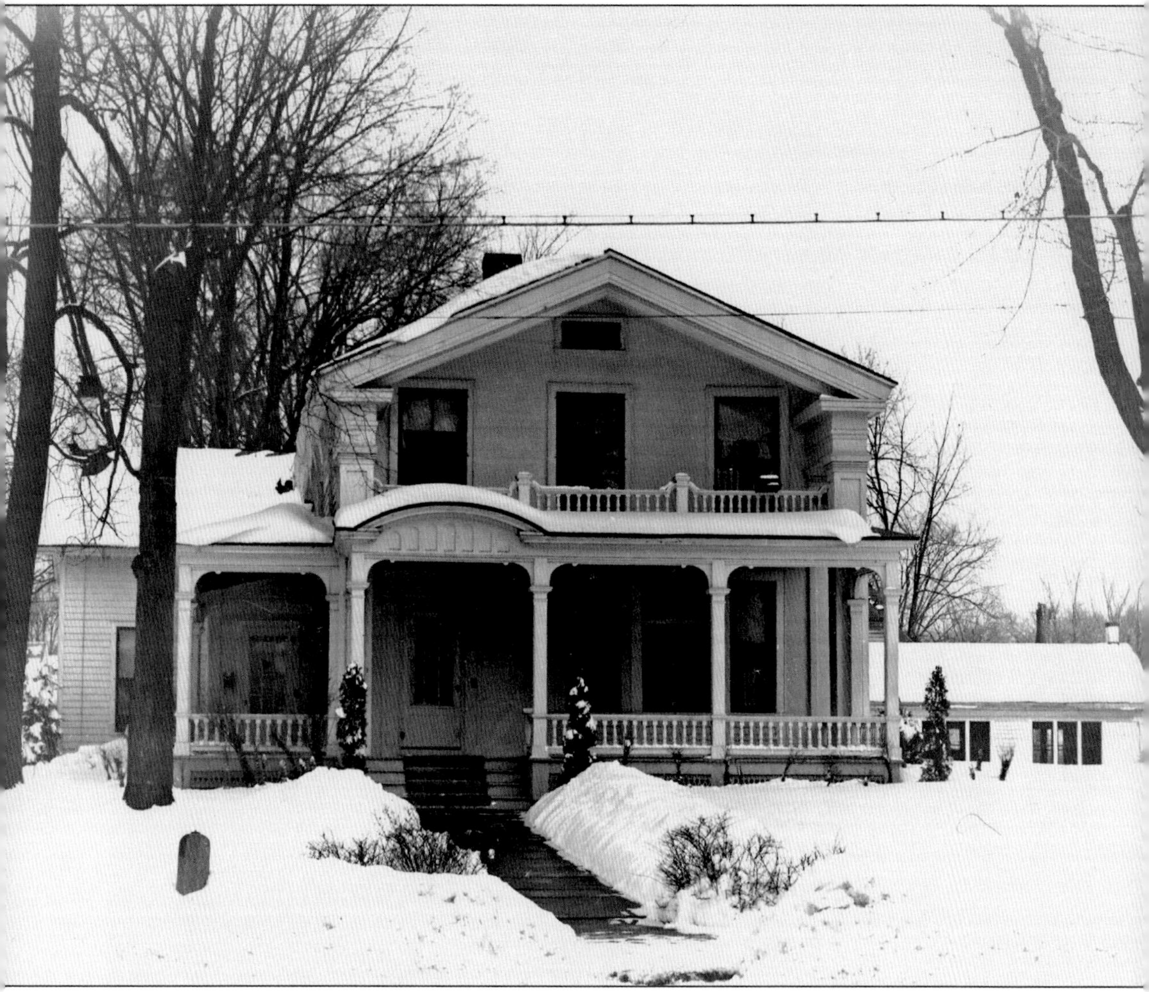

Alonzo Morgan, 1799–1889, came to Glens Falls from Vermont in 1813 to live with his stepfather, Henry Spencer, and learn saddle and harness making. Henry Spencer's business failed, and Alonzo was left with the failure. He bought and sold properties and was able to develop new streets throughout the village. He is responsible for making the village a truly vibrant, flourishing place to live. His Greek Revival–style home on Maple Street (shown with external changes) was near the center of his developments on Center, Maple, Lawrence, and Oak Streets. He also developed the areas around Elm and Park Streets. He served as president of the Glens Falls Insurance Company and helped establish the first library in the Rogers and Cowles Store at the corner of Park and Glen Streets. Although Morgan spent a great deal of time developing various areas of the village, he was opposed to the creation of a public water system. More than anyone, he was responsible for the rapid development of Glens Falls.

Jones Ordway, 1818–1890, (also known as Jonas) began working as a woodsman but also did canal work. He was married in 1835 and had two children. Five years later, he went into the hotel business, farmed, and lumbered in the North River area. He bought woodlands in four different counties and in 1873 organized the Morgan Lumber Company as a successor to the Abraham Wing mill. He was president of the Glens Falls Gas and Light Company. In 1890, he donated $50,000 toward a YMCA at 151 Glen Street that would "meet the needs of young men and boys." It opened in 1892 and was named Ordway Hall in his honor. The Ordway home was at 86 Warren Street (below). His monument is the tallest in the Glens Falls Cemetery, but alas, his name is misspelled on it.

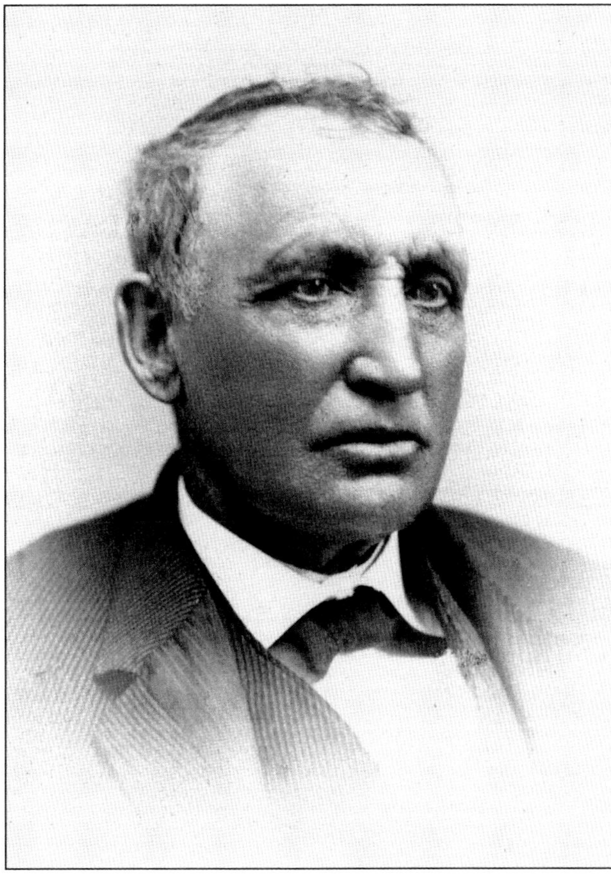

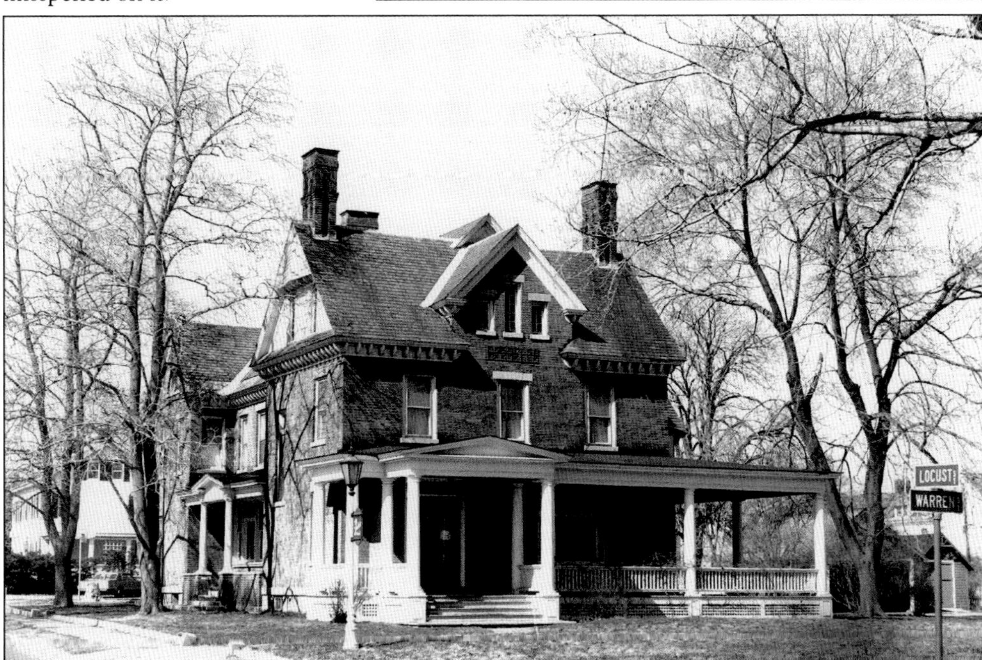

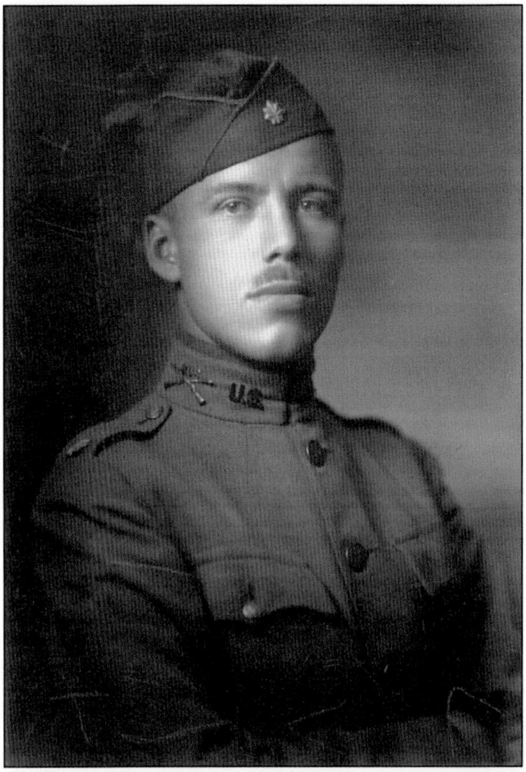

Robert Patterson, 1891–1952, was born in Glens Falls and graduated from the Glens Falls High School and later from Union College and Harvard Law School. He practiced law for a year and then volunteered as a private in the army on the Mexican border. Two years later on the French front, he received a Purple Heart, the Silver Star, two citations for gallantry, and the Distinguished Service Cross.

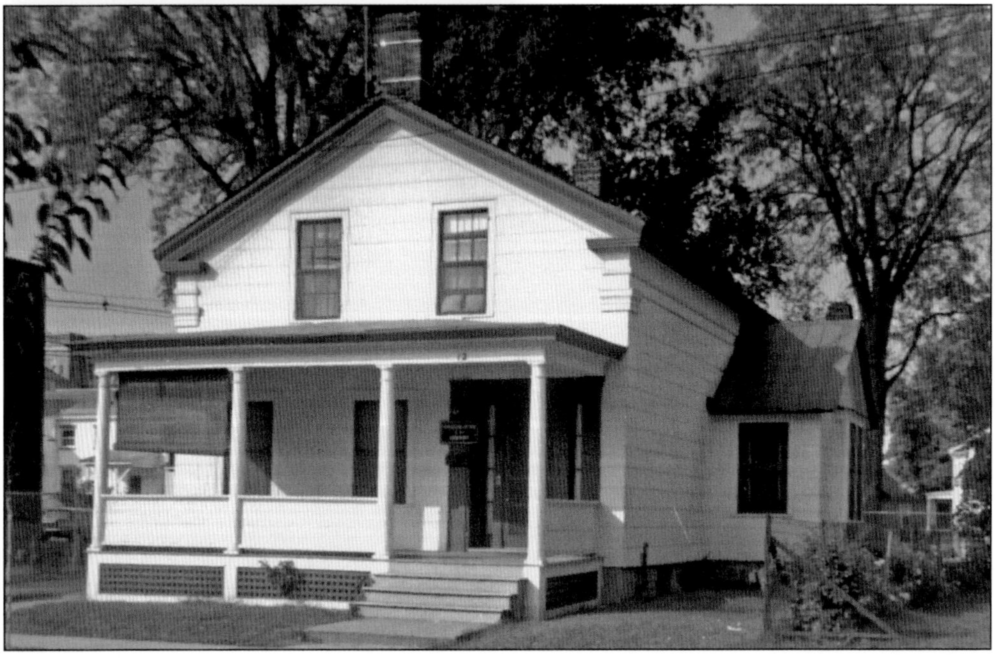

Patterson's young life was spent at 12 Center Street (shown), which is on the National Register of Historic Places, but the family moved to 69 Warren Street, where he lived for many years. That home was torn down to build the U.S. post office that contained the army recruiting office. That facility was named the Robert P. Patterson Army Reserve Center.

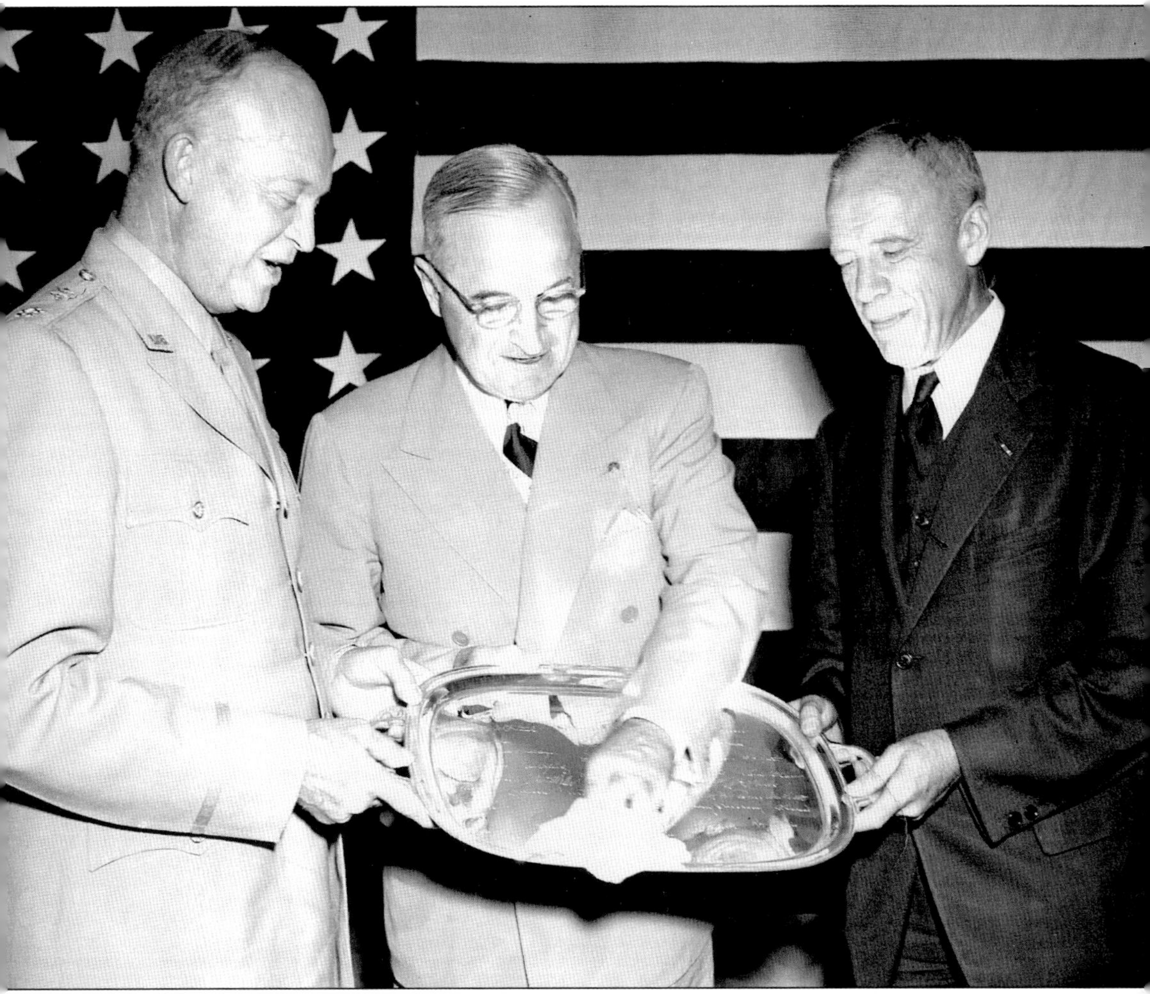

Patterson became a federal district judge in 1930, appointed by Republican president Herbert Hoover. Democratic president Franklin Roosevelt raised him to the circuit court of appeals in 1939. He resigned his position to volunteer in the military. In 1940, he was summoned to the White House and elevated to the rank of undersecretary of war. Pres. Harry S. Truman offered him a choice of becoming a justice on the U.S. Supreme Court or secretary of war in 1947. Patterson chose the more challenging military position. He is remembered for his focus on duty to his country. He was responsible for Glens Falls being named "Hometown U.S.A." in a series of *Look* magazine articles. At a farewell banquet in the Pentagon building in Washington, D.C., Truman (center) and Gen. Dwight D. Eisenhower (left) both honored Patterson (right) on his retirement with a silver tray. Truman referred to Patterson as "a good and loyal soldier." Patterson died in a plane crash while landing in New York City and is buried in Arlington National Cemetery.

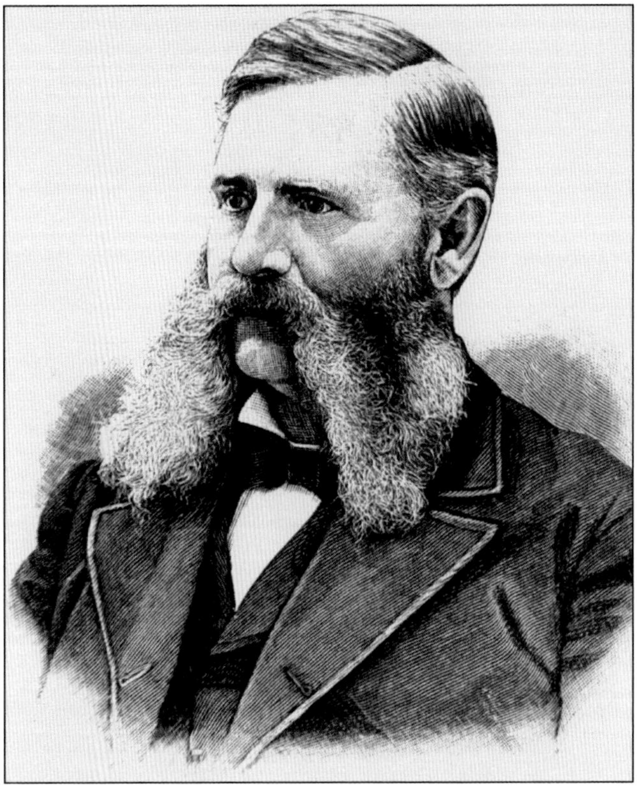

Buell Streeter, M.D., 1832–1900, started working as a child. He was a blacksmith apprentice, a farmhand, and a driver on the Erie Canal. After completing his schooling in 1859, he began practicing medicine and surgery. During the Civil War he was a surgeon in the 4th New York Cavalry, then medical director in the Army of the Shenandoah. He saw action at Bull Run, Cedar Mountain, and Gettysburg.

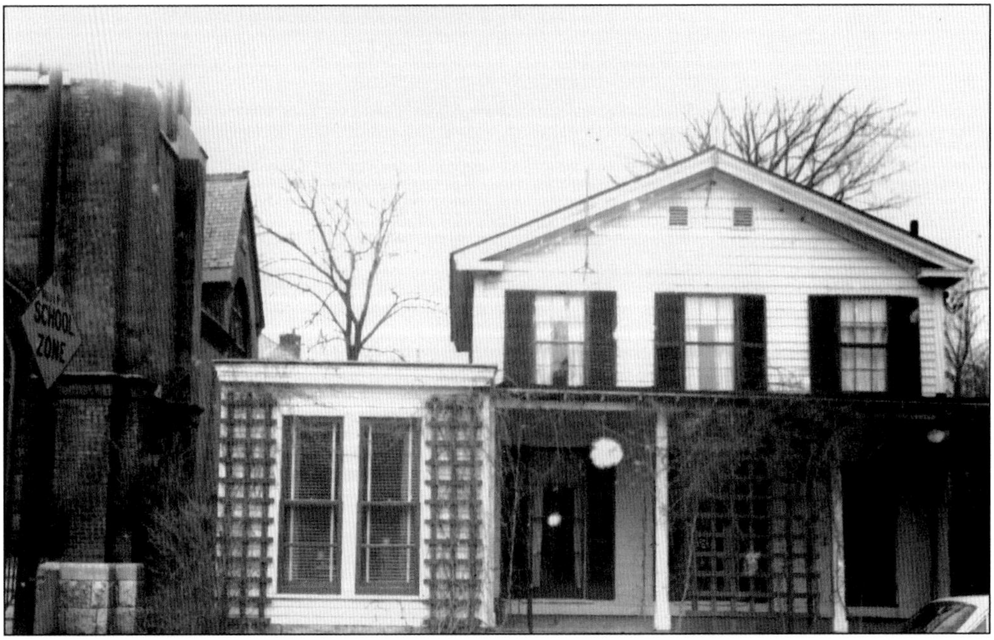

After the Civil War, Dr. Buell Streeter set up practice in his home on Maple Street (shown). He was the Warren County coroner for several terms. He was also president of the Warren County Medical Society, Glens Falls Board of Education, and Warren County Agricultural Society. He was a founder of the Glens Falls Union School and one of its trustees for several years.

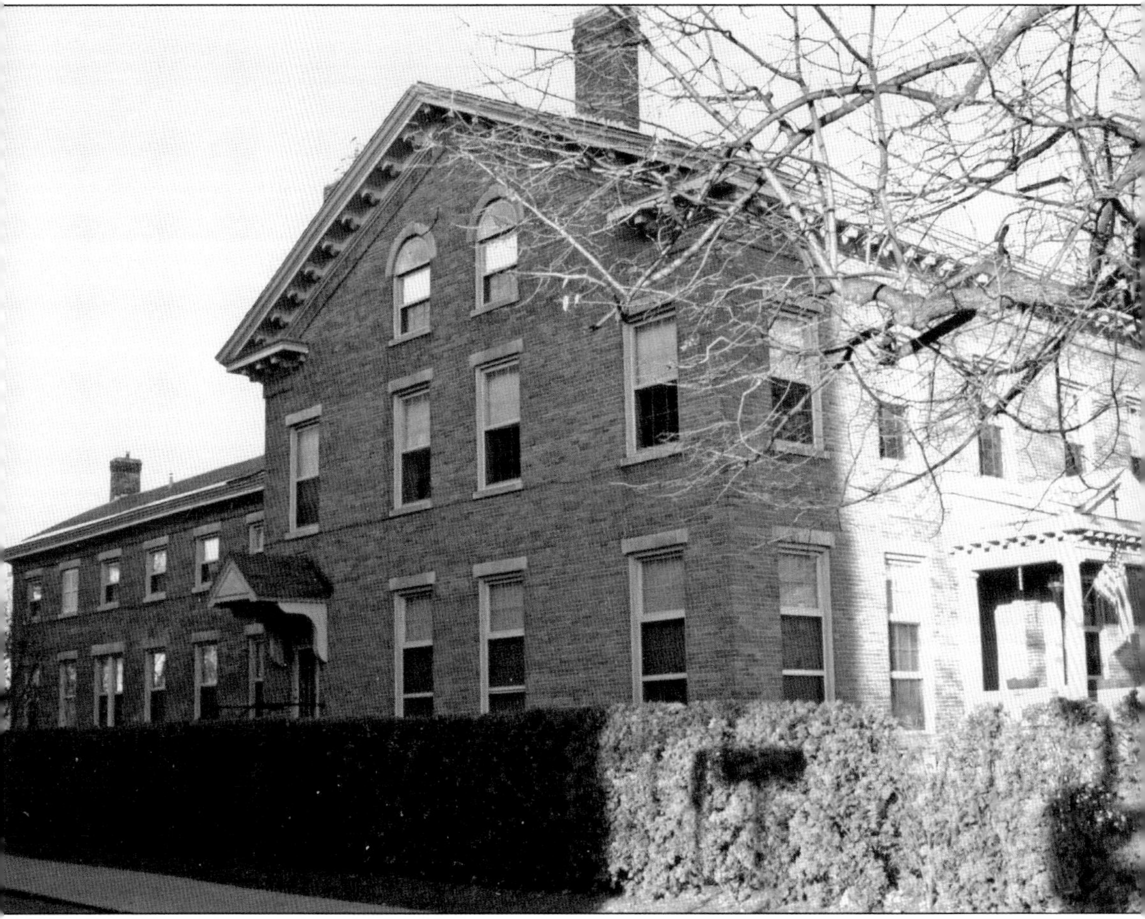

Lemon Thomson, 1857–1920, received his medical degree from Albany Medical College in 1882 and studied surgery in Vienna and Berlin. He returned to Glens Falls and started a hospital in the Colvin Building. When the building burned in 1900, he moved to Bay Street but soon moved to the house at 40 Warren Street. This was considered one of the first hospitals in Glens Falls. While at this location, he returned to Europe three times to continue his studies of surgery. The building is now the rectory of St. Mary's Church (shown). An interesting note about the site is that it survived the 1864 fire that leveled more than 100 building in Glens Falls, but it is said to have scorched beams in the attic to attest to its nearness to the flames. Thomson was also interested in real estate, owning a business block at the corner of Elm and South Streets, along with the Thomson-Bullard Block on Warren Street, and was part owner of the Land-Cement Brick Company. Thomson's daughter married John Alden Dix, future governor of New York State.

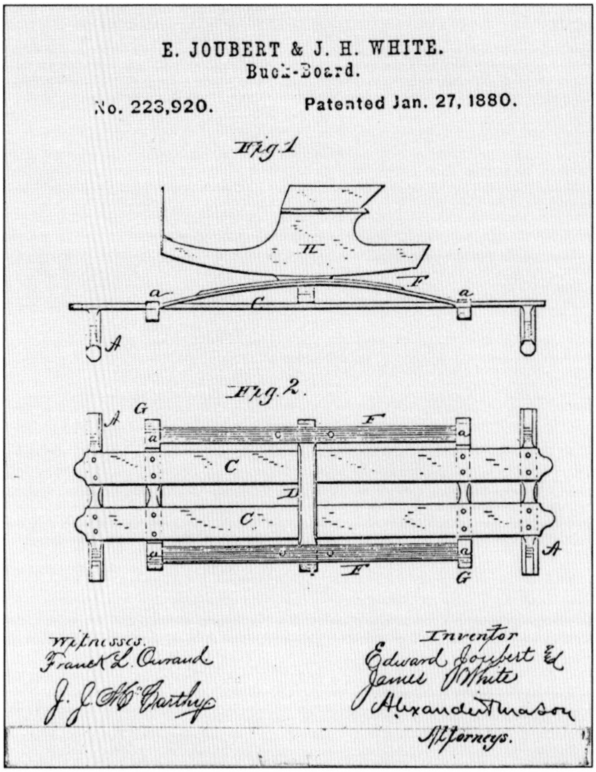

James Huyler White, 1836–1916, came to Glens Falls at the age of 10. He apprenticed for seven years to Edward Joubert, a skilled carriage maker, with whom he later became a partner. Soon after the production of the first "Glens Falls Buckboard," he became the company salesperson. White was considered an influential citizen in the community.

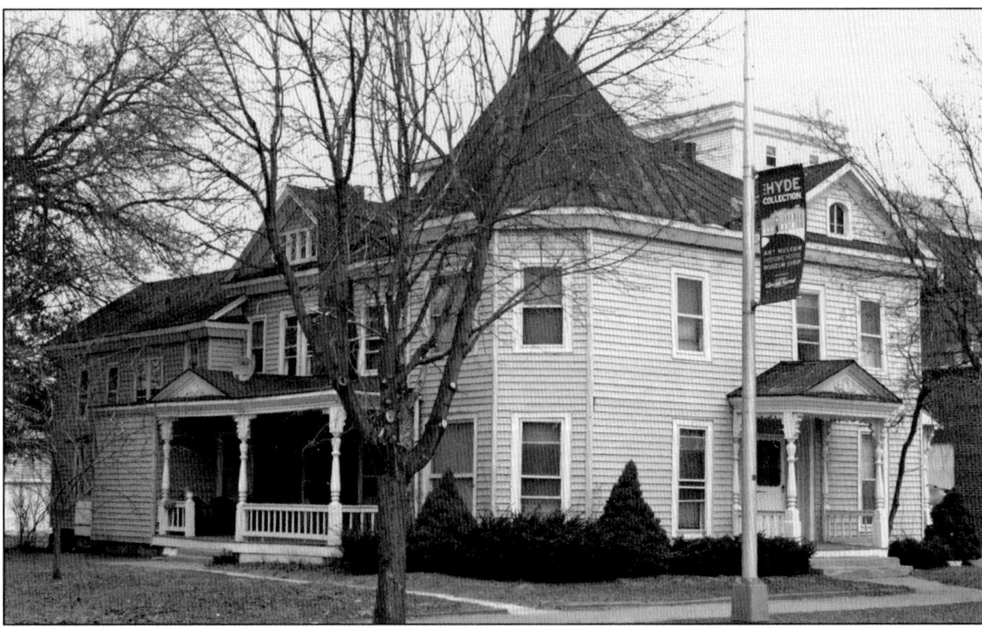

Joubert and White manufactured their line of buckboards at their building on Warren Street beginning in 1864. Their construction made them favorites of the elite in the United States and Europe because of an incorporated suspension system that created a comfortable ride. Carriages were sold to European nobility and prominent families in the United States (see page 71 for the names of families). White lived on Warren Street next to the Glens Falls Academy (shown).

Abraham Wing, 1721–1793, was one of first Quaker settlers in Glens Falls. He built a mill on the Hudson River and owned a tavern at the comer of Warren and Ridge Streets. The area was called Wing's Falls. The land, part of the original Queensbury Patent, had been called "the Corners." Wing's home was a farm on Warren Street on the site of what would become the Glens Falls Home.

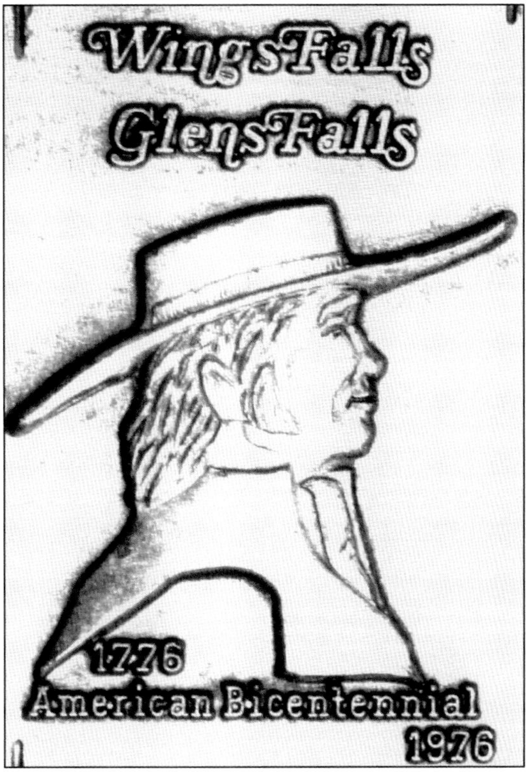

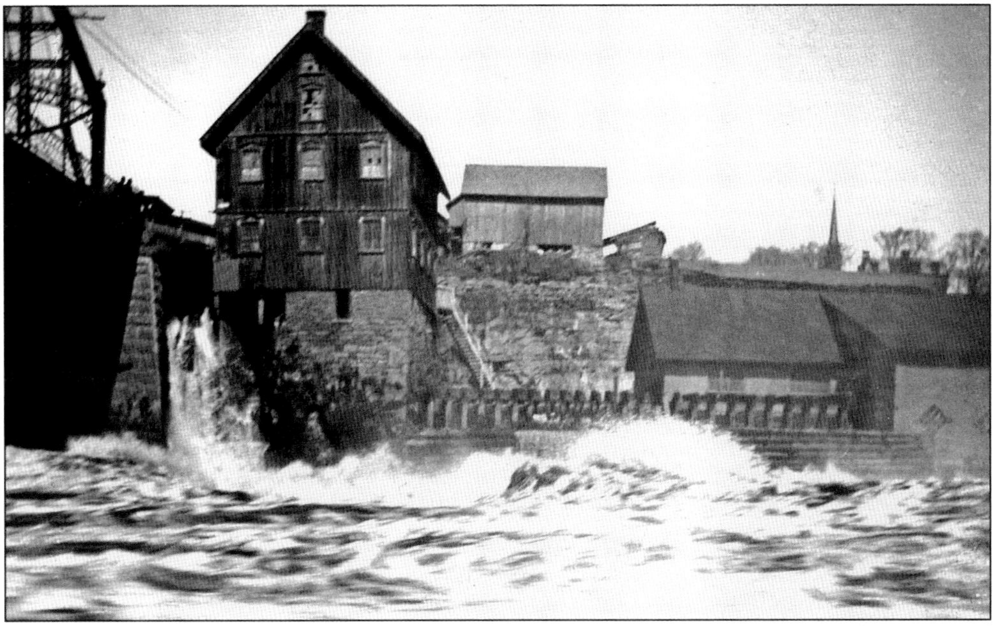

At an early town meeting, Wing was elected moderator, overseer of the poor, and treasurer of the village. He married Antis Wood and had nine children. During the Revolutionary War, Quakers refused to fight for either side. They relocated to an area of Connecticut but returned with additional Quakers when the fighting was over. Wing built one of the first of many mills on the Hudson River (shown).

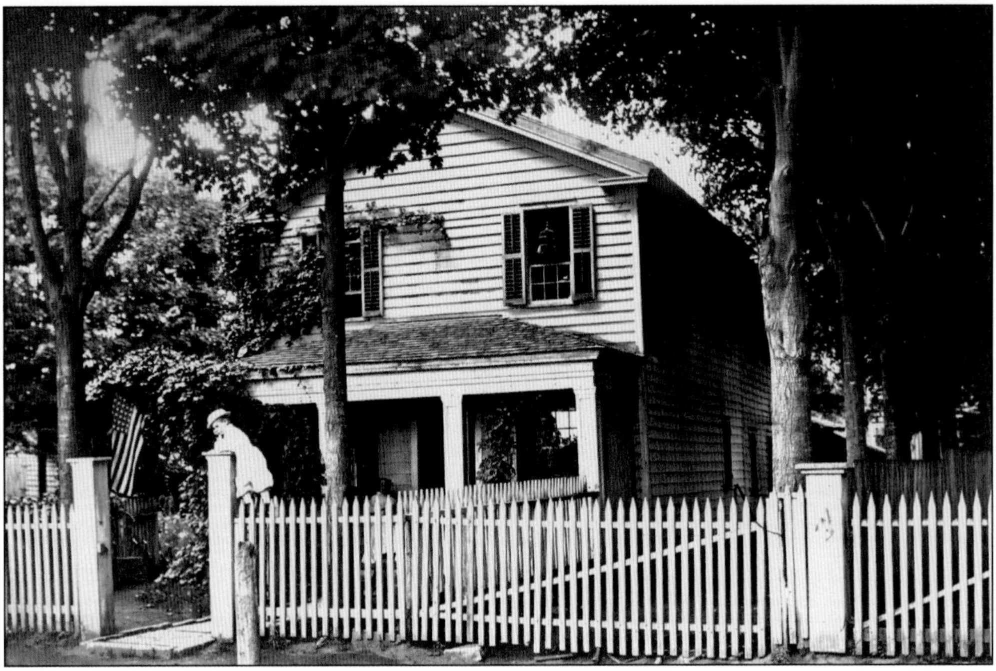

Halsey Wing, 1809–1870, was the great-grandson of Abraham Wing, founder of Glens Falls. He was a partner in the Abraham Wing Saw Mill and the Jointa Lime Company. He was the first Warren County judge as well as an important businessman. His first home was on Jay Street (shown), where he started his family.

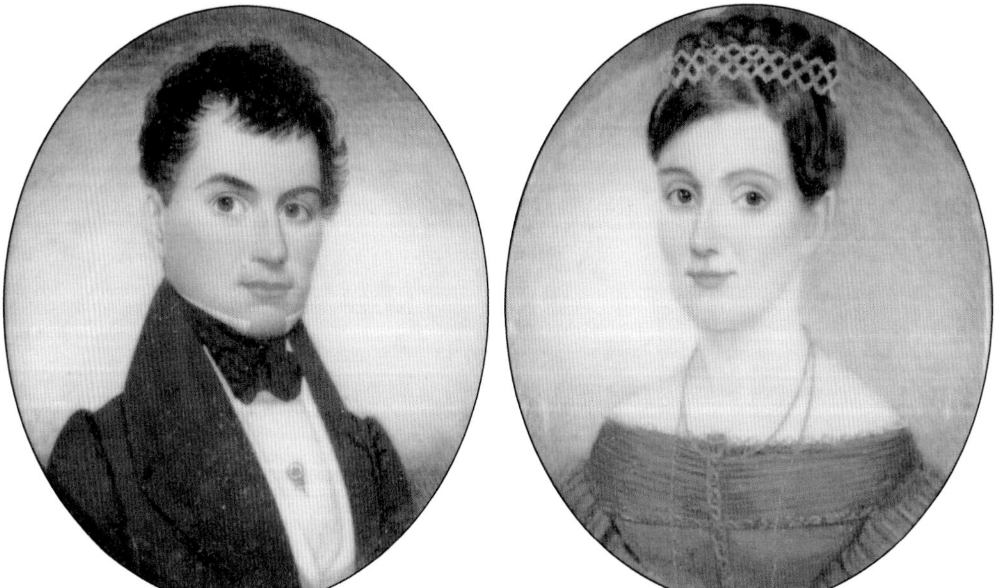

Harriet Rogers, 1815–1887, married Halsey Wing and had six children. She was the president of the Warren County Women's Sanitary Commission and organized the Ladies' Patriotic Association during the Civil War. Their sons, Edgar and George Henry, were both killed as a result of the Civil War. She was active in erecting the Civil War monument in town. The photographs show their painted wedding portraits from 1835.

Four

THE NORTH

The north end of town was where the founding fathers hoped to establish a settlement. However, that was not meant to be. Starting with farms in the area, it developed as a residential area with large and stately mansions gracing the elm tree–lined main street. It was the area of town where the city-owned cemetery developed, but at that time it was the outskirts of town. Lumberman and philanthropist Henry Crandall began buying up farms in the north end of the village and established a park there named after him. A stream was dammed, and ponds large enough to support motor launch travel were created. The park afforded space for huge winter festivals that competed with Lake Placid. When the village became a city, tennis courts and ball fields were established to further enhance the property. Several of the millionaires had their homes along Glen Street. This chapter will feature some of the people who made this part of town their home as well as Crandall Park, the Glens Falls Cemetery, and Union School No. 1. The people included are Annetta Barber, George Bayle, Edward Bemis, Edward Birdsall, Samuel Boyd, David Champlin, Daniel and Emily DeLong, Irving Griffing, J. Robert McMullen, Celia Micks, Bronco Charlie Miller, Estelle Palmer, and Augustus Sherman.

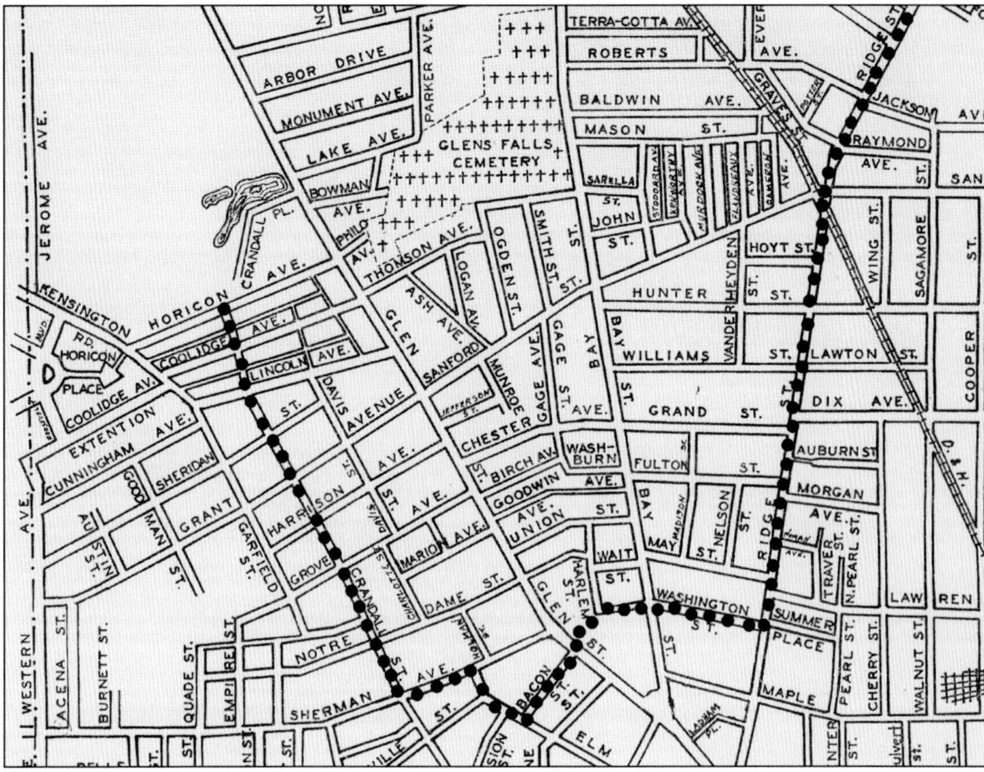

For the purpose of this chapter, the north will refer to the U-shaped area of the town, including Washington Street as its base, going north on the west side of Ridge Street and proceeding west to Crandall Street and then going north to the limits of the city, including Crandall Park.

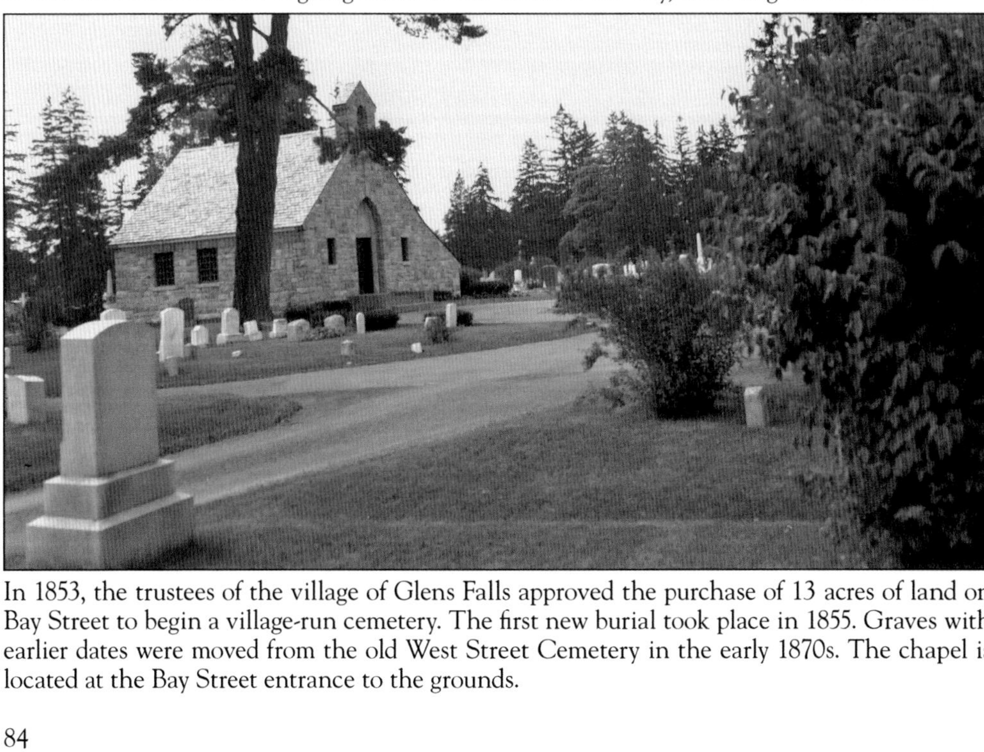

In 1853, the trustees of the village of Glens Falls approved the purchase of 13 acres of land on Bay Street to begin a village-run cemetery. The first new burial took place in 1855. Graves with earlier dates were moved from the old West Street Cemetery in the early 1870s. The chapel is located at the Bay Street entrance to the grounds.

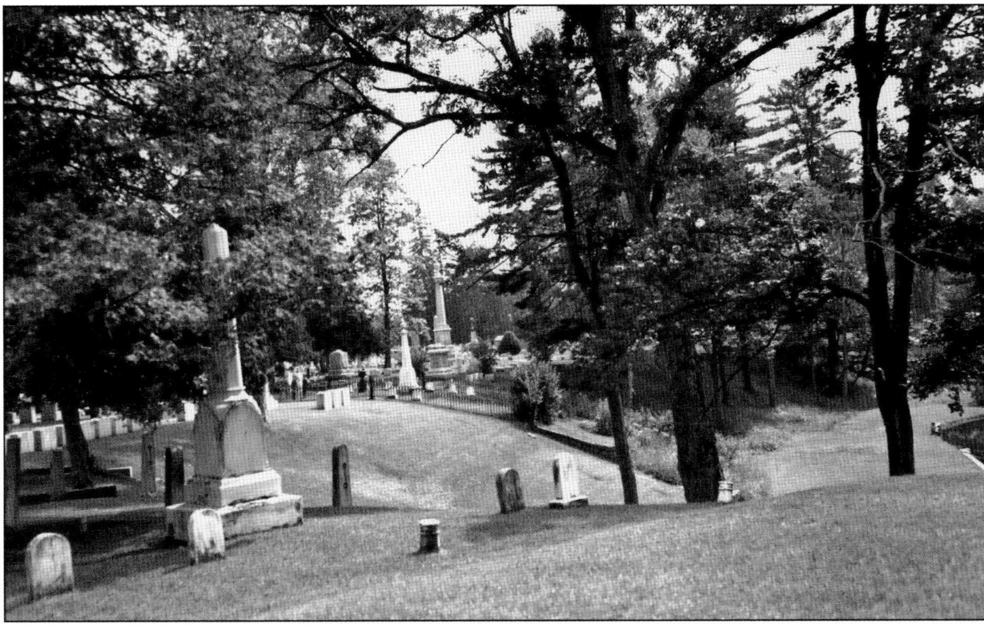

Victorian cemeteries developed with parklike settings. Large expanses of lawns and native trees were kept to make the cemetery a pleasant place. Funerary designs reflected the feelings about death at the time. Over 12,000 burials are found in the cemetery, but it has been able to maintain a natural feel. As of 2004, it is on the New York State and National Register of Historic Places. (Glens Falls Cemetery Collection.)

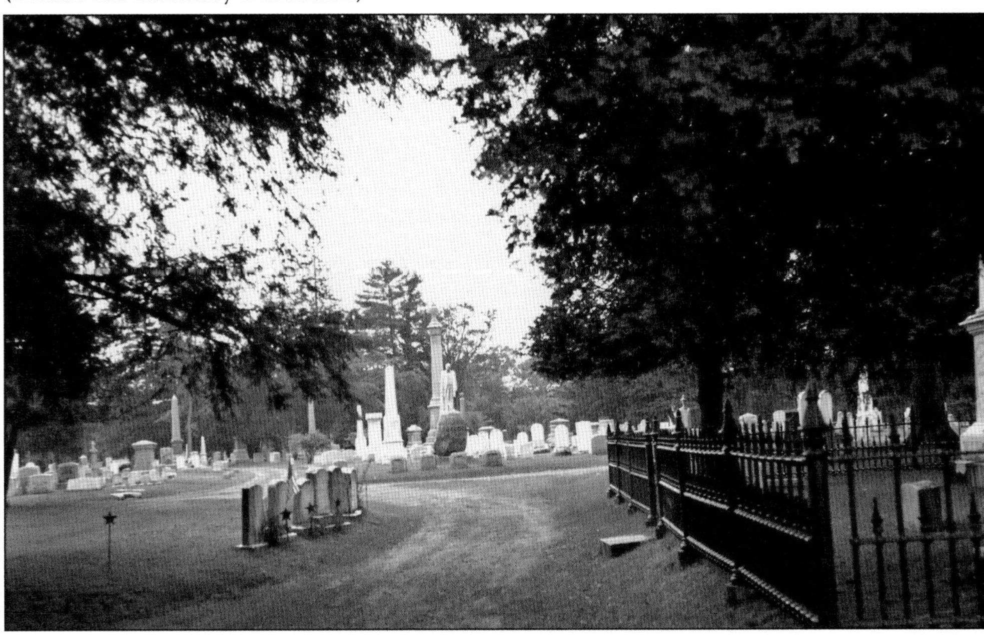

Family plots were enclosed with fences, and visitors came to sit and even picnic with their departed family members. Some notables buried there include Edward Bemis, the DeLong family, Harry Elkes, Jeremiah Finch, Charlotte Hyde, Russell Little, Bronco Charlie Miller, Jones Ordway, Samuel Pruyn, and Augustus Sherman. It is the only municipally run cemetery in the city. (Courtesy of the Glens Falls Cemetery Collection.)

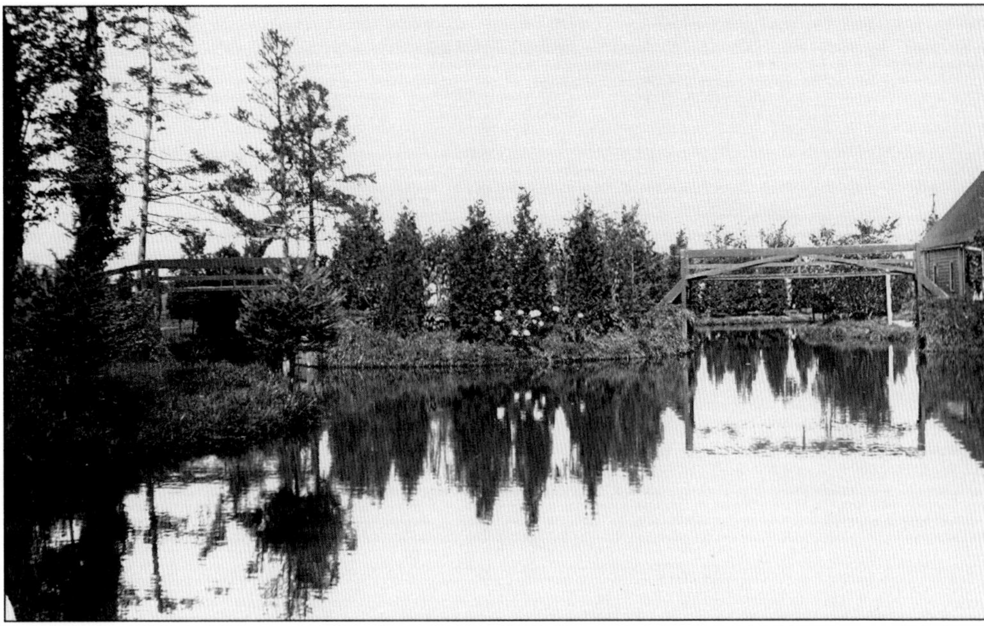

One of the major features of the north end of Glens Falls is Crandall Park. In 1880, Henry Crandall, retired lumberman and philanthropist, began buying tracts of farmland that he converted into a public park. Much land was purchased from Cole's woods for about $30,000 with his idea to provide a place for children to play. At the time, one pond was so large a motor launch operated on it.

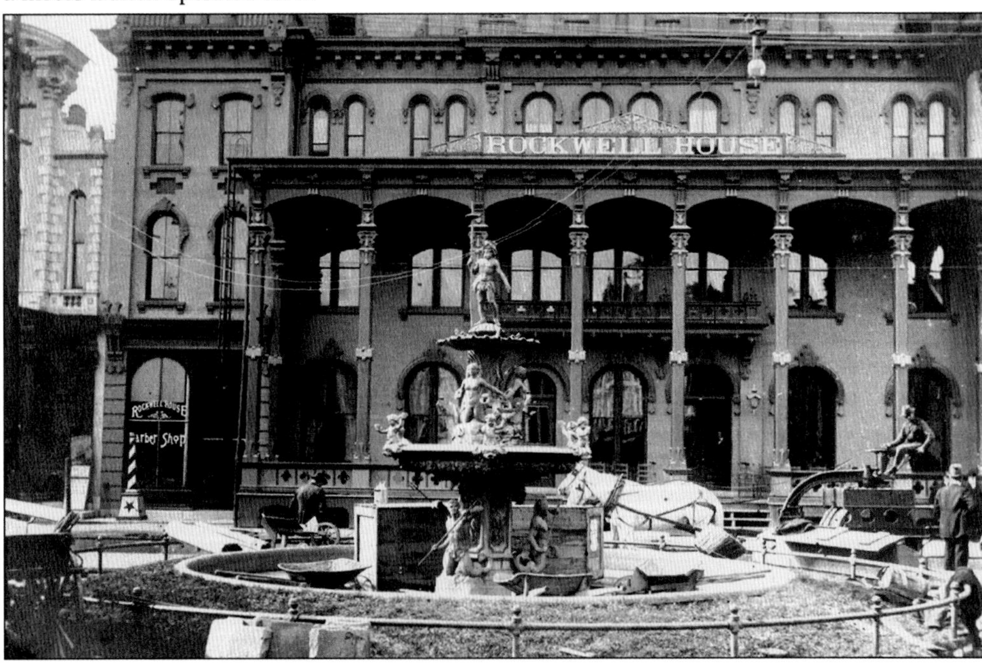

When trolley service appeared in the downtown section of the village, the ornate Neptune Fountain in front of the Rockwell House had to be moved. Its new home was in Crandall Park. It remained there from 1898 until World War II, when it was removed and the metal was melted down for use in the war effort.

Henry Crandall erected a large obelisk in the park with his log mark star on the top. Around the base was stone curbing laid out also in the pattern of a star. Trees were planted parallel to the curbing following the star pattern. Inside the base of the obelisk are the tombs of Crandall and his wife Betsy. His name appears, but she is listed simply as "his wife."

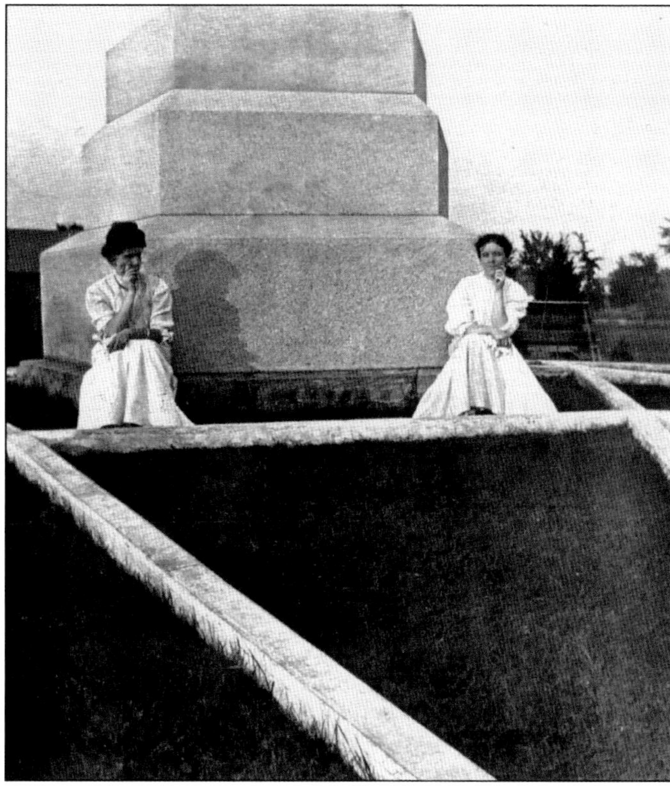

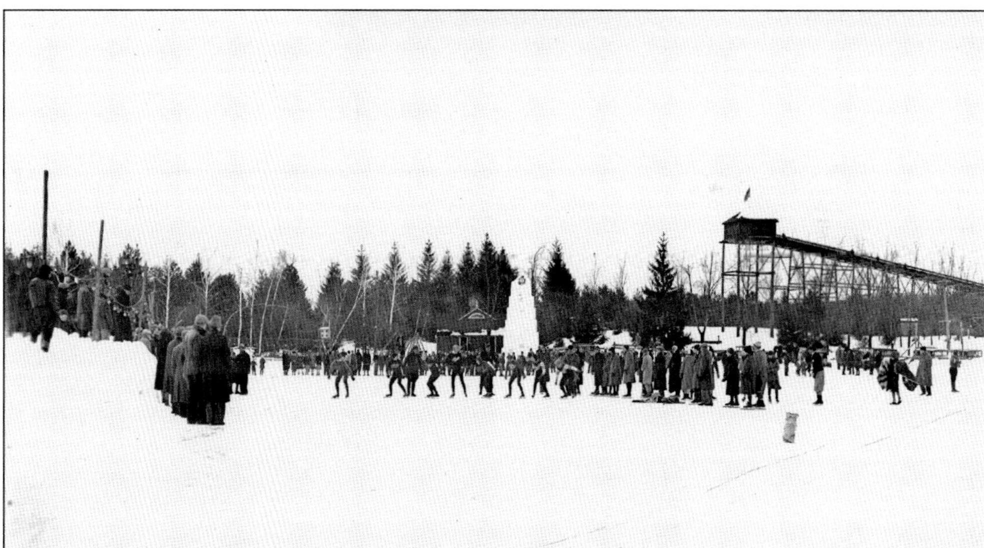

About 1927, the Outing Club organized winter activities in the park. Included were skating, hockey, tobogganing, and dogsledding. The highlight was a toboggan run rising 50 feet into the air and running 250 feet from the field house toward Halfway Brook. A national sports magazine reported Glens Falls as a winter sports center along with Lake Placid and Tupper Lake. Events such as this continued until 1932.

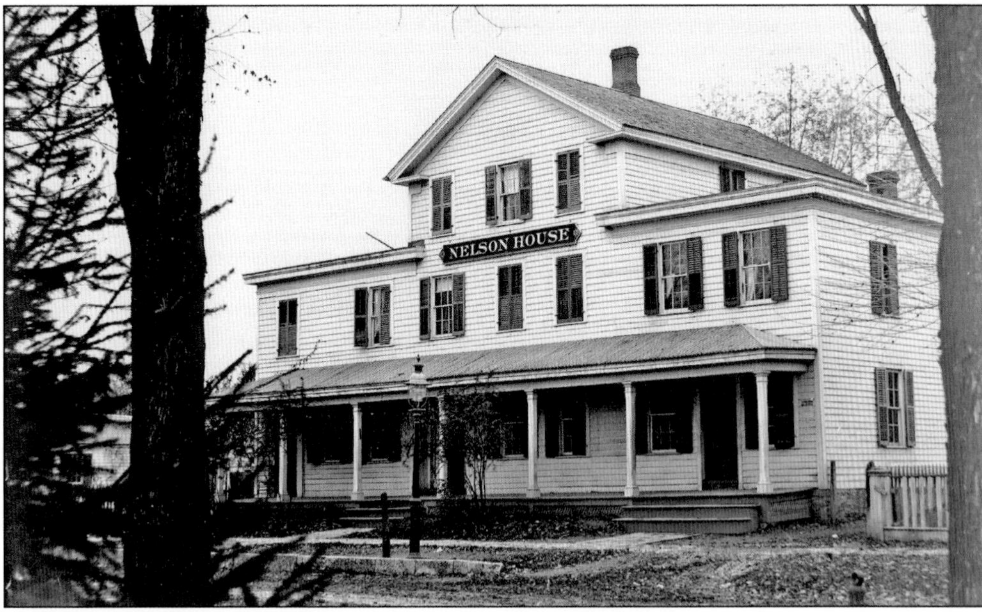

In 1925, land was purchased from the owners of the Nelson House (above) at the corner of Bay and Washington Streets to build the Glens Falls Hebrew Association's community center building. Dedicated on February 14, 1926, the building became the center of Jewish activity in Glens Falls. Included in the building are classrooms, an auditorium, the Hebrew Free School, a library and reading room, social rooms, and a large basement used for social functions. Sara Tefilo, the orthodox Jewish congregation organized in 1892, conducted services for a number of years in the community building. It had moved from its building on Jay Street into the center as an economical move. The facility is now known as Congregation Shaaray Tefila, seen below.

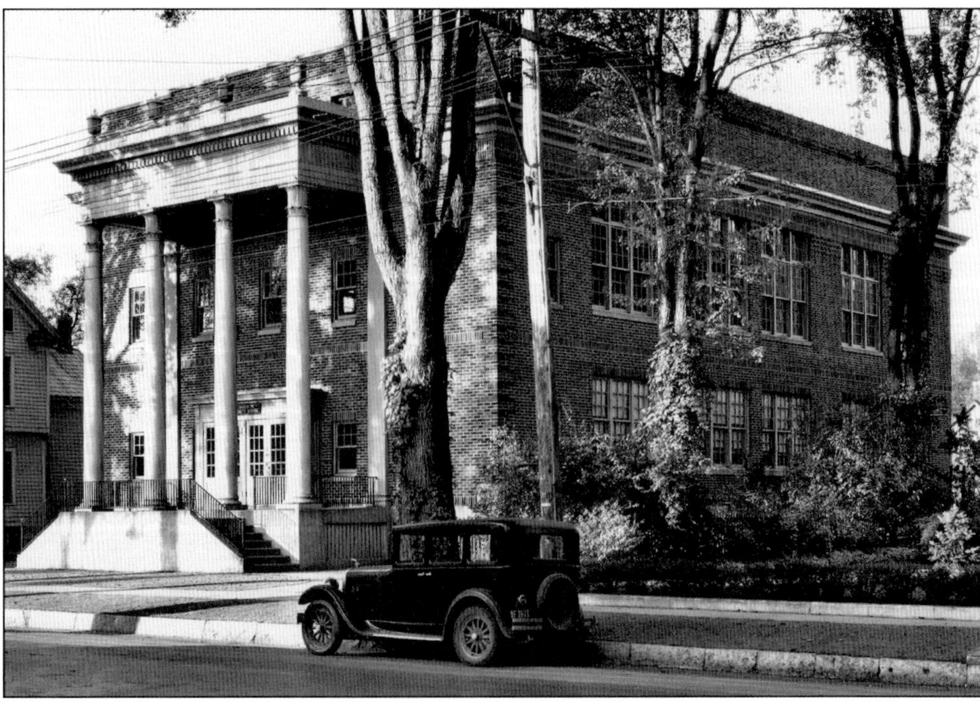

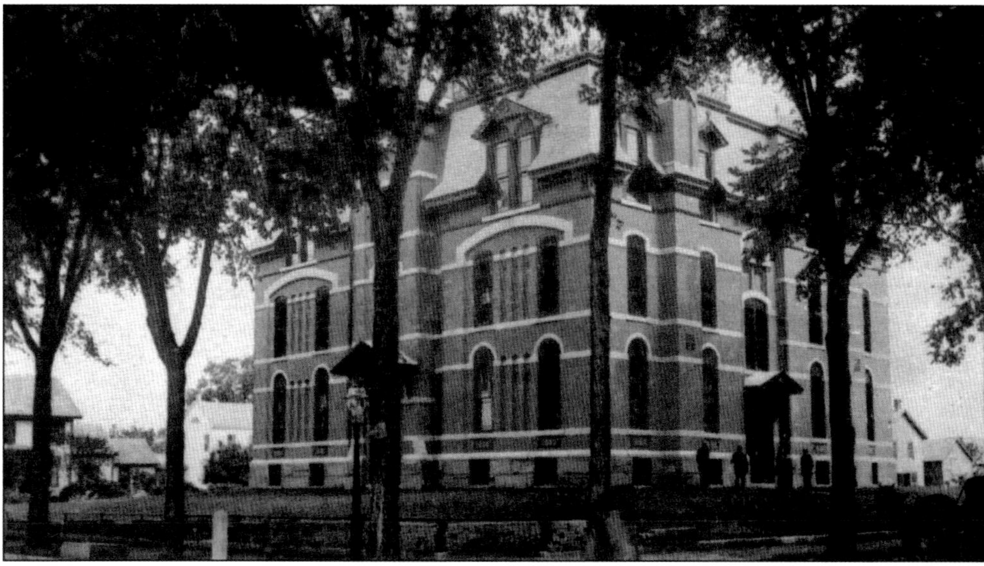

In 1884, a three-story brick building opened as Union School No. 1 on Glen Street, capable of housing 500 students. This started the united public school system. The building served as the design for schools to be developed in Glens Falls. Classrooms and small auditoriums were on the first floors, and the bathroom facilities were in the basement, giving rise to requests for "going to the basement."

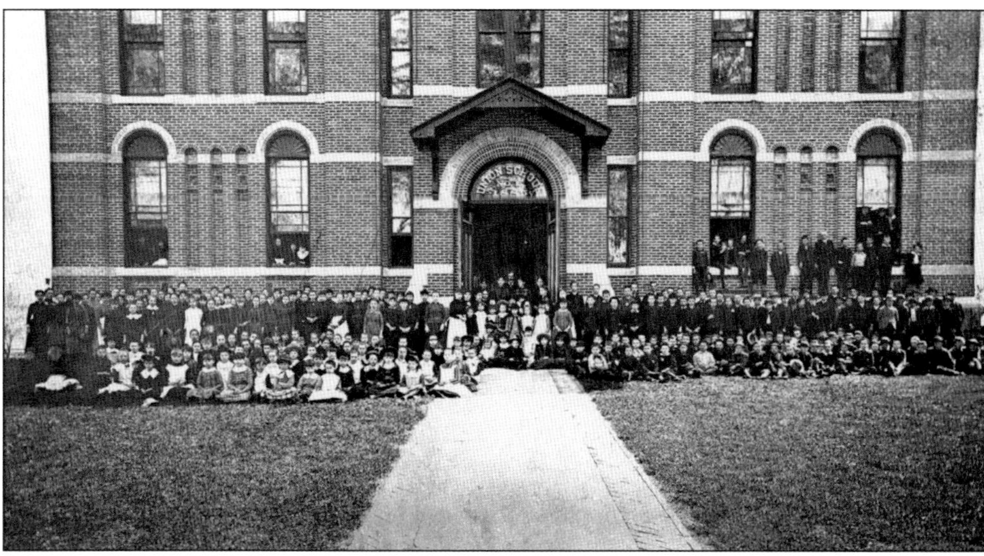

The Union School No. 1 is often referred to as a high school, but it originally held elementary grades one to eight as well. When enrollment increased in 1900, some primary grades were moved into the Lockhart building at 24 Union Street. When the school burned in 1902, high school students were housed in the village hall on Ridge Street until the new facility was completed in 1906.

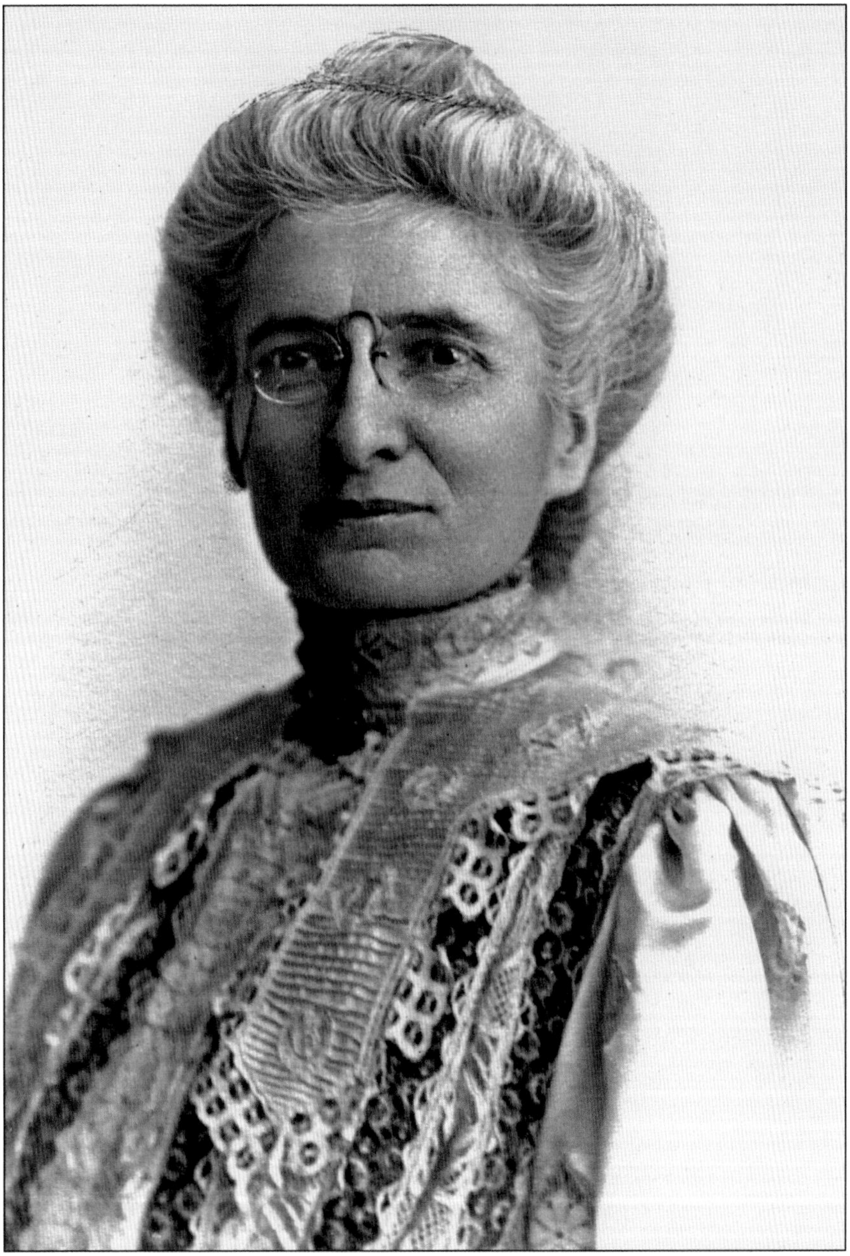

Annetta Barber, 1859–1945, was born in the Chazy area of the Adirondacks. She graduated in 1898 at the age of 40 from Women's Medical College, New York City. Her first practice was at 11 Birch Avenue, Glens Falls, but soon moved to 261 Glen Street, where she ran a private hospital. Next she moved to 8 Notre Dame Street, where she specialized in maternity and critical care patients. Dr. Barber was noted for being one of the first women doctors in Warren County and for doing her house calls on a bicycle. In 1904, she served as a member of the Humane Society in Glens Falls, which at the time, dealt with not only abused animals but also children. She was responsible for getting the children to religious services on Sundays. She was very active in several civic organizations in the area. When she retired, she resided in the Glens Falls Home for Women on Warren Street but died in Ogdensburg and is buried in her hometown of Chazy.

George Bayle, 1860–1939, at age six, was the oldest of three children when his father died. He started working by age 12 for Robbins and DeLong. From there he went to B. B. Fowler's where he swept floors and was the night watchman working his way up to bookkeeper. He left Glens Falls for four years to work for several establishments in New York City, gaining business experience.

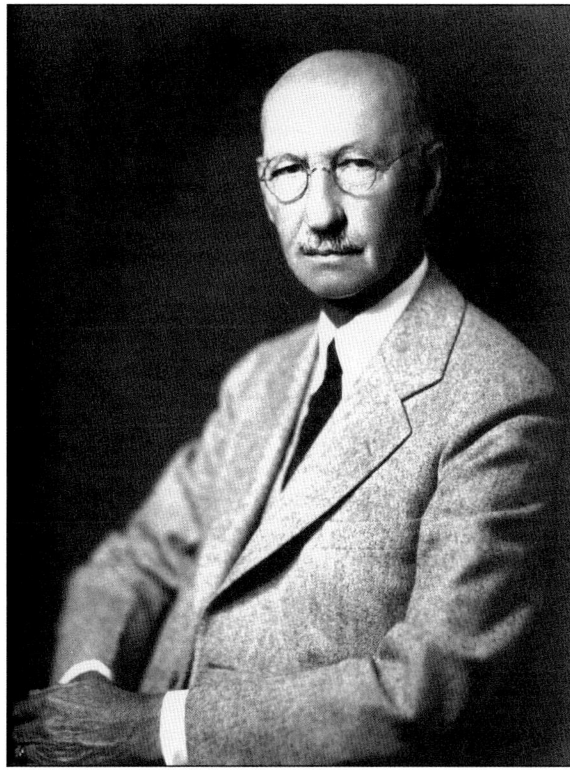

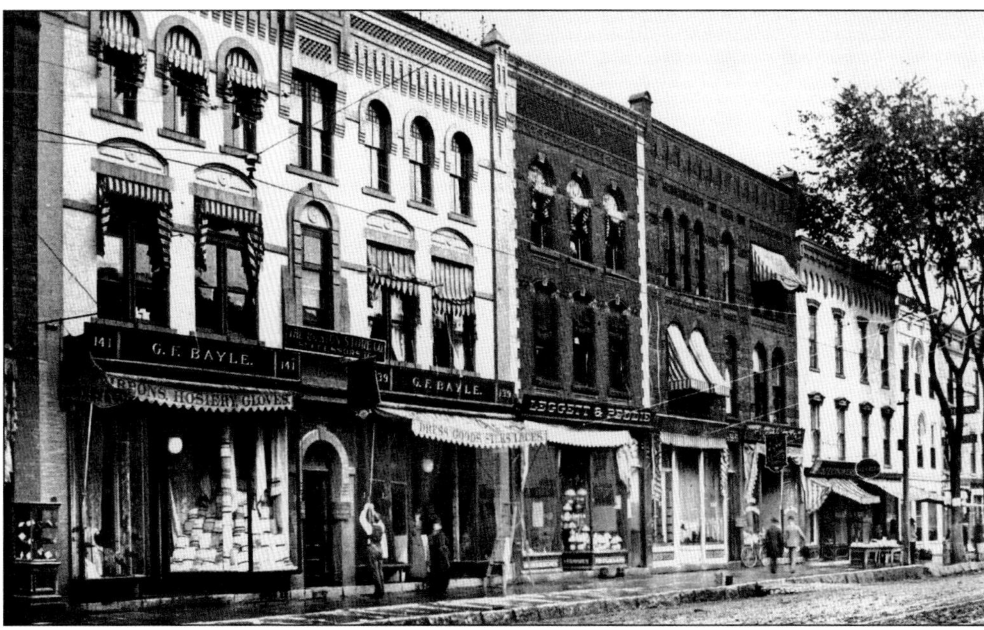

Upon returning to Glens Falls in 1884, Bayle opened the George F. Bayle and Company dry goods store on Glen Street, which later became the Boston Store. Ten years later, Bayle became vice president and general manager of New England's largest mercantile business, Denholm-McKay Company. In 1897, he went back to New York City to be the general manager of a large department and dry goods store. (Courtesy of the Bayle family.)

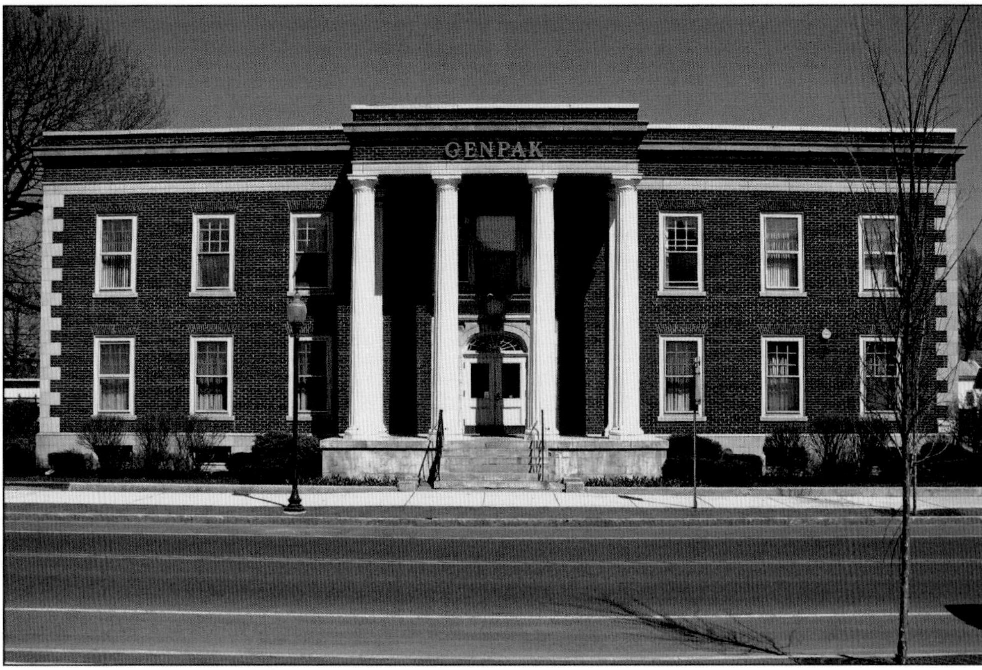

Coming back to Glens Falls, Bayle became president of Glens Falls Portland Cement Company, working there until retirement. Being civic minded, he was on the boards of education, Glens Falls Insurance Company, Glens Falls Post Company, First National Bank, and Glens Falls Hospital. He helped facilitate the building of the Queensbury Hotel, Westmount Sanitarium, and Warren Street Knights of Columbus building, now Gen Pak headquarters (shown).

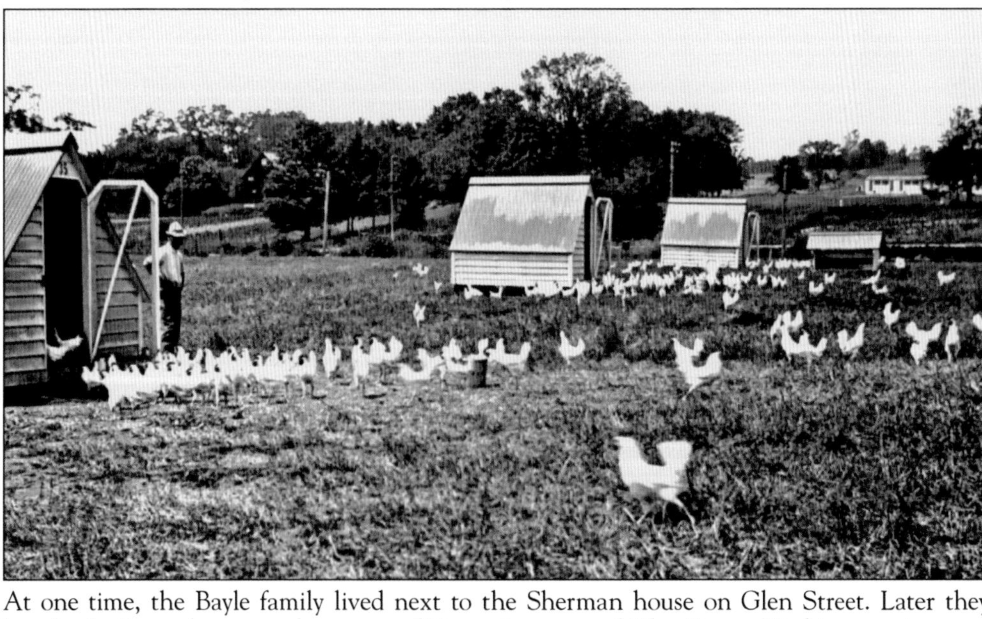

At one time, the Bayle family lived next to the Sherman house on Glen Street. Later they bought the Pruyn house on the corner of Grove Avenue and Glen Street. His biggest enjoyment was raising chickens on a 52-acre farm he purchased on Country Club Road. About 2,000 eggs were collected daily that were sold locally and to hotels and restaurants in Albany and New York City. (Courtesy of the Bayle family.)

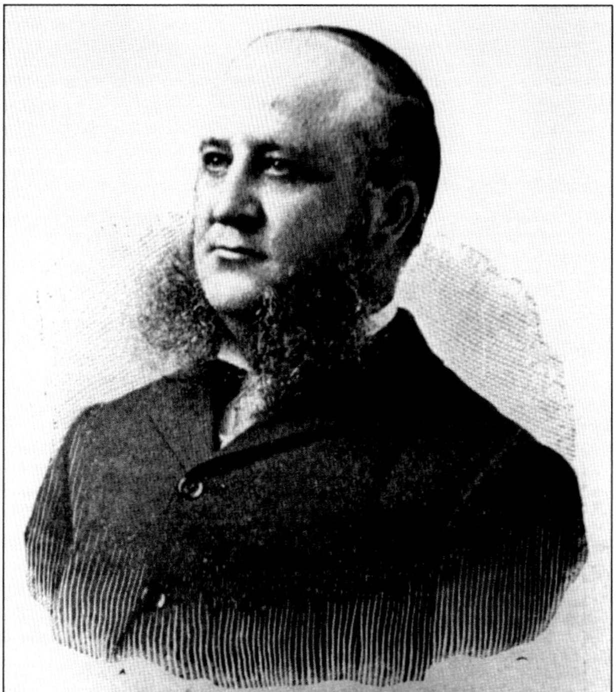

E. H. BEMIS, EYE SPECIALIST.
(From Photo Feb., 1897.)

Edward Bemis, 1849–1901, was born in Vermont but attended schools in New Hampshire. He learned medicine with Dr. Rowland Gray of New York City. After medical studies, he became interested in diseases of the eyes, thus beginning an optician's practice. He came to Glens Falls in 1872 where his efforts became renowned throughout New York and New England.

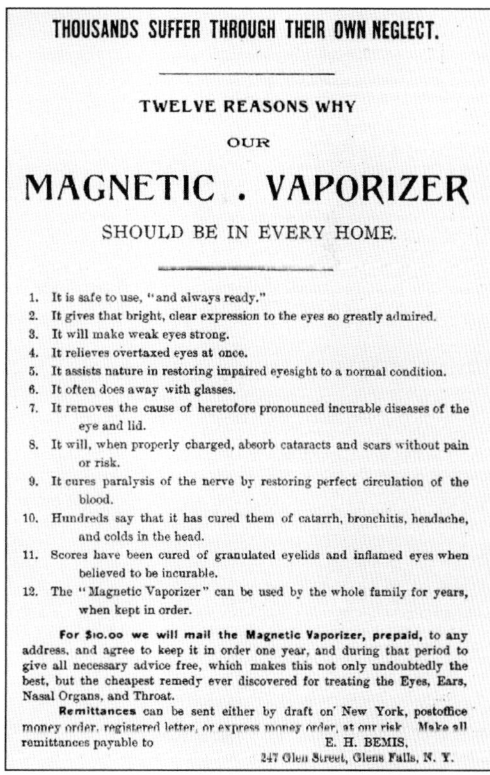

THOUSANDS SUFFER THROUGH THEIR OWN NEGLECT.

TWELVE REASONS WHY

OUR

MAGNETIC . VAPORIZER

SHOULD BE IN EVERY HOME.

1. It is safe to use, "and always ready."
2. It gives that bright, clear expression to the eyes so greatly admired.
3. It will make weak eyes strong.
4. It relieves overtaxed eyes at once.
5. It assists nature in restoring impaired eyesight to a normal condition.
6. It often does away with glasses.
7. It removes the cause of heretofore pronounced incurable diseases of the eye and lid.
8. It will, when properly charged, absorb cataracts and scars without pain or risk.
9. It cures paralysis of the nerve by restoring perfect circulation of the blood.
10. Hundreds say that it has cured them of catarrh, bronchitis, headache, and colds in the head.
11. Scores have been cured of granulated eyelids and inflamed eyes when believed to be incurable.
12. The "Magnetic Vaporizer" can be used by the whole family for years, when kept in order.

For $10.00 we will mail the Magnetic Vaporizer, prepaid, to any address, and agree to keep it in order one year, and during that period to give all necessary advice free, which makes this not only undoubtedly the best, but the cheapest remedy ever discovered for treating the Eyes, Ears, Nasal Organs, and Throat.

Remittances can be sent either by draft on New York, postoffice money order, registered letter, or express money order, at our risk. Make all remittances payable to

E. H. BEMIS,
247 Glen Street, Glens Falls, N. Y.

Bemis's practice grew immensely, and it is reported his income was over $30,000 annually in the Glens Falls office. He patented a new cure, called "Magnetic Vaporizing," where a jet of air was forced into the eye to break blood vessels. When that healed, the eye problem was supposedly solved. He took care of cataracts, glaucoma, detached retinas, weeping eyes, and so on.

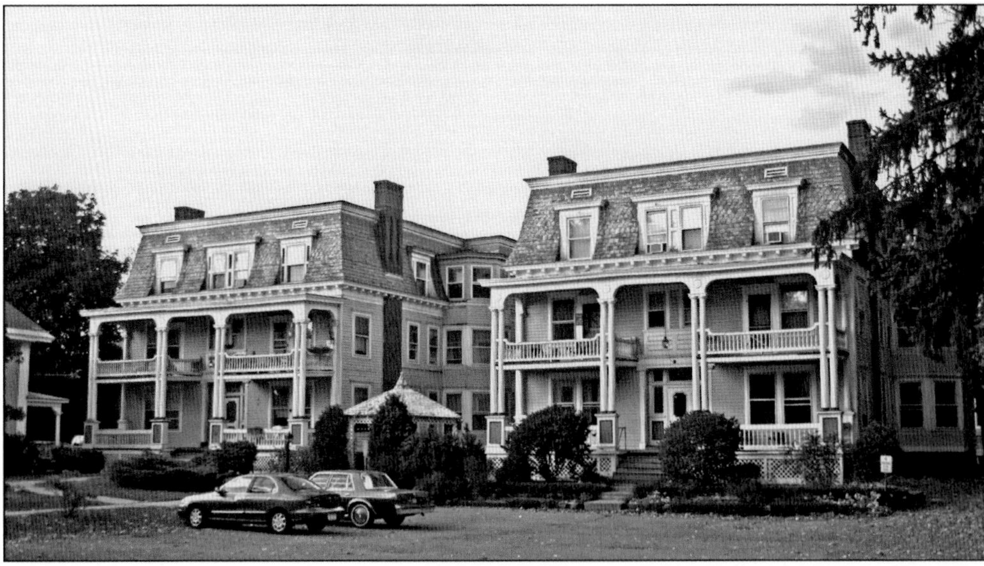

Dr. Edward Bemis owned many large apartment buildings (shown here in 2008) to house his patients and their relatives while in Glens Falls for treatments. He ran a farm to also provide fresh food for the guests. The patients came from 23 states and 3 countries. They added $135,000 to the local economy yearly.

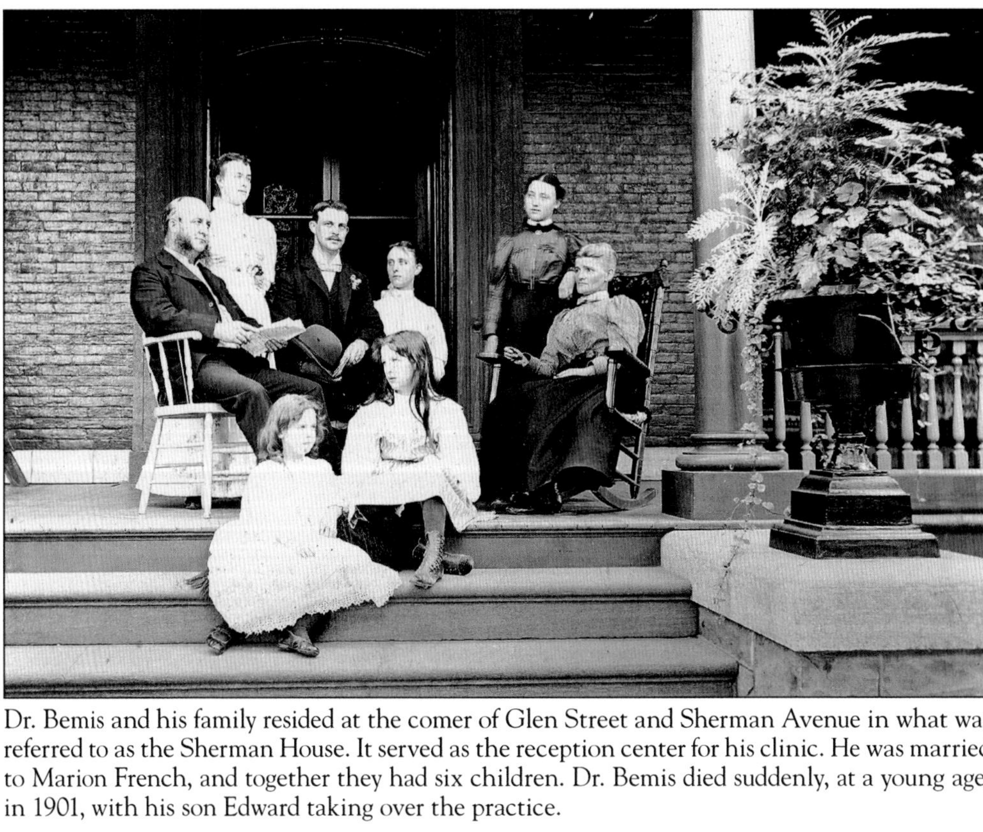

Dr. Bemis and his family resided at the comer of Glen Street and Sherman Avenue in what was referred to as the Sherman House. It served as the reception center for his clinic. He was married to Marion French, and together they had six children. Dr. Bemis died suddenly, at a young age, in 1901, with his son Edward taking over the practice.

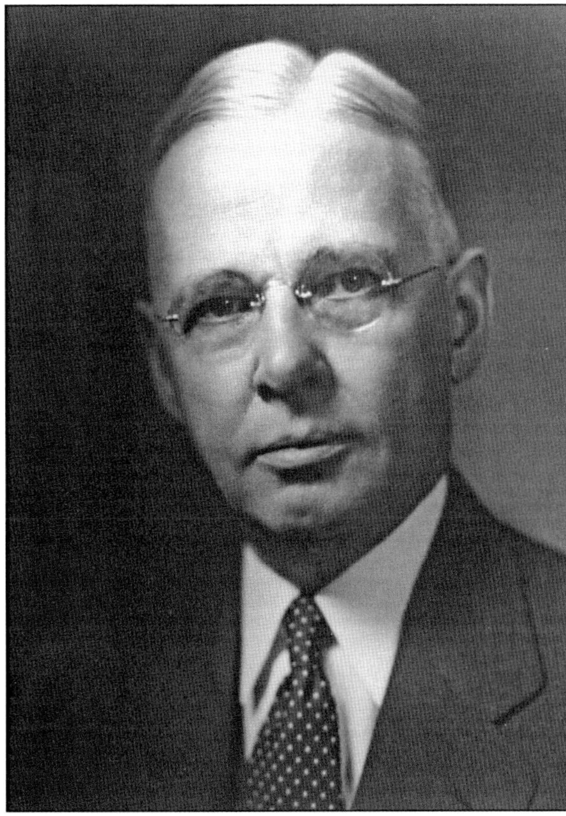

Edgar Birdsall, M.D., 1876–1964, was born in Brooklyn and moved to Glens Falls with his family in 1884. He attended the Glens Falls Academy and went on to New York Medical College and Flower Hospital in 1899. He began a practice in Brooklyn but returned to Glens Falls, setting up an office, seen below, with his physician father in the Colvin Building. He was town physician for Queensbury as well as coroner. Dr. Birdsall established the first radiology department in the Glens Falls Hospital and was a member of the department for about 50 years. Pres. Franklin Roosevelt commended him for his work with the program Eyes for the Navy, with its development of binoculars, telescopes, and spyglasses for military purposes. He remained chief of the radiology department at the Glens Falls Hospital from 1922 to 1959.

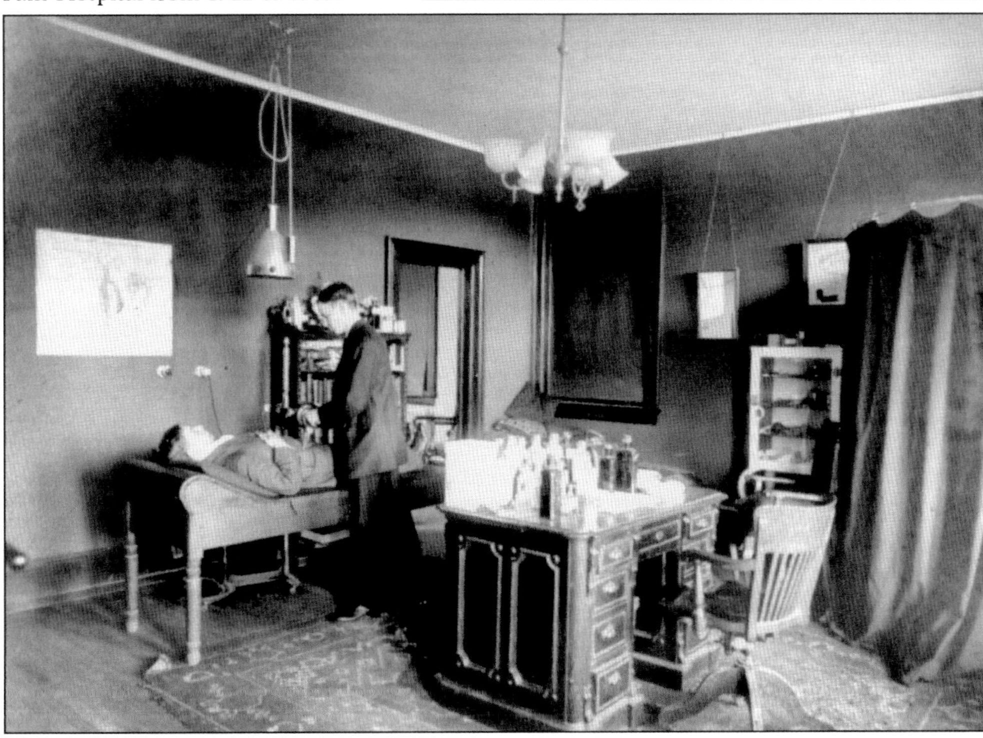

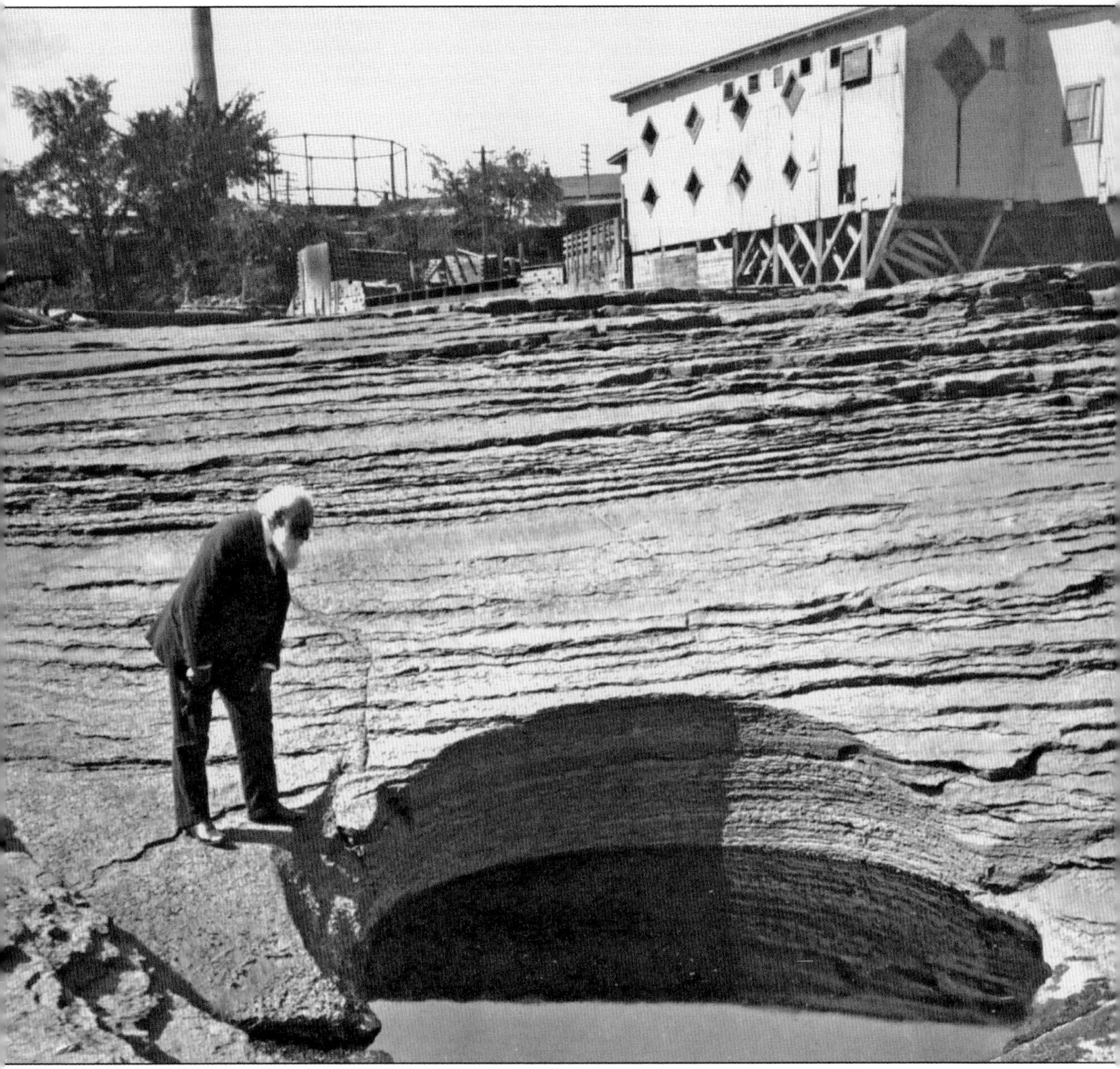

Samuel Boyd, 1843–1934, came to Glens Falls with his family as a child. They lived at the corner of Park and Elm Streets, which at the time was sparsely settled. One of their neighbors was lumber baron James Morgan. During Boyd's lifetime he worked at many trades. He was a painter and paperhanger for 40 years, owned a bookstore on Warren Street, and worked as a post office clerk and an accountant for local merchants. Boyd married Katherine TenEyck and had five children. They owned a house and seven acres of land on Chester Street where he pastured a cow. After retiring at age 79, he wrote the book *In the Days of Old Glens Falls*, based on memories and research of the city. One of his memories included fighting the major fire of 1864 that destroyed a large part of the village. He is shown overlooking a pool near the entrance to Cooper's Cave.

David Champlin, 1786–1872, came to Queensbury around 1817, bought a 1790 farmhouse and property on the Plank Road, and founded the Champlin Tannery located on Halfway Brook. It operated from 1820 to 1870. According to the 1865 agricultural census, he owned 15 acres of improved land and 7 acres of unimproved land valued at $1,000. He and his wife, Esther, had eight children.

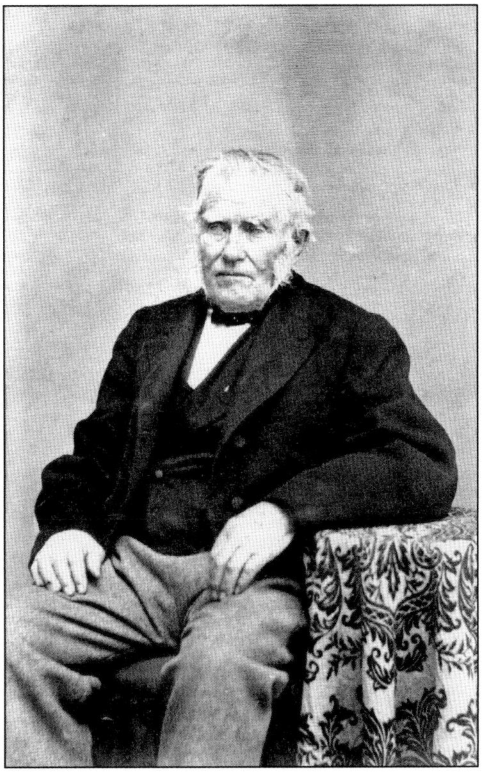

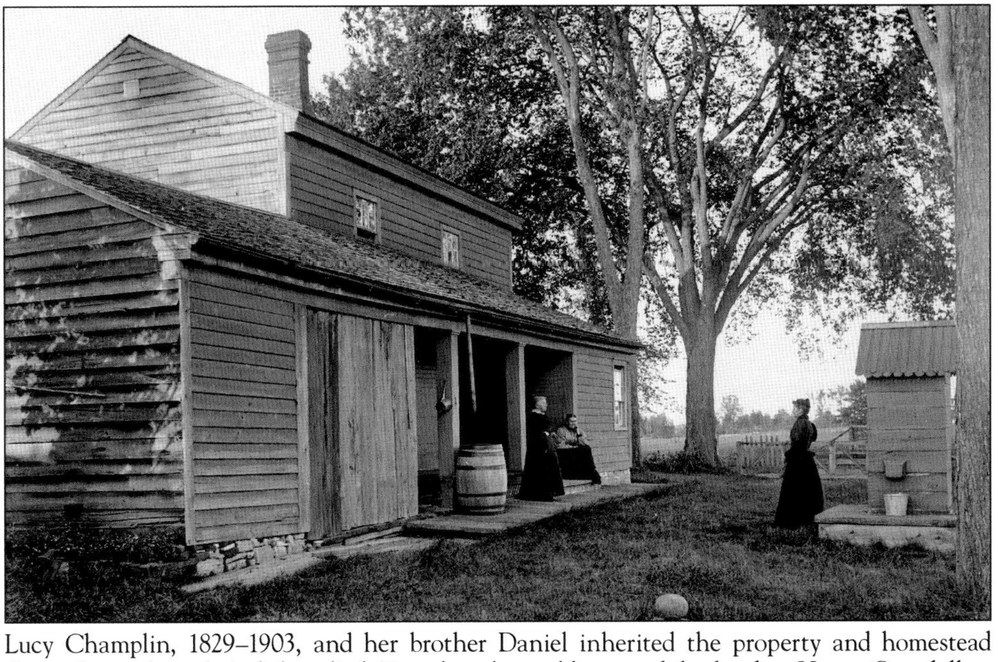

Lucy Champlin, 1829–1903, and her brother Daniel inherited the property and homestead shown here when their father died. Together they sold most of the land to Henry Crandall to be incorporated into Crandall Park. The family home was eventually sold to the Chitty family, whose daughter Marion was a noted historian in the area. The house was eventually moved to Glenwood Avenue, where it stands today.

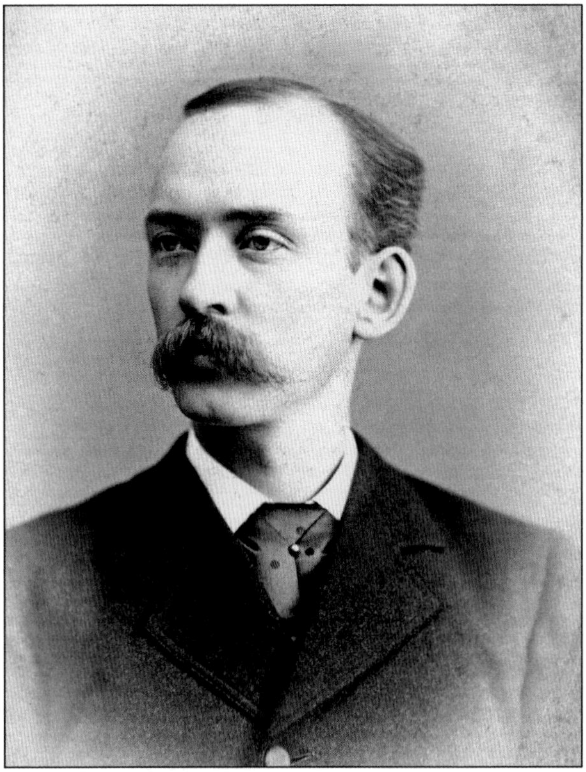

Daniel Peck DeLong, 1850–1914, moved to Glens Falls, was educated at the Glens Falls Academy, and worked for seven years in a dry goods store. When his brother-in-law Harvey Coffin died, he purchased the Coffin Brickyard and renamed it the Glens Falls Brick and Lumber Company. Clay came from the source he renamed Brickyard Pond, now Hovey Pond. The business grew to 45 acres and was producing five million bricks a year. DeLong married Emily Tearse, who was descended from the Campbell family and Sarah McNeil, who is buried with Jane McCrea, massacred during the Revolutionary War. While her husband was a prominent businessman, she was involved in the Aid Society, the Women's Civic Club, and the Woman's Missionary Society. She was instrumental in establishing the Glens Falls Home for Women on Warren Street.

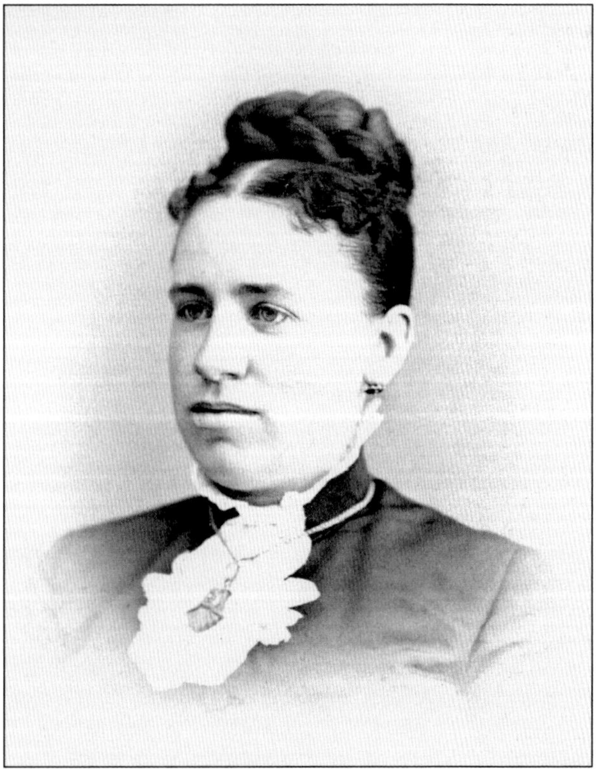

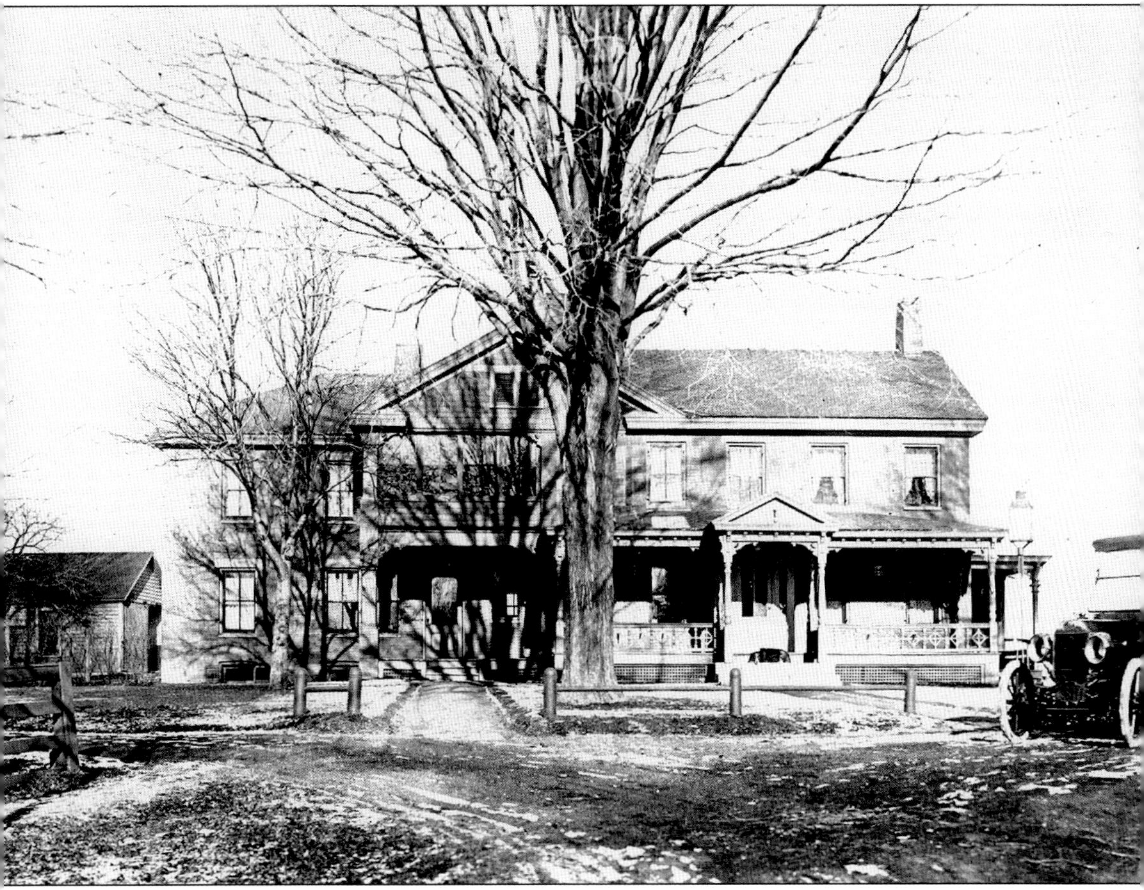

Daniel and Emily Delong first lived on Glen Street across from the DeLong family home, then on Bay Street near his brother Cutler. When the brick business prospered, they were able to build a beautiful mansion, seen here, on Glenwood Avenue in the 1890s. Daniel and his wife had six children, but two died at a young age. They were members of the Presbyterian Church on Glen Street for over 80 years, where Emily sang in the choir for 25 of them. Around the same time, Emily's brother William married Daniel's sister, Elizabeth. Daniel was active in the local Democratic Party and elected town supervisor for the Town of Queensbury. He was also a member of the New York State Assembly representing Warren County. DeLong served as a vice president of the Glens Falls Trust Company. The Daniel DeLong home on Glenwood is now an antique center.

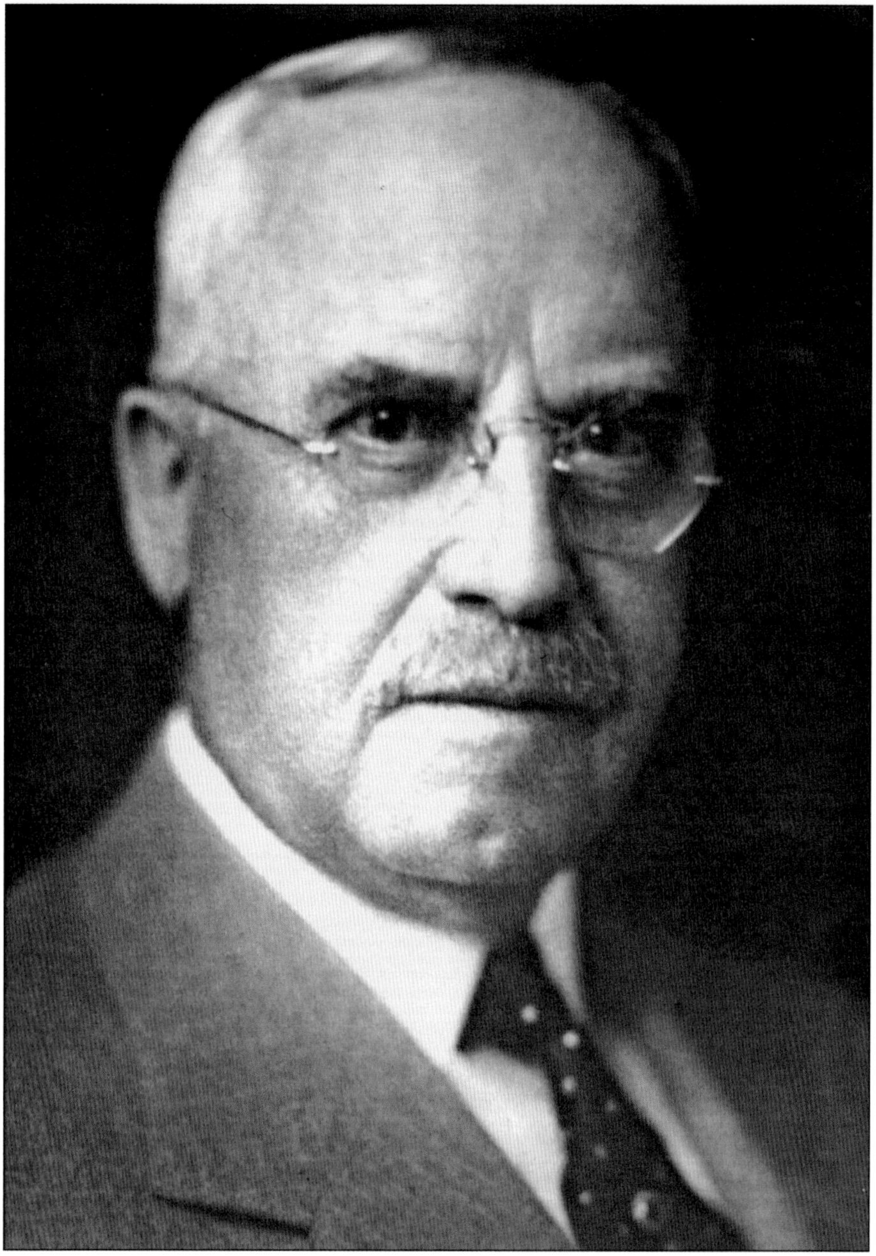

W. Irving Griffing, 1859–1941, came to Glens Falls from Greenwich in 1875. He worked as a private driver and drove a stage between Glens Falls and Fort Edward. In the 1880s, he survived the terrible small pox epidemic that struck Glens Falls. He maintained a stable of trotters and pacers that were entered into local races. In 1904, Griffing and business partner Morgan Leland built a livery stable along with a carriage and buckboard repository on the site of the McGregor estate on the Glen Street hill. In 1913, J. E. Sawyer Company bought and expanded the building. Griffing was also in the real estate business. He had the Glens Falls Post Company on the corner of Park and Glen Streets built as a rental property. He was a lifelong Democrat and was a village trustee before being elected mayor of the city in 1912, 1914, 1920, and 1934, all two-year terms. He lived at the northern corner of Lincoln Avenue and Glen Street at the time of his death.

J. Robert McMullen, 1871–1946, known as J. R., was born soon after his parents arrived from Ireland. Educated in Glens Falls, he studied business in New York City. McMullen and his partner Walter Leavens began the McMullen-Leavens Company as a shirt factory in 1902. Twenty years later, Leavens died, leaving the business to J. R. Because of the Feeder Canal and railroad spur to Glens Falls, customers around the world had access to his products. By 1935, the company saw a decline in the shirt industry, so it started making women's shirtwaist dresses. With marketing and sales in New York City, McMullen accumulated great wealth and built a huge estate with expansive gardens (seen below) on Glen Street. In 1939, Troy Shirt Makers Guild evolved as a shirt-making operation. The company continued after his death, closing for good in 1996.

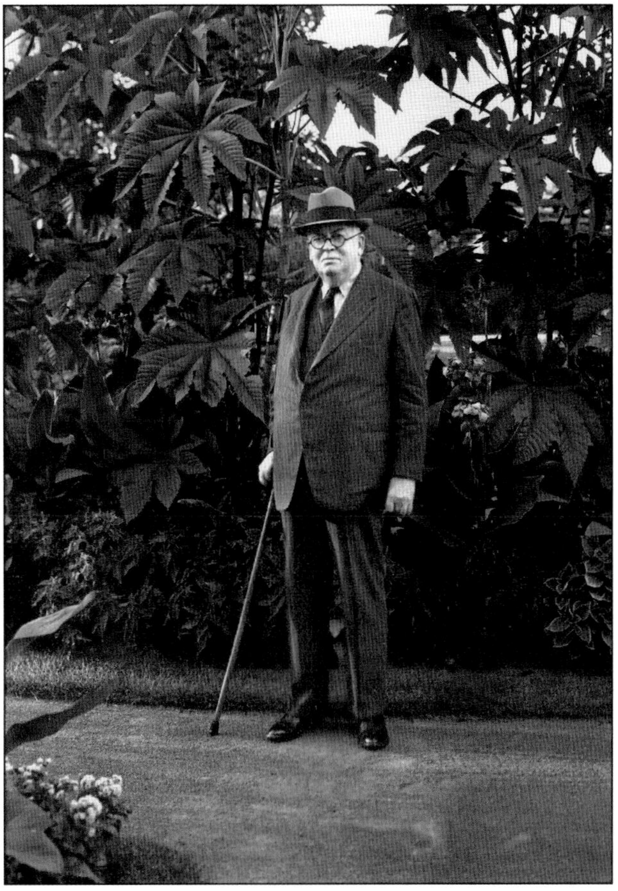

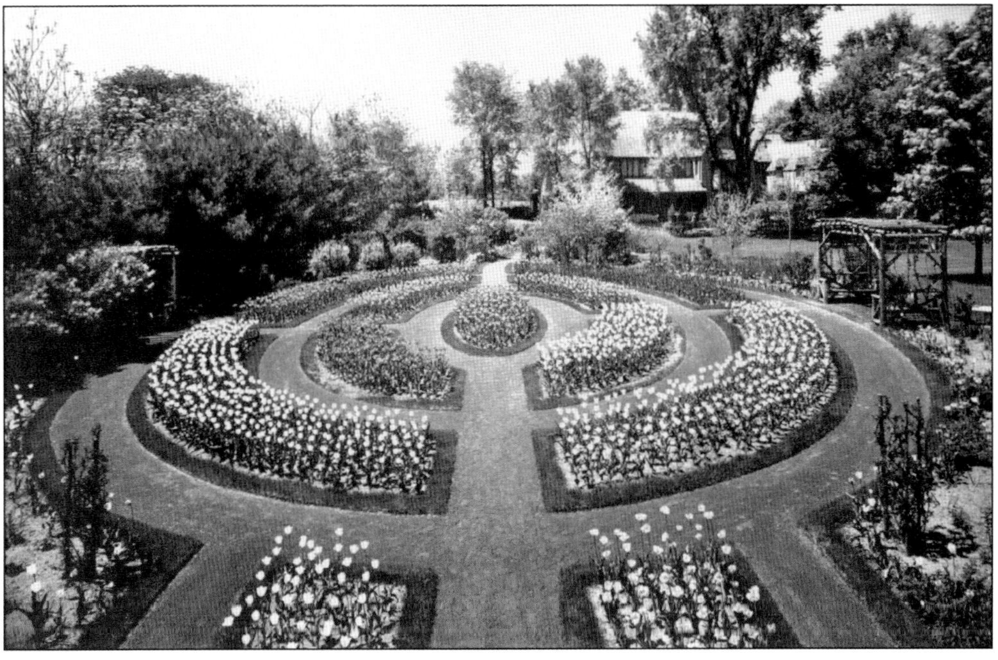

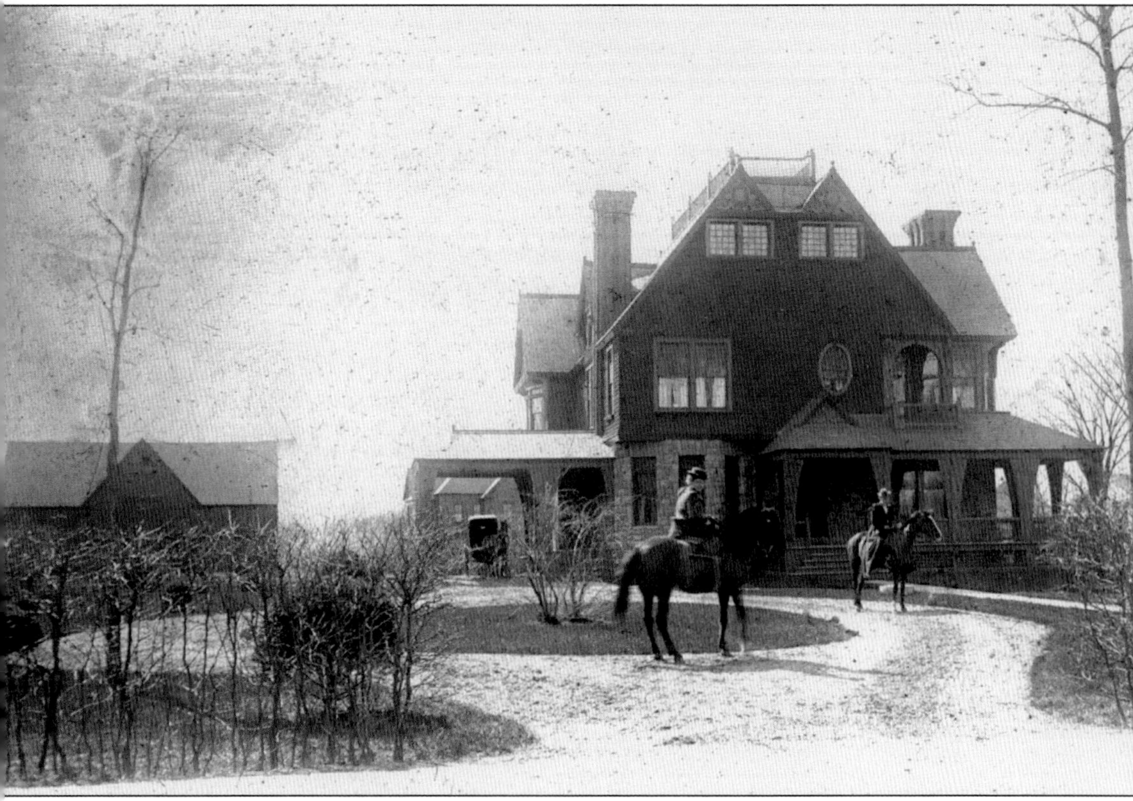

Celia Micks, D.O., 1880–1970, was born in Nebraska and graduated in 1905 from S.S. Still College of Osteopathy in Iowa. She started her practice in Middletown, New York, where she lived with her husband, also a doctor. Micks came to Glens Falls in 1917 and opened her office at the corner of Glen and Notre Dame Streets. At one time, she lived in the Birdsall residence on Ridge Street (shown). During World War I, the deadly influenza epidemic kept her busy day and night. Micks traveled to Schuylerville, Greenwich, Warrensburg, and Schroon Lake to care for patients. She later married Fred Colburn, who owned the Rialto Theater Block where her office was then located. She served as a member of many Glens Falls clubs and organizations, becoming known as a caring mother, wife, and doctor 24 hours a day.

Charles Mortimer Miller, 1850–1955, told the story that he was born in a covered wagon in Hot Creek, California. Miller and his brother were actually born in New York City and at the ages of 9 and 10, considered juvenile delinquents, were put on a "school ship" to California to get them off the streets. Miller jumped ship, got away, and became the youngest Pony Express rider at age 11.

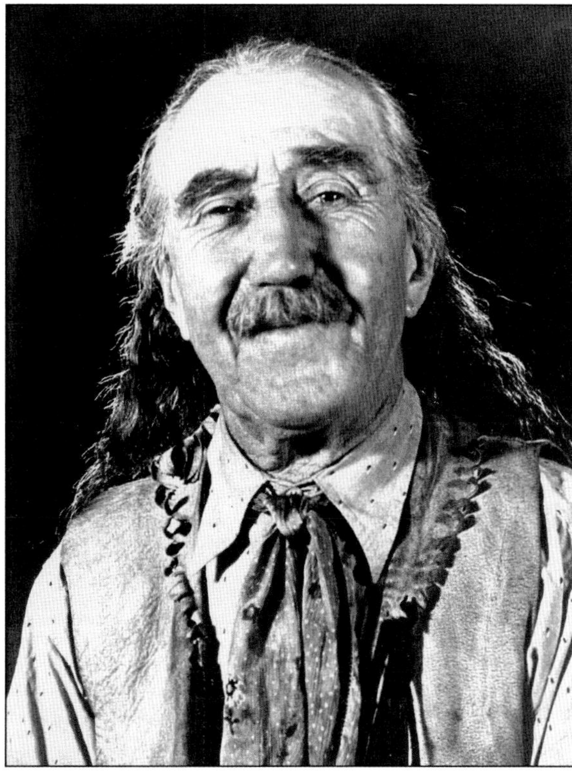

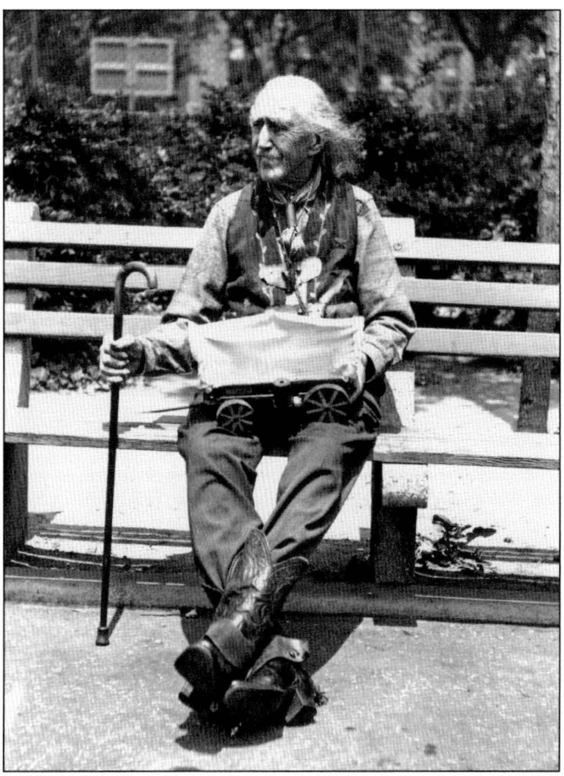

Miller joined Buffalo Bill's Wild West Show in 1885. He broke and trained horses for Theodore Roosevelt and the U.S. Army, while earning the nickname Bronco Charlie. Miller missed the Civil War, but tried to enlist in the army during World War I and was turned away as he was 68 years old. He went to Canada and enlisted in the 18th Hussars, lying about his age.

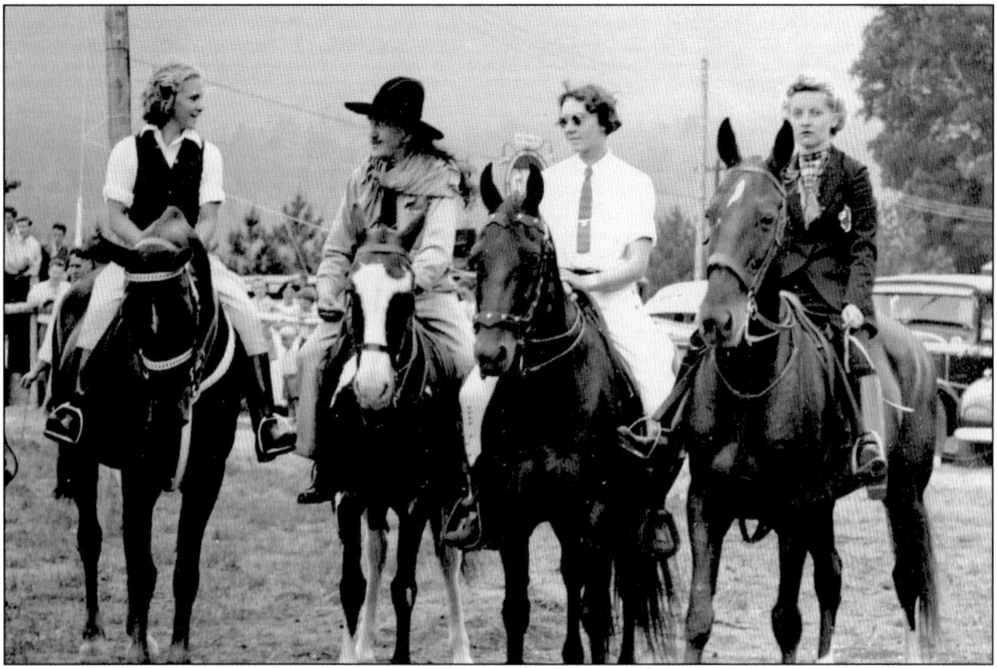

Charles Mortimer Miller came to Glens Falls with one of his shows. He met Carrie Potter and was married in the home of her grandfather Bethuel Witherill on Glen Street. Carrie lived at 9, now 12, Thomson Avenue with the children while Charles toured with the Wild West Show. During one of his local shows, Miller (second from left) rode with the late Charlotte "Polly" Wiswall (second from right).

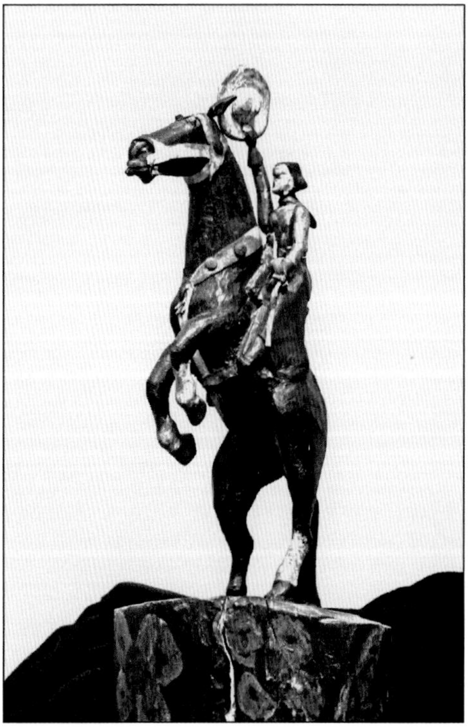

During his retirement years, he carved small rodeo figures, some of which are found in the collection at the Chapman Historical Museum in Glens Falls. His last great achievement was riding his favorite horse, Pole Star, from Patchogue, Long Island, to San Francisco, delivering a letter from Mayor Jimmy Walker (New York) to Mayor Angelo Rossi (San Francisco). He died at the age of 105 and is buried in Glens Falls.

Estelle Palmer, 1875–1956, was extremely active in the Red Cross during World War I. Referred to as Daisy, she was known for her enthusiasm and sincerity in any endeavor with which she was involved. She was especially patriotic and was seen marching in parades and encouraging citizens to become active in such ventures. She would have been considered a social activist, as she spent a great deal of time photographing areas of Glens Falls that she considered to be problematic. One concern was about tobacco advertising found on local playgrounds (seen below). Many of her photographs are in the archives at the Chapman Historical Museum. In later years, failing health caused her to become a recluse, but she still continued to keep informed of current events. Palmer planned a simple funeral so her friends would not be inconvenienced.

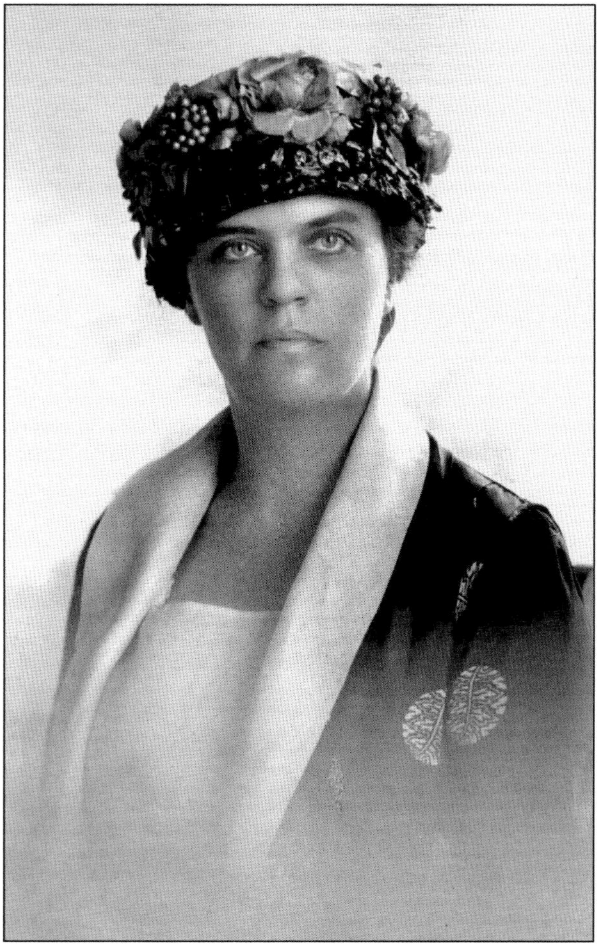

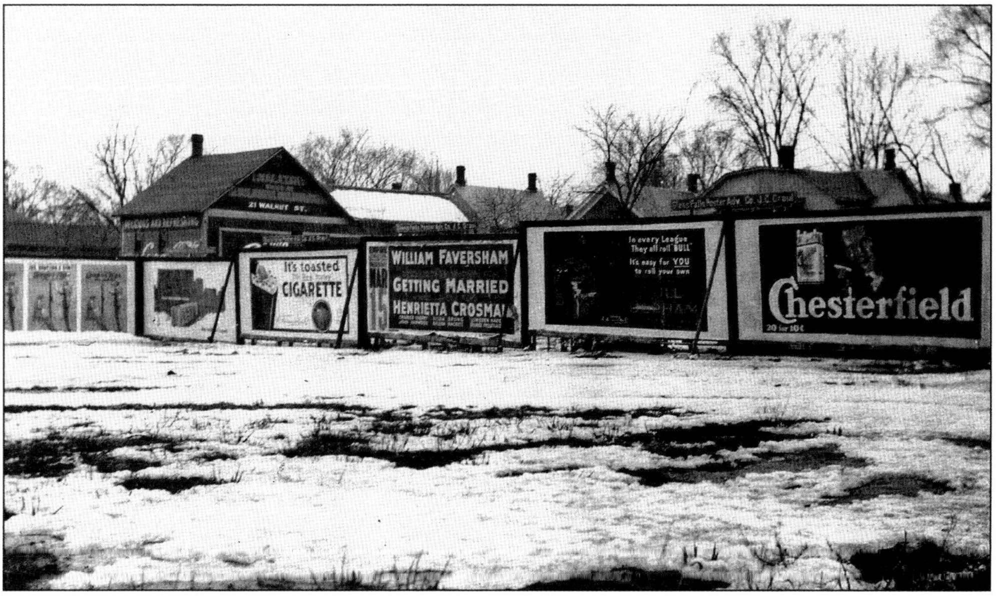

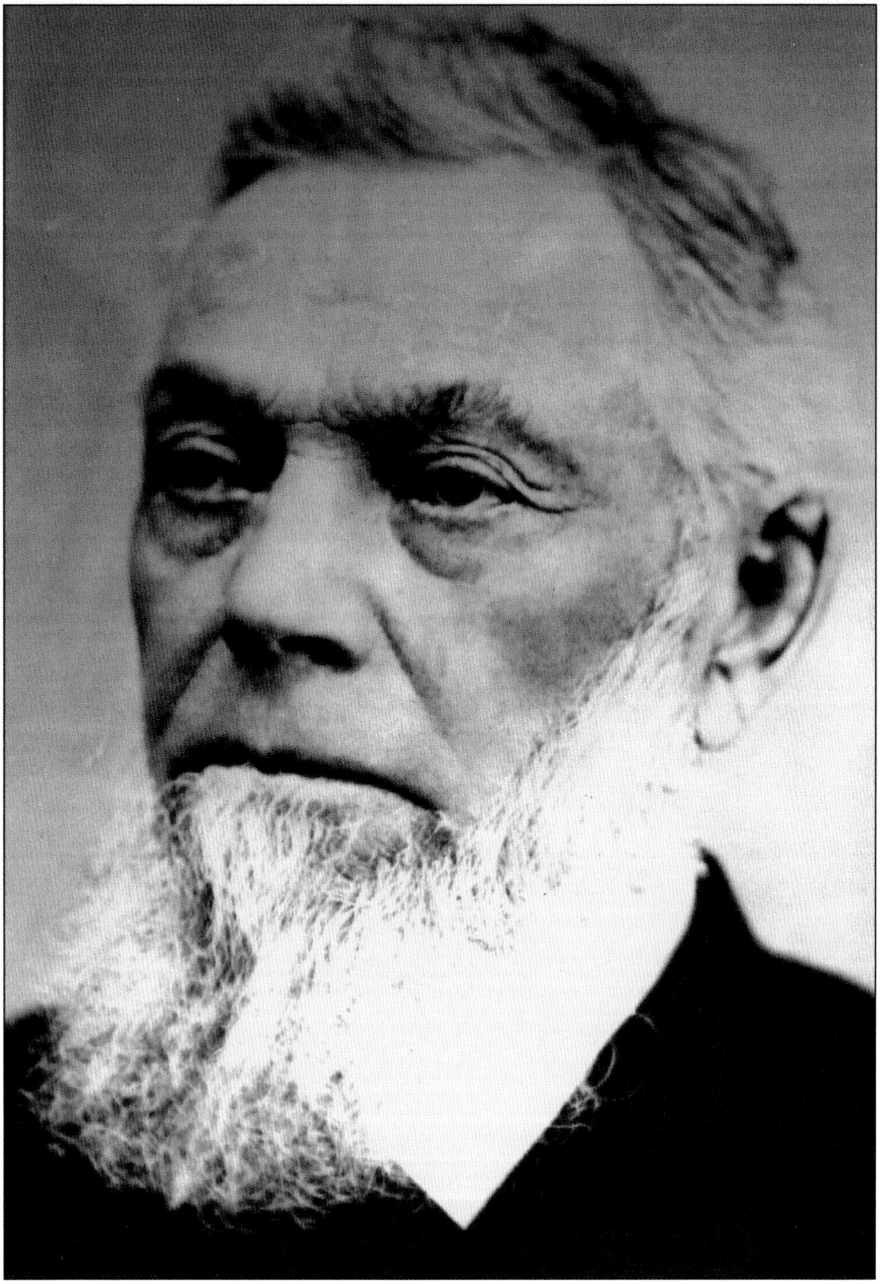

Augustus Sherman, 1801–1884, only spent one year in school in Arlington, Vermont. Moving to the area at the age of 15, he floated logs down the Hudson River from Corinth to the Big Bend area of Glens Falls and on to Roger's Island in Fort Edward. By 16, after his father's death, he took over the family business. He ran a mill with two saws and a gristmill in Luzerne but still rafted lumber to market. He purchased large tracts of land in the Adirondacks. In 1824, Sherman married a teacher, Nancy Weed. They had nine children, three dying very young. By 1840–1841, he sold all his Luzerne businesses and in 1842 consolidated all his lumber interests in Glens Falls. His wife Nancy died in 1848, and he married Charlotte Conkling in 1856. They had four more children. Charlotte taught him to read after their marriage.

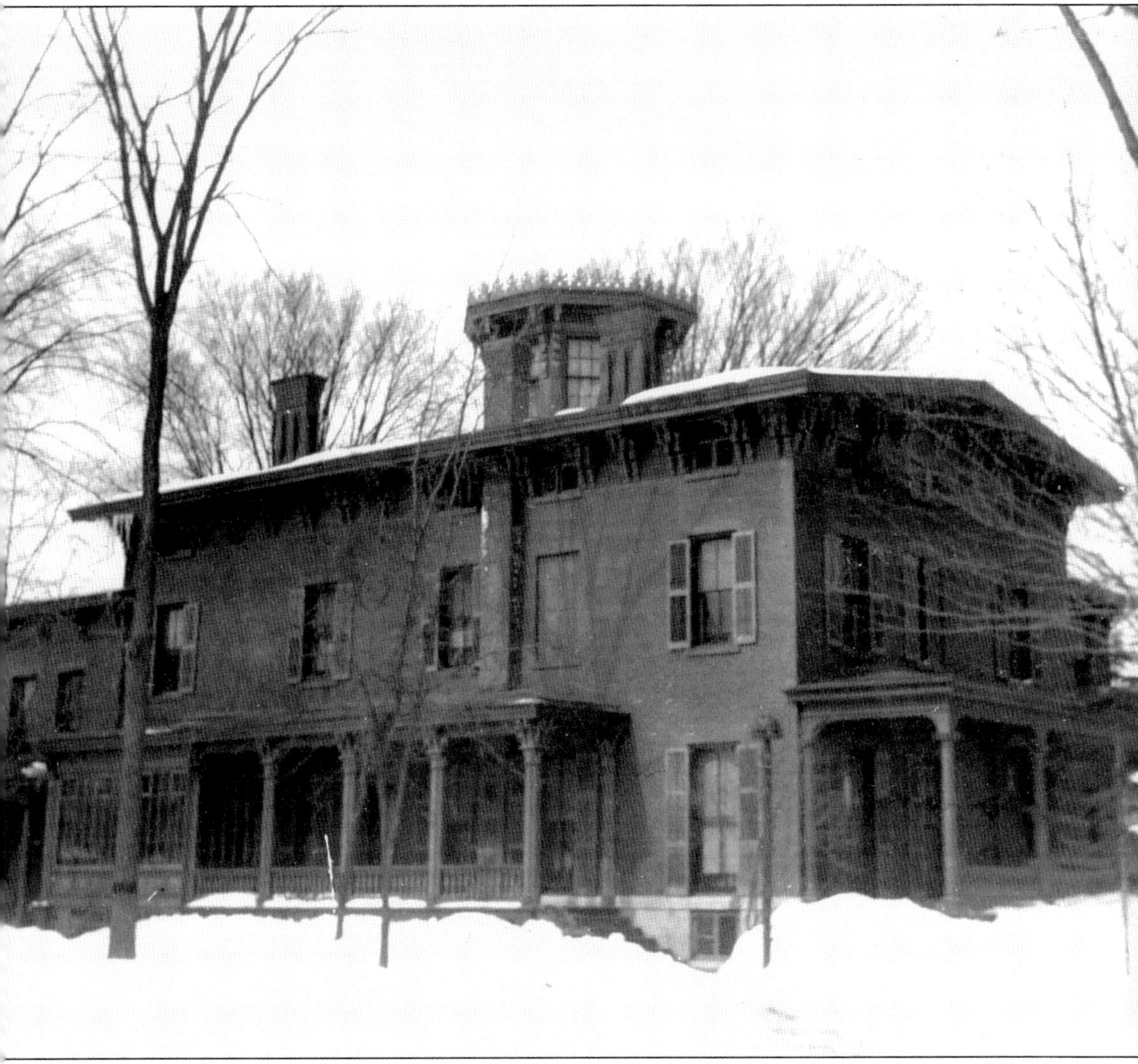

Sherman's home was in the style of an Italian Victorian villa, seen here on the northwest corner of Hawkeye (now Sherman) and Glen Streets. His property went north up Glen Street to Grove Avenue, west to Quade Street and south to Orville Street. In 1884, the home was sold to Henry Lapham, and in 1897, it became part of the Bemis Sanatorium. For 26 years, Sherman was president of the Commercial Bank, which later became the First National Bank. He owned the first boat on the Feeder Canal and was the first president of the Glens Falls Paper Mill Company and the Bald Mountain Lime Company. He was the manager, director, or trustee of every money corporation in Glens Falls. Prior to his death, he transferred most of his property holdings to his son Darwin, who had married Calvin Robbin's daughter, Marion. When Sherman died, he was considered the wealthiest man in Warren County.

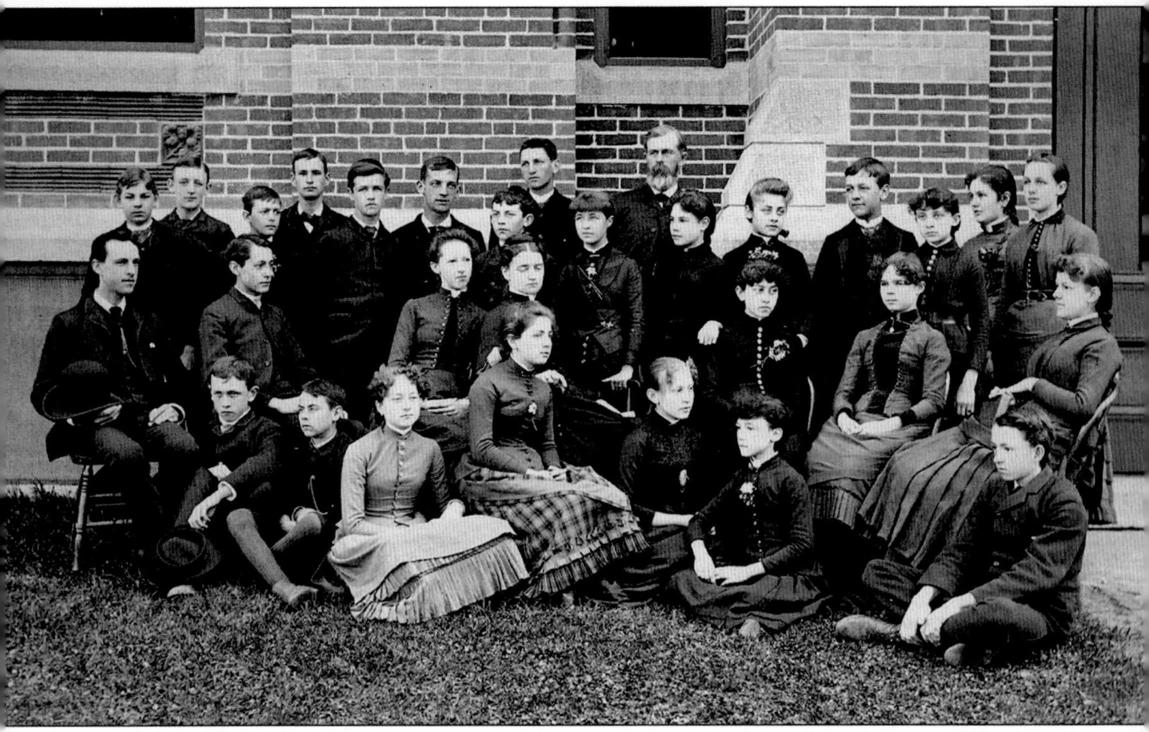

Sherman Williams, 1846–1923, was born near Cooperstown and graduated from Albany Normal School and settled in Flushing as a teaching principal. At age 36 he came to Glens Falls to face the challenge of forming a Union Free School District. He sought to obtain buildings with space to increase enrollment, repair old buildings, and employ adequately trained teachers. Children between the ages of 8 and 14 were expected to go to school for 8 consecutive weeks out of an academic year of 14 weeks. Corporal punishment was used to maintain discipline and most teachers were only high school graduates. When the canal closed for the season, a teacher might expect an additional 40 to 50 students to enroll for the winter months. Improved hiring practices dropped classroom averages to 56 pupils. During Williams's term as superintendent, a new building was built on Glen Street that was to become the prototype for all future buildings. He is shown here with a beard in the back row with a graduating class from Union School No. 1. He helped develop confidence in public school education.

Five

THE WEST

Today the west side of town is thought of as the exit to the interstate. However, it was and still is a typical residential neighborhood. This was the area inhabited by French Canadians who supported St. Alphonsus Catholic Church with its French-speaking clergy. It was also home to many Jewish families in town. One of the first union schools was set up in this neighborhood. When Solomon Parks gave his home to start the first community hospital, it anchored that facility in the west end. Extreme wealth in the area contributed to the development of the fairgrounds, and later a mile-long track for thoroughbred racing. Several "moneyed" men owned racehorses and were part of the grand circuit. Because there were still local volunteer fire departments, the open spaces in the west end allowed for competitions and community enthusiasm for these events. These spaces were also home to the annual visit of the circus. This chapter will show the activities of the area as well as some of the "anchors" found there. They include the circus, fairgrounds, Mile Racetrack, Glens Falls Hospital, St. Alphonsus Church, and Union Free School No. 2. People will be Philetus Allen, Merritt Ames, John Bazinet, Harry Elkes, Walter Garrett, James Holden, Annie Hull, Solomon Parks, Samuel Pruyn, and Seneca Ray Stoddard.

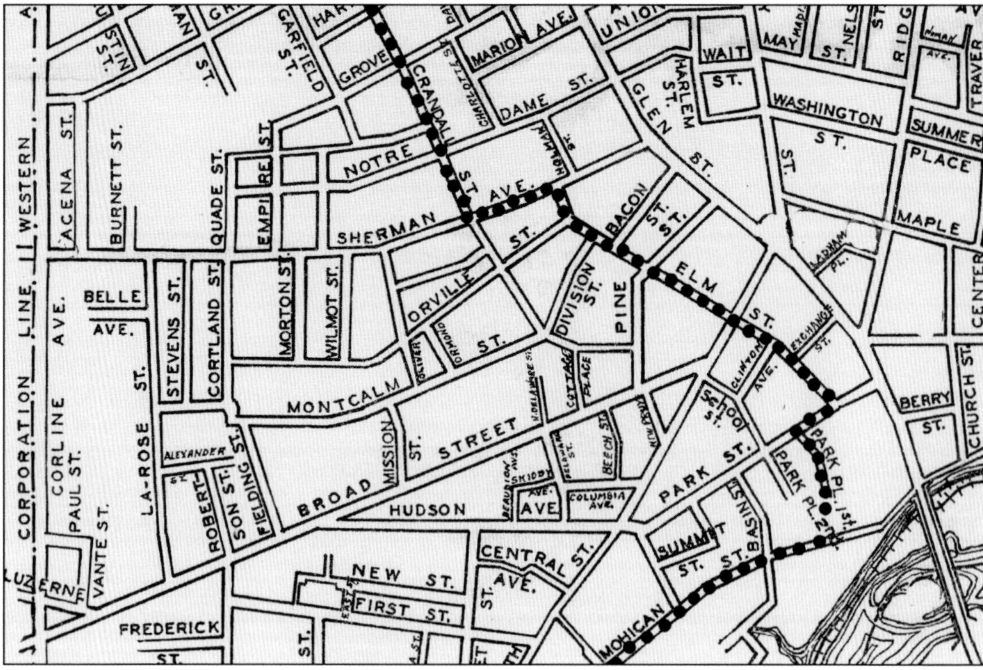

The west end in this chapter will refer to the area beginning north of Mohican Street, up to Park Street, on to Elm Street, then north to Sherman Avenue, and then north again on Crandall Street to Crandall Park. Presently this is a typical family-oriented neighborhood with small independent businesses and redeveloping controlled-income housing.

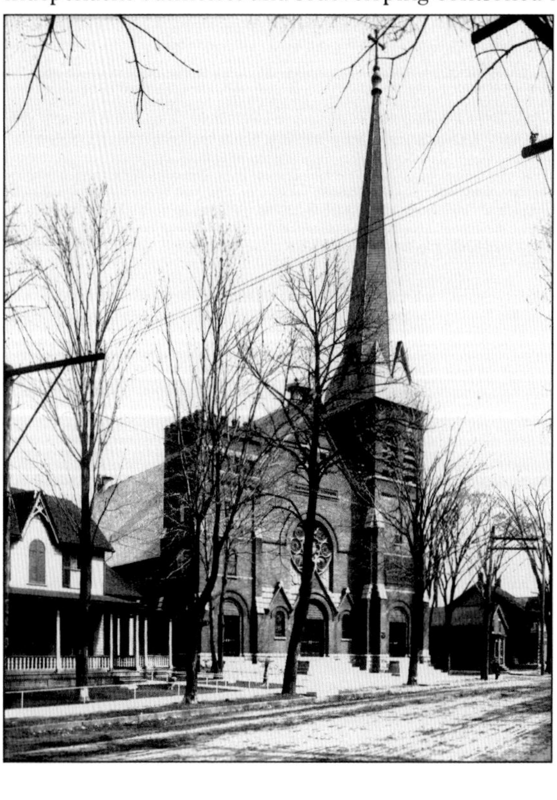

St. Alphonsus Church was the anchor for Roman Catholics in the west end that settled there from Canada. They were French speaking, and the parish priest delivered the mass in that language. The parish began with services in private homes, then in a smaller building that was enlarged periodically, and finally to the grand brick church, seen here, that opened in 1888.

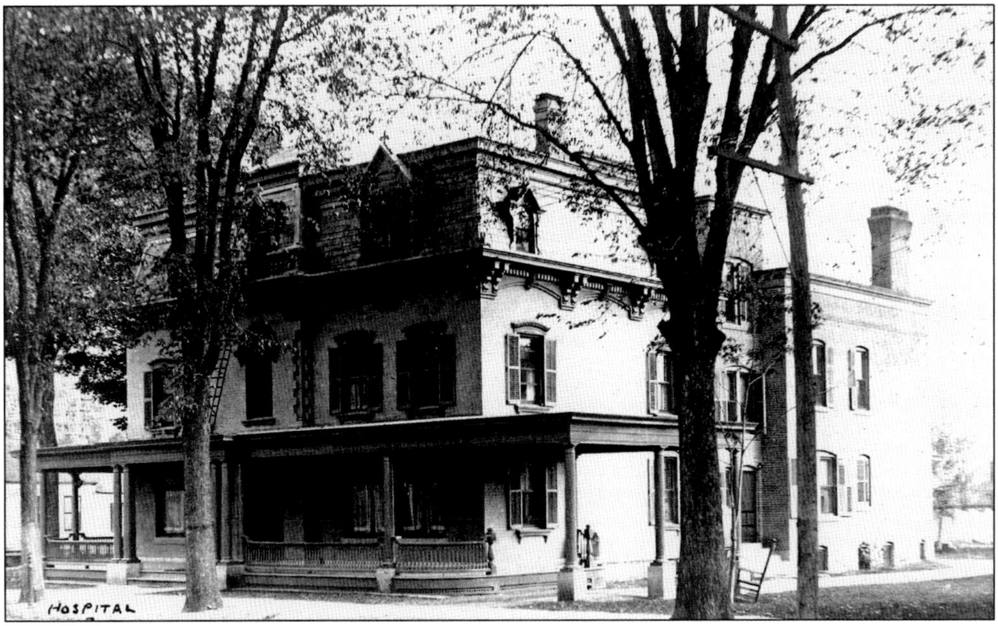

Solomon Parks, originally from south Glens Falls, donated his brick home at 34 Park Street for use as a community hospital in 1899. It opened as the Parks Hospital for medical care in November 1900, named in his honor. The space provided room for the care of 22 patients.

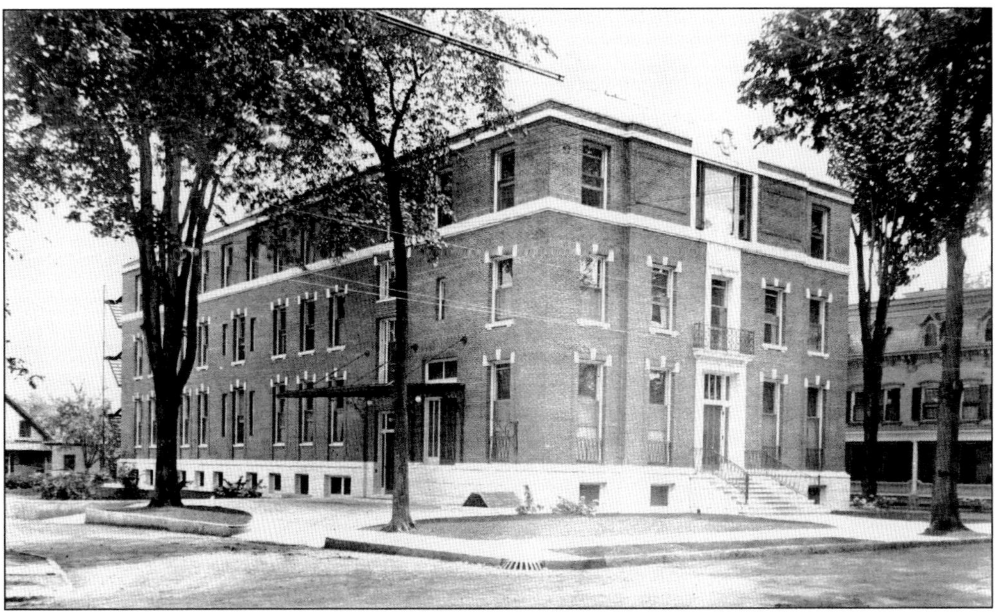

In 1903, a training school for nurses was established. It served the community well until 1932, with over 200 graduates when it was torn down to make room for an expanded facility, seen here. It rapidly outgrew its space, and a new building opened in 1938 with spaces for 150 patients but could handle up to 200 in an emergency. This building became the north wing during future expansions.

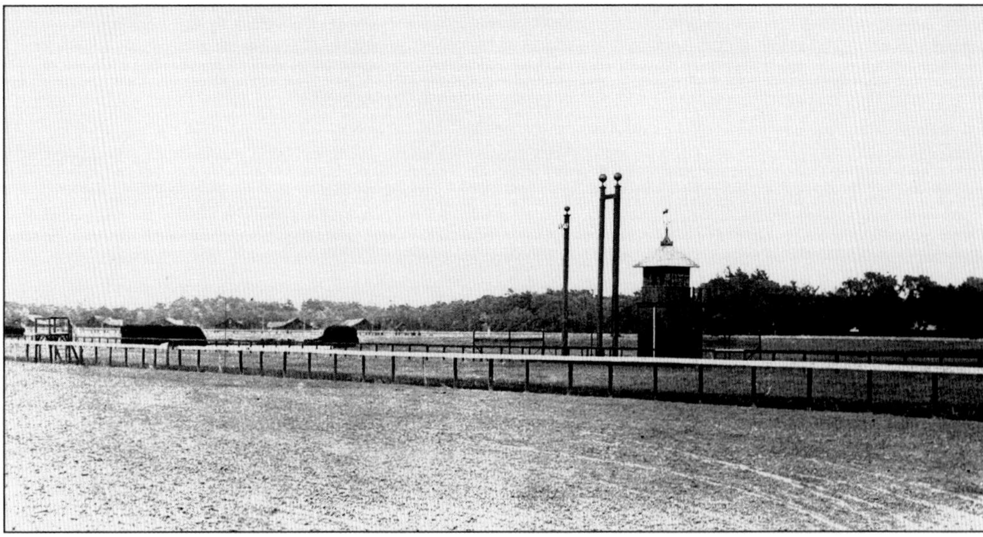

In 1869, a group of influential Glens Falls citizens purchased 28 acres of land in the area of what is now Glen Street, Lincoln Avenue, Kensington Road, and Crandall Park. The Warren County Fairgrounds developed, including a half-mile track for harness racing and several fair buildings and a grandstand that was located on present-day Coolidge Avenue.

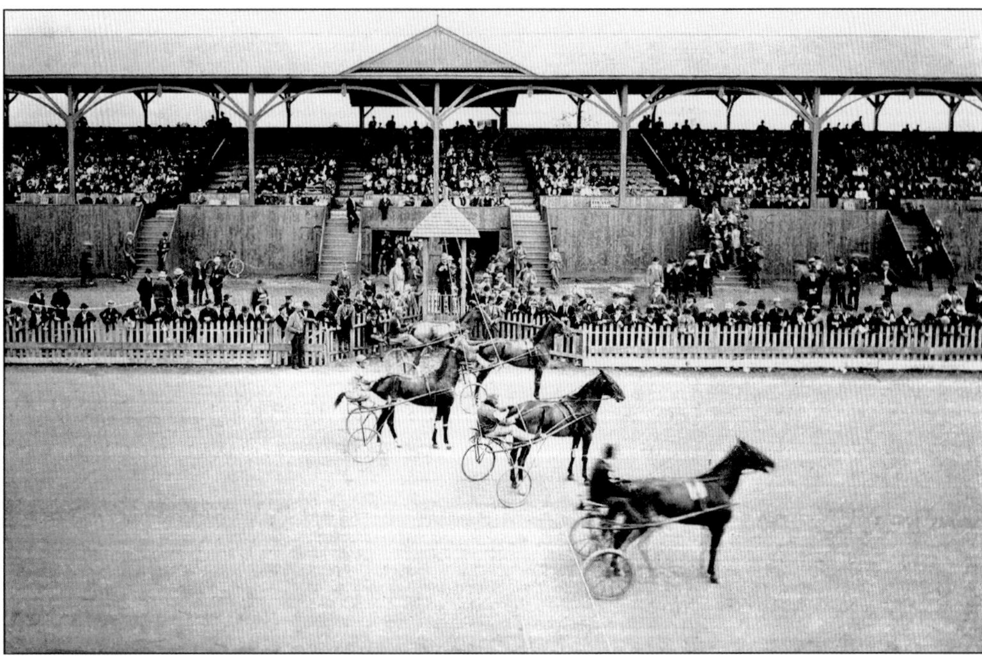

In 1893, additional acres were purchased and a mile track was established. This track was part of the grand circuit and considered one of the fastest in the country. This remained in use until 1902. After that time, Russell A. Little and Arthur Sherman purchased the land and developed residential lots now known as Broadacres. Today's Western Avenue was called Mile Track Boulevard as it led to the track.

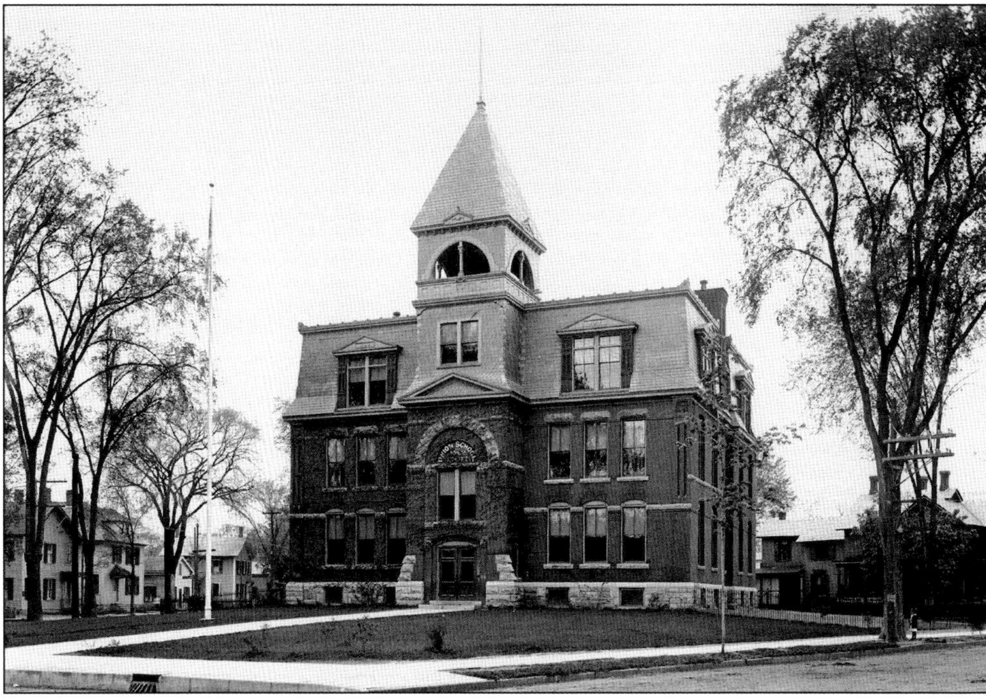

In 1823, a two-room schoolhouse was built at the corner of South and West Streets. It was enlarged in 1863, and then in 1892, the three-story, 12-room brick building known as Union Free School No. 2 was opened and called the South Street School. It held classes for kindergarten through grade seven with 12 teachers. At one point there were 640 eligible school-age children in the district, but only 374 were enrolled, with the average attendance a mere 101. Because of the open space in front of the school, Union Square, named because of the union school there, local fire departments from South and West Streets were able to stage competitions. At the time when there were no mechanical entertainments, these competitions attracted large crowds. Since volunteers manned most fire departments, support by excited families was greatly appreciated.

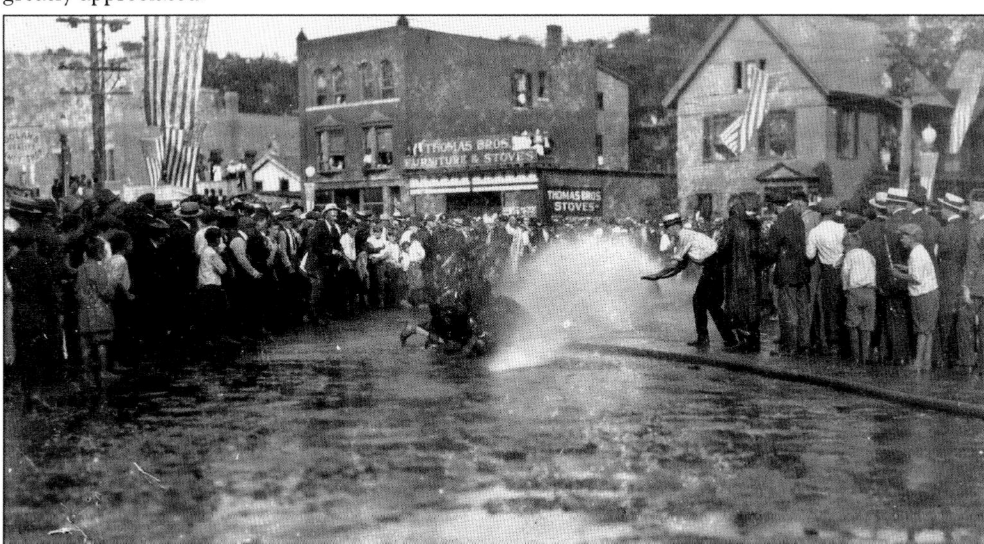

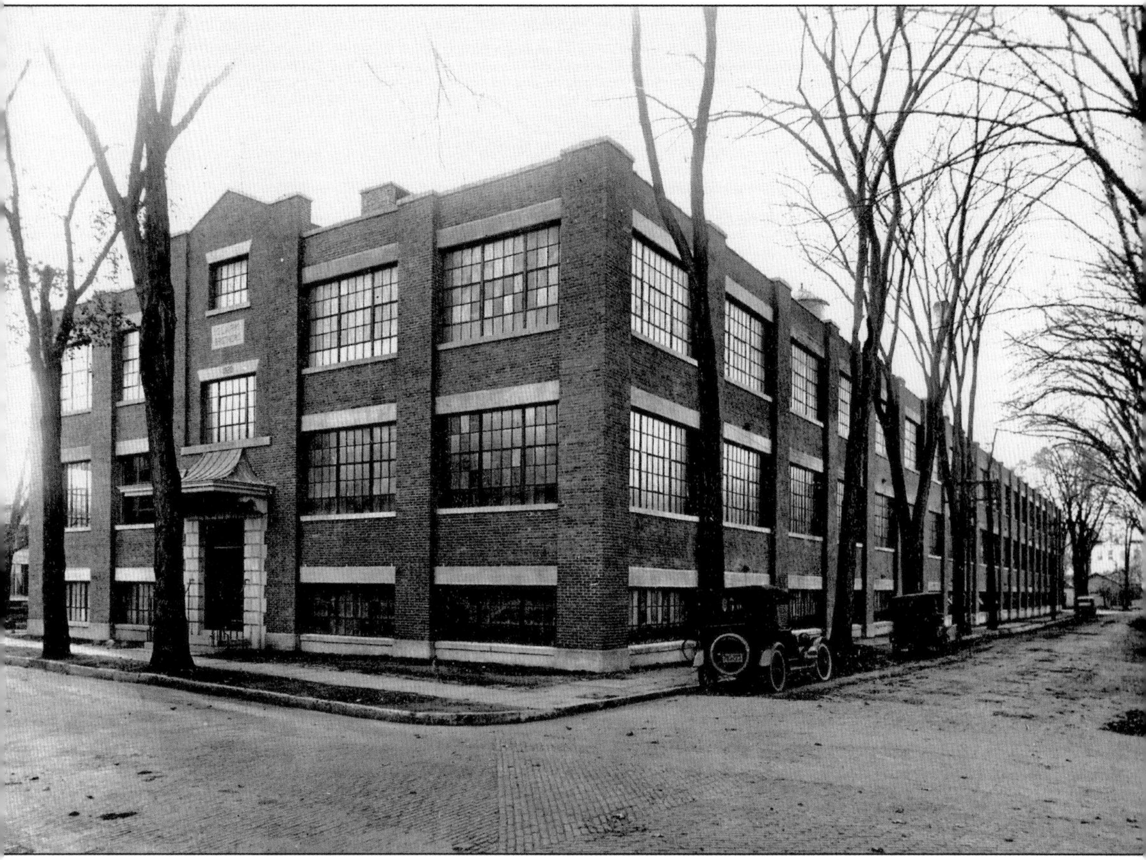

Robert G. and Alfred S. Clark came to Glens Falls in 1919 to establish their textile business. They purchased a lot on the corner of Elm Street and Clinton Avenue from Samuel Pruyn and broke ground in early 1920. By October, the entire facility was operational as the Clark Brothers Glove Company. All yarns arrived in a raw state, and dying, cutting, weaving, stitching, finishing, boxing, and packing was done in-house. The plant produced the finest-quality silk gloves as well as underwear. The company operated 24 hours a day, but the 350 employees were able to use a well-furnished recreation room during their breaks. During World War II, there was a boycott of German-made goods, so the Clark Brothers factory prospered. After the war, the Reciprocal Trade Agreement allowed Germany, France, and Italy to take over 60 percent of the leather glove production and 60 percent of the American silk glove market went to Japan. This was the beginning of the demise of Clark Brothers. It closed in 1959, and the building is now being converted into upscale condominiums.

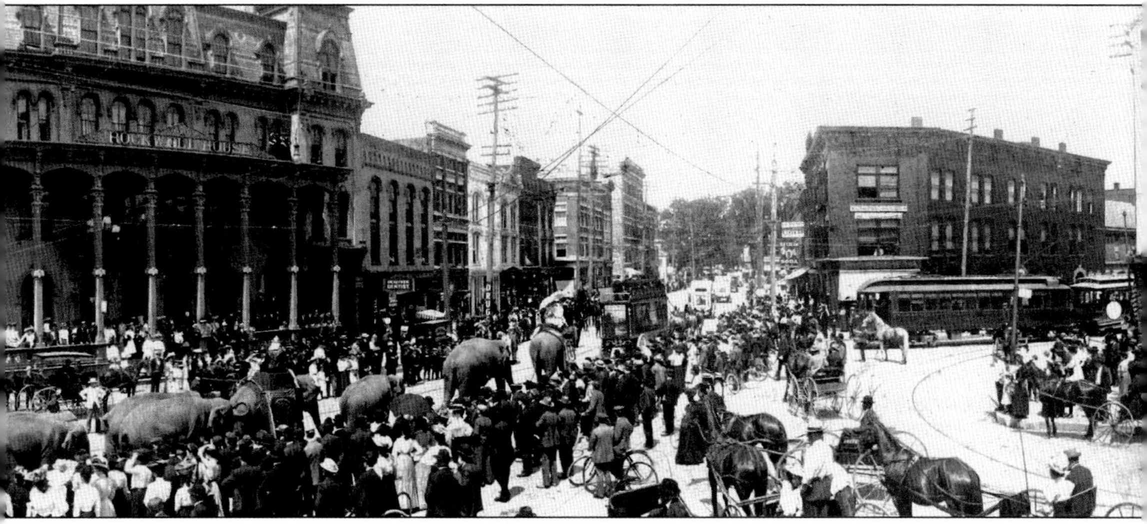

From the end of the 19th century through the mid-20th century, the circus came to Glens Falls. It was staged in the west end of town in the area of the present-day Hannaford store. Prior to setting up the huge circus tents, an introductory parade was held through the town. Arriving at the train station on Maple Street, the various carts with animal cages were assembled into a parade that went to Warren Street and then north on Glen Street before turning west to the show grounds. People lined the street to watch this annual spectacle. Of particular interest were the elephants that "marched" freely with their trainers in the street (shown). Clowns and acrobats moved through the crowds, building excitement for the shows that were to come during their stay. Late in the 1900s, the show was moved indoors to the civic center, but the circus decided that this venue was too small and ended its visits to the city.

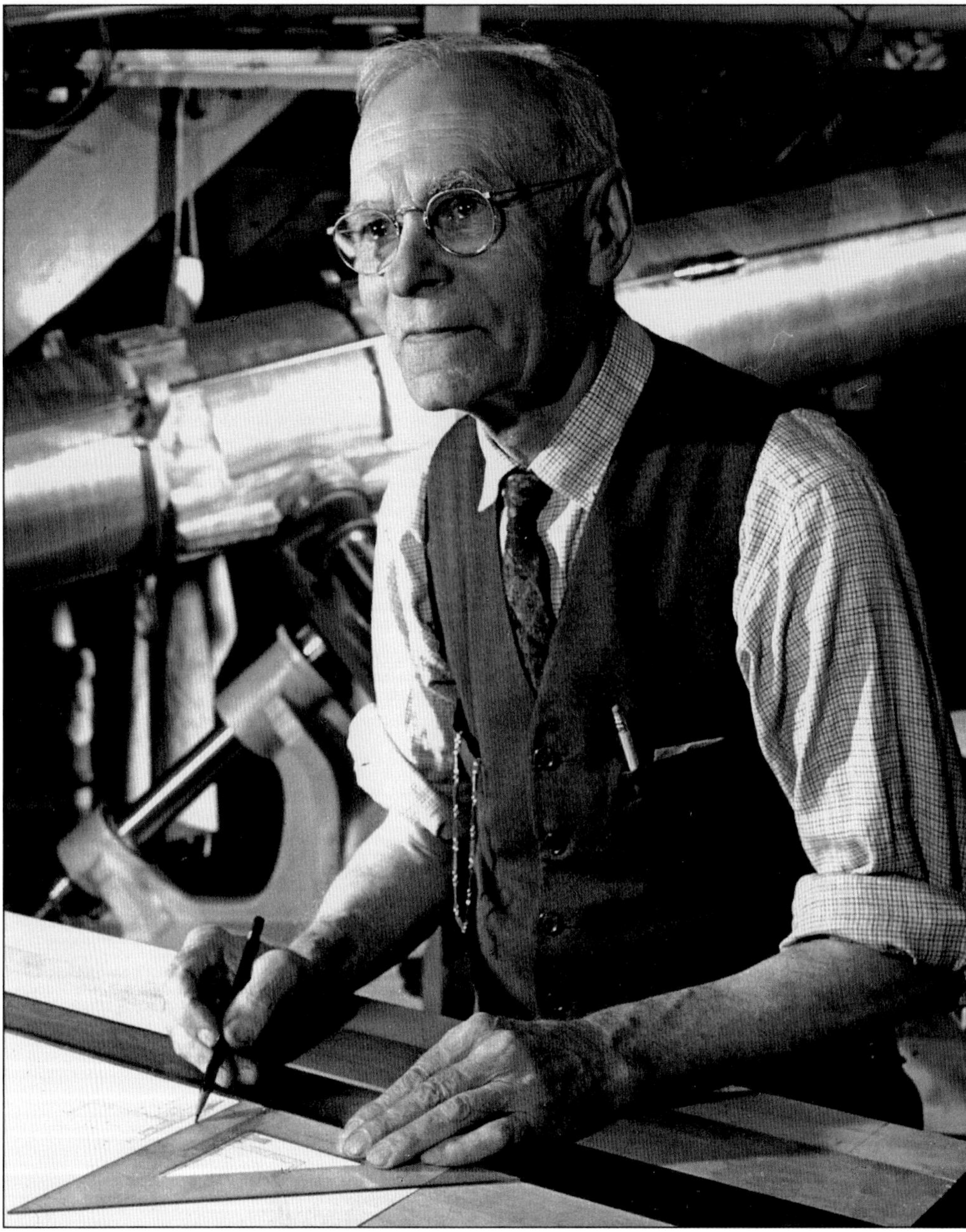

Philetus Allen, 1874–1957, was employed as a painter and paperhanger for William Austin, a local decorator. Later he worked for Wilmarth and Son furniture store in the finishing department for 30 years. A perfectionist in everything he did, he restored fine furniture, repaired antiques, and replaced ornate scrollwork on picture frames. He was also considered an artist in watercolor and oils. Allen designed, had built, and lived in the houses at 8, 18, and 26 Coolidge Avenue. His last house was at 45 Sheridan Street where, as an amateur astronomer, he became well known for the telescopes he built. Many Glens Falls residents peered at the stars through the instrument when it was set up in his yard. Classes of local children came to look through the telescope and have astronomy lessons. Even though his formal education ended with high school, he became an expert in this field and shared his information freely.

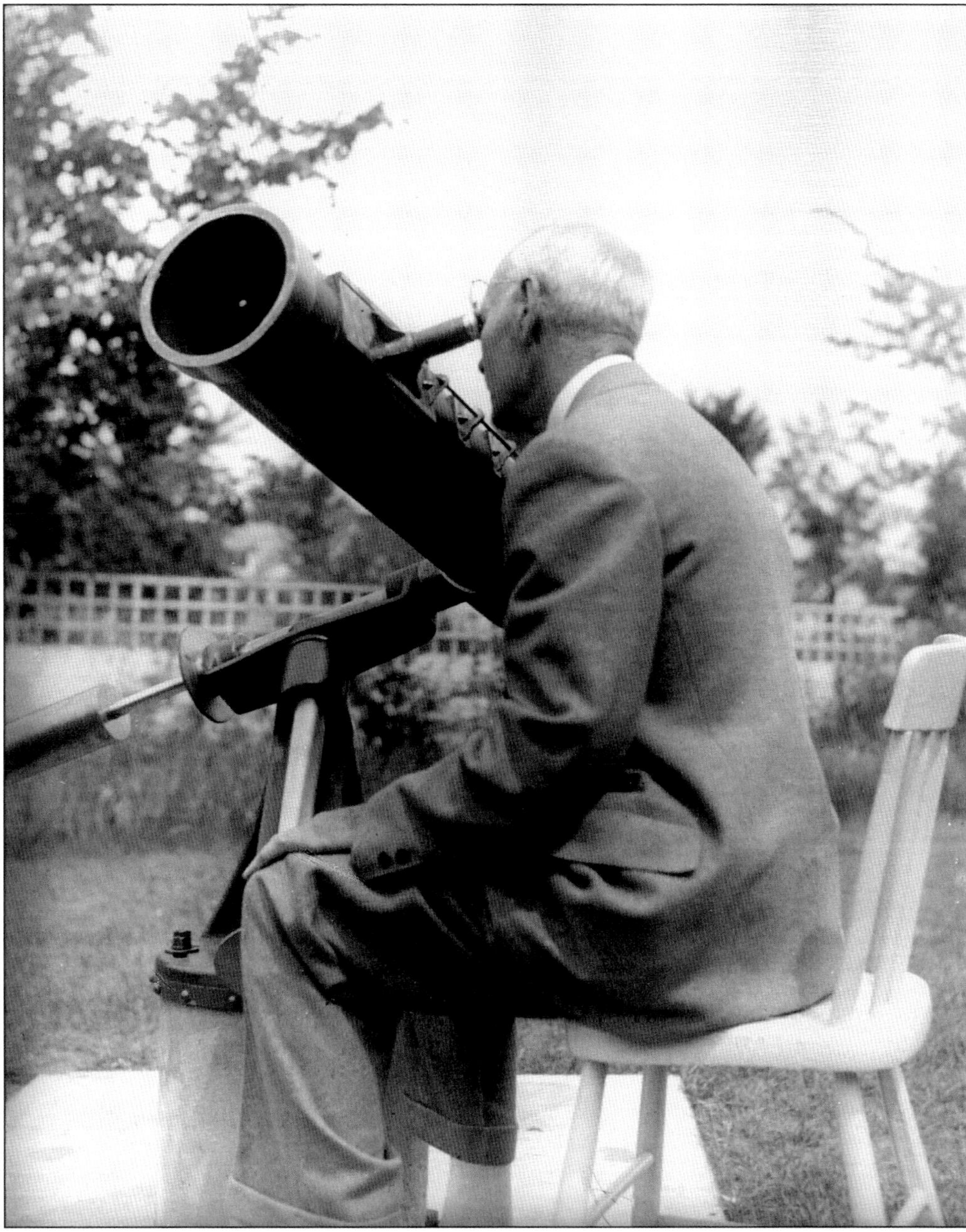

Allen received national attention in scientific circles regarding his construction of telescopes. One telescope was 200 times more powerful than the human eye. All parts of his instruments were made by hand, including its six-inch mirror that took him three months to grind and polish. He was able to complete a telescope in about eight months. His masterpiece was one with a 12-inch mirror. His reflector type telescopes had no lenses except in the eyepiece. The principle parts were a mirror, a prism, and an eyepiece that gives the true coloration of the stars. His 10-inch telescope was bought by Princeton University. Allen often wrote letters to the editor of a local newspaper explaining what to look for in coming events in the sky. An article was written about him and his works in the *Scientific American* around 1948.

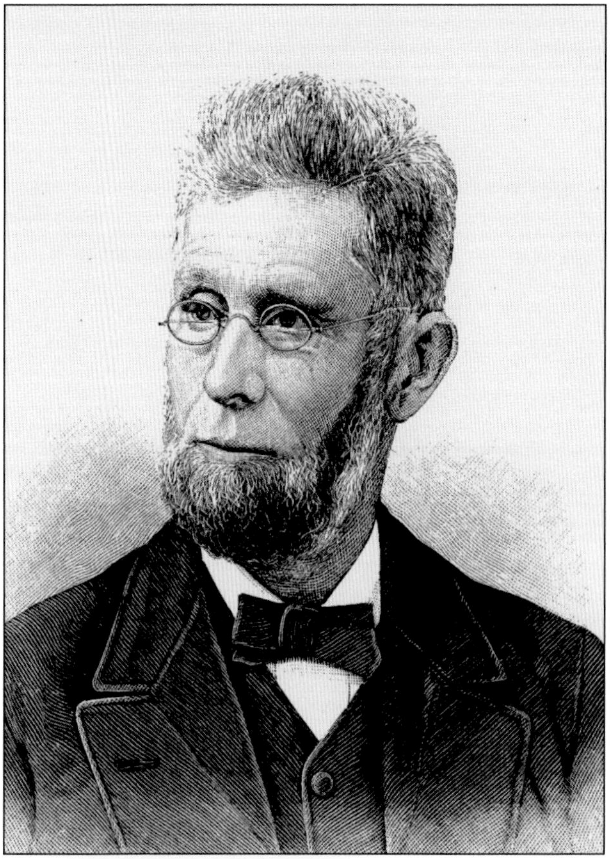

Merritt Ames, 1825–1914, was born in Poultney, Vermont, coming to Glens Falls in 1846. As an excellent orator, avid Bible student, and militant Christian, he was able to give lectures in churches in several states. He studied chemistry and astronomy on his own. Ames became a professional photographer and was friends with George Eastman. While developing his own lantern slides, he realized he was throwing away wastes from the developing process that contained silver. After experimentation, he began collecting this residue from photographers around the country. Opening a plant on Sherman Avenue (below), he purified the wastes into silver nitrate to be reused by photographers, silver for the U.S. Mint, and for making mirrors and medicine. When business boomed, he was able to purchase silver from the U.S. Mint as an investment instead of selling it to them.

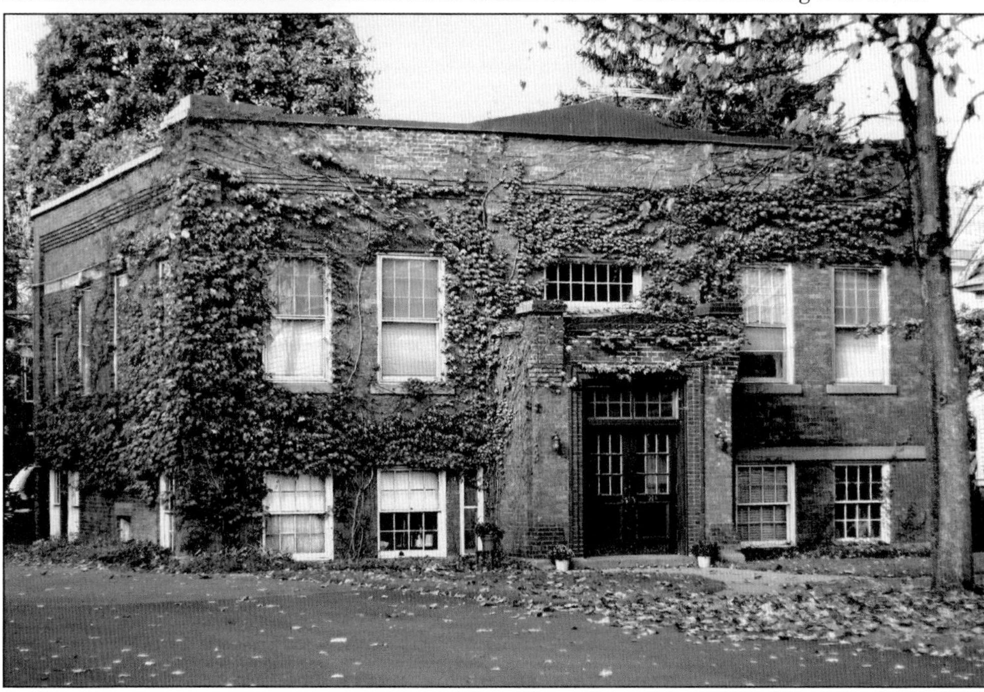

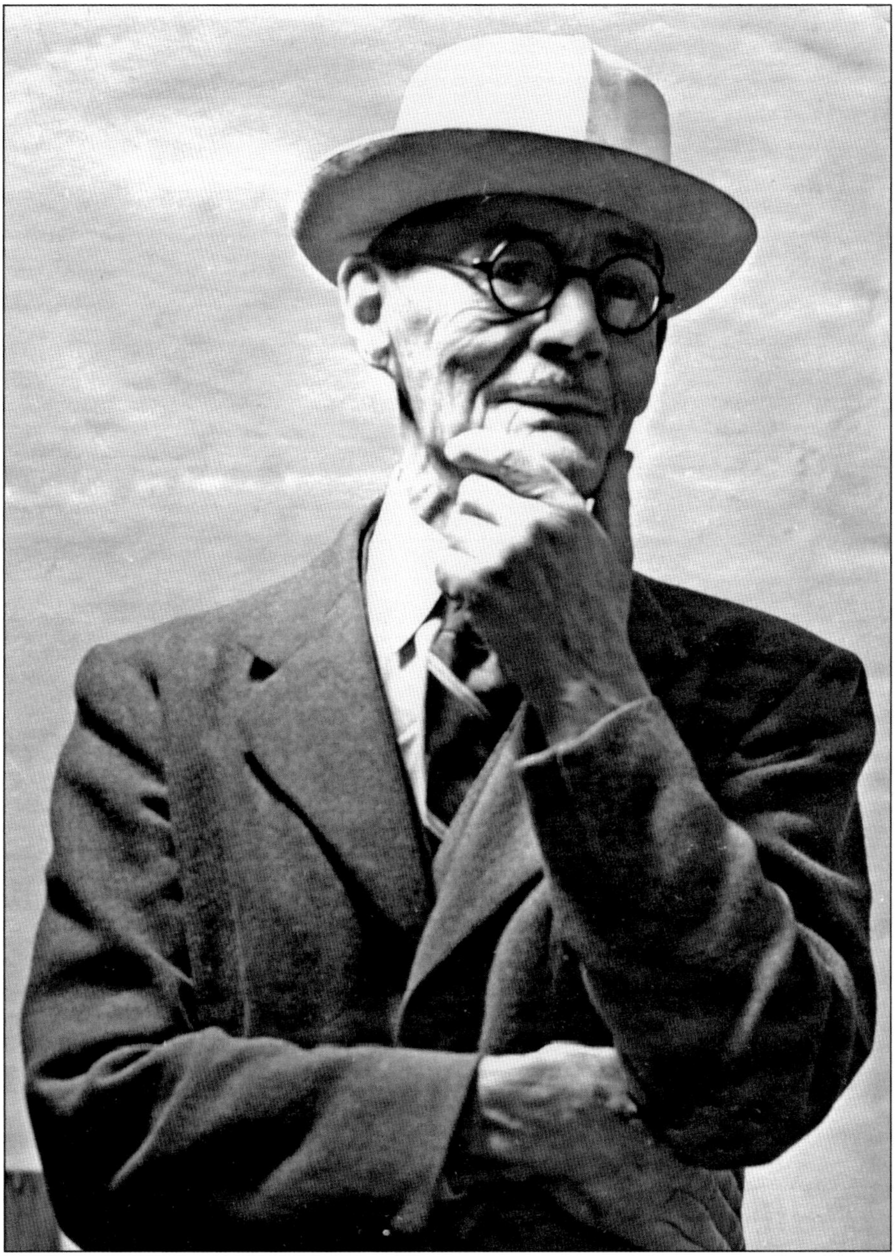

John Bazinet, 1867–1953, came with his family to Glens Falls in 1868. He attended the old brick school in Union Square that was to become the South Street School. Later he worked as a blacksmith and paymaster with the Glens Falls Portland Cement Company. He started his political career as village treasurer in 1907. He was the city's first chamberlain and then was Warren County's treasurer for three terms. Bazinet served as fourth ward councilman and member of the water board and zoning board of appeals. He served as mayor for five consecutive terms beginning in 1940. He was involved with many local social organizations, including charter member and grand knight of the Knights of Columbus and charter member and chaplain of the Glens Falls Elks Lodge 81, Benevolent and Protective Order of Elks. He was also a member of the Canadian Republic Society and St. Alphonsus Church.

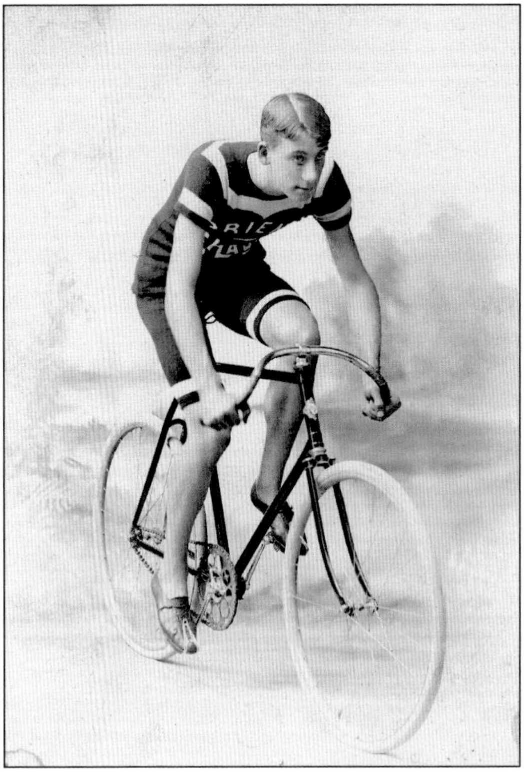

Harry Elkes, 1878–1903, moved to Glens Falls with his family when he was a teenager. They lived on Orville Street and then Grove Avenue. His father, Harry, an ex-athlete and trainer, coached him along with Leona, a famous French bicycle racing champion. Part of his training was cycling up and down Glen Street hill. Harry was the Lance Armstrong of his time, breaking records in Europe and at home.

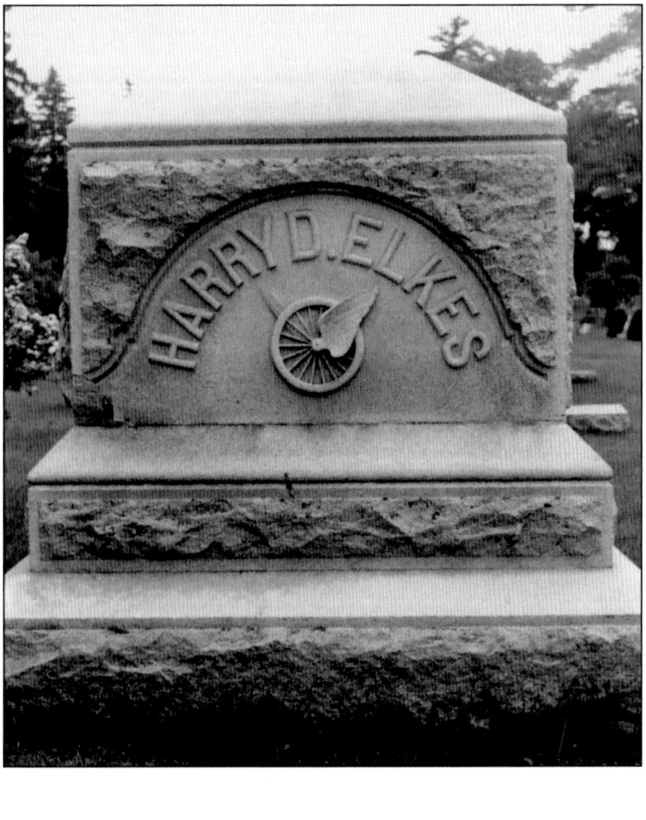

Elkes won the National Paced Championship in 1900 and 1901. He teamed up with the great sprinter Floyd MacFarland to win the 1902 New York Six Day Race. Elkes broke records at distances of up to 25 miles. At the Charles River board track, the chain brake tangled in his rear wheel, throwing him in front of a pacing motorcycle. He died instantly. Elkes is buried in the Bay Street Cemetery.

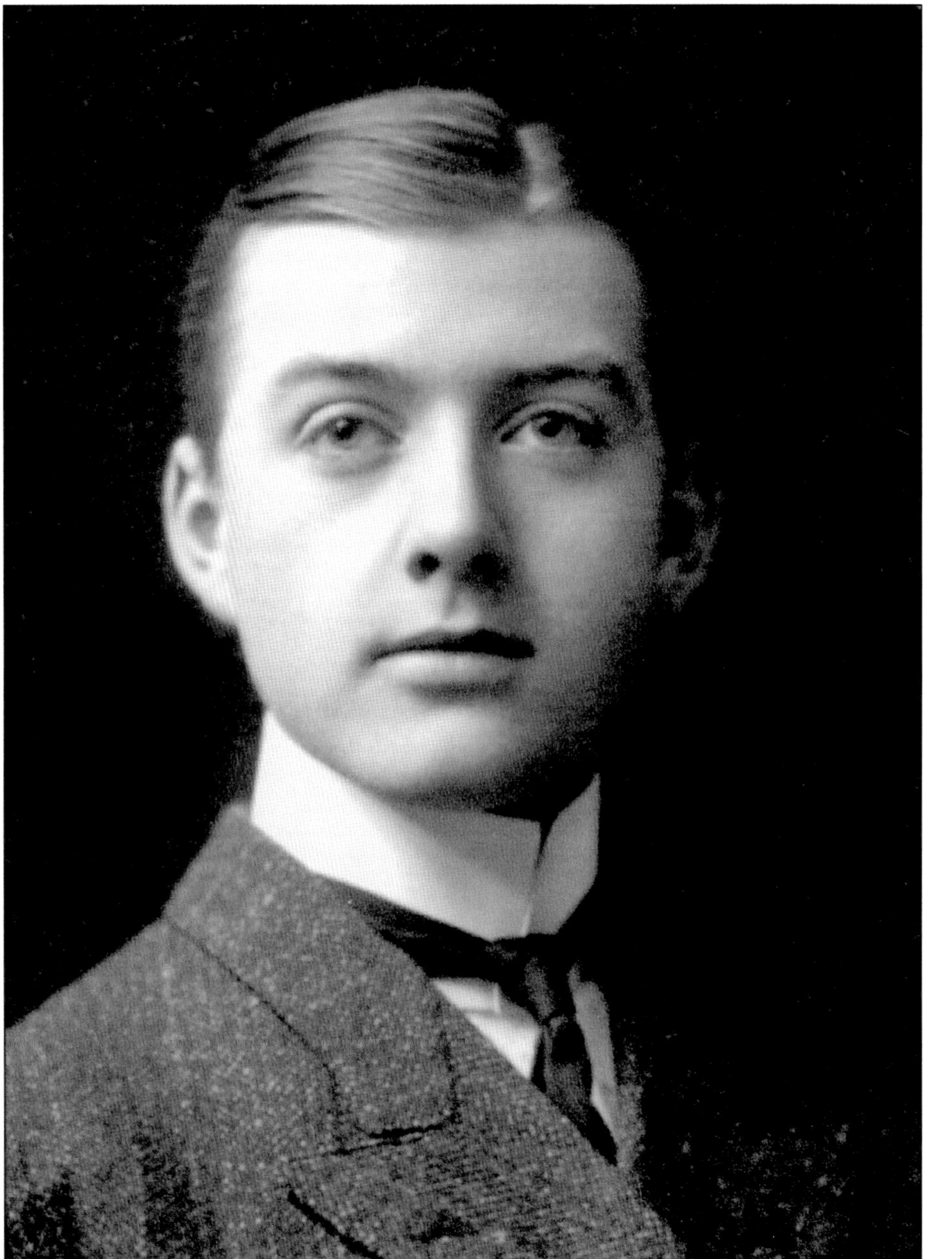

Walter Garrett, D.D.S., 1882–1972, attended public schools in Glens Falls, graduating as president of his class in 1898. However, at age 10 he started violin lessons, and when he was 18, he gave violin lessons in Glens Falls, Greenwich, and Saratoga Springs. He played the violin in the first orchestra of the Empire Theater and later led the orchestra. Garrett played in the Baltimore Symphony while studying dentistry at Baltimore Medical College. He graduated magna cum laude in 1910, later joining the dental staff at the Glens Falls Hospital, remaining there for 20 years. He resigned that position in 1946 but continued his private practice until his retirement in 1961. Dentistry runs in the family as his father James and son Richard were both dentists, and presently his grandson Richard Jr. is practicing. (Courtesy of the Garrett family.)

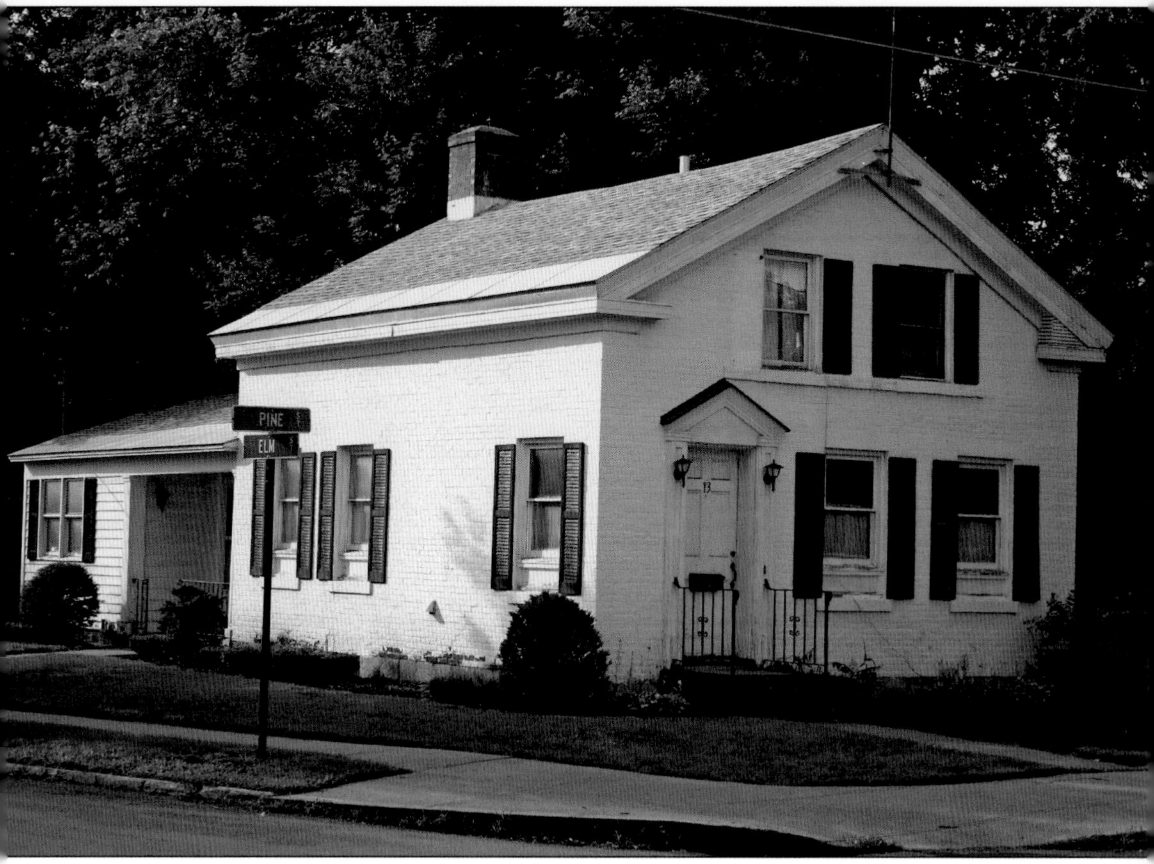

Annie Melissa Hull, 1877–1948, received her early education in Glens Falls, entering New York Medical College and Hospital for Women and graduating in 1903. Dr. Hull began her practice in her family home, Oak Forest, in Queensbury, and then moved to the corner of Pine and Elm Streets in Glens Falls. House calls were made from there for 40 years. She was the health and truant officer for the Queensbury School District. She served the poor and rural folks of the area. Dr. Hull often brought homegrown vegetables to her patients and would take their dirty laundry home to clean. She never neglected an emergency need. In 1914, she bought her first automobile to make house calls easier. Dr. Hull never sent bills, believing that if people had the money, they would pay. She died peacefully in her sleep at home.

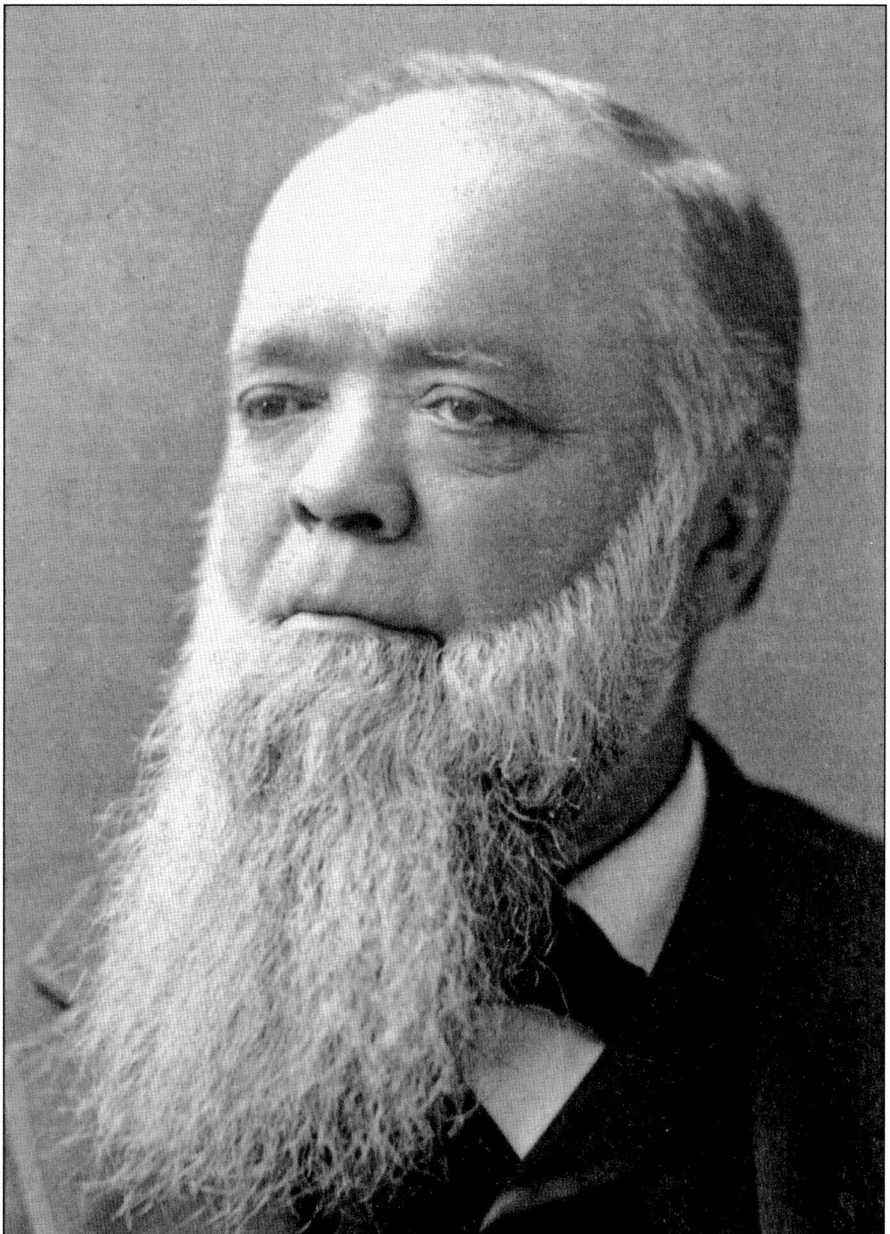

Solomon Parks, 1827–1900, a South Glens Falls native, built a sawmill and bridge across the Hudson River in Fenimore. He became overseer of the Glens Falls Paper Company and was considered a genius at manufacturing paper. Parks's company used straw and rags for manufacturing purposes. This provided an opportunity for local farmers to sell their straw at a profit. The company produced about 20 tons of print paper a week. The business included his son Fred as foreman. Parks was Glens Falls village president in 1877. He offered his home at 48 Park Street to be used as a community hospital. He died before the grand opening. That might have been a good thing as people regarded the hospital as an avoidable place. They believed that doctors experimented on rather than treated patients. His legacy is alive today as his original family residence in South Glens Falls is the Parks-Bentley Place, home of the historical society.

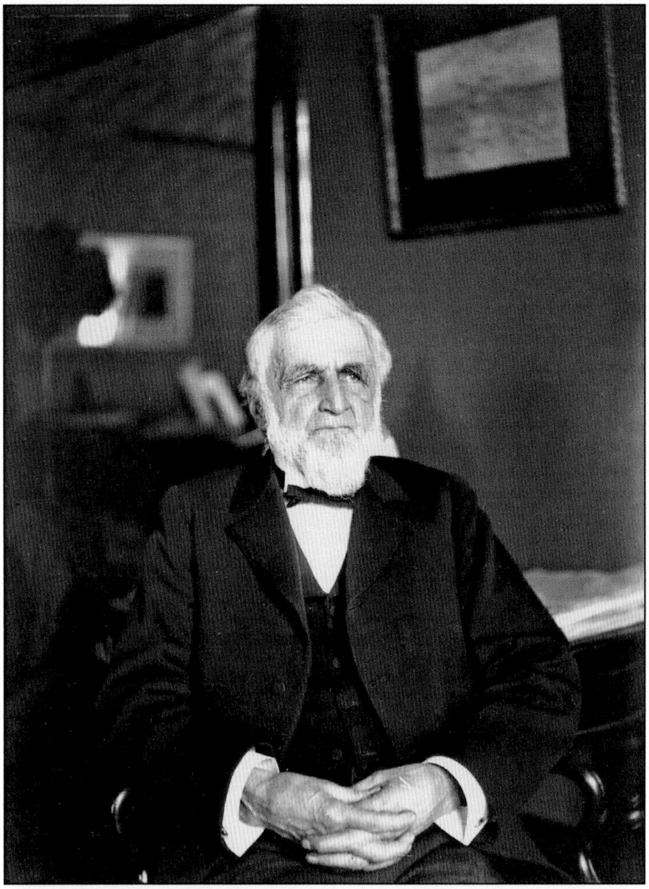

Samuel Pruyn, 1820–1908, left the family farm at age 30 to work in a lumber mill. He held many jobs within the lumber business. When he felt he had saved enough money, he married and bought his first house at 11 Bay Street. Together with Jeremiah and Daniel Finch, he formed a partnership, buying the Glens Falls Company in 1865. The company engaged in the sale of lime, lumber, grains, and marble. It later became the Finch Pruyn Company. He had a keen memory and kept business details in his head, not in ledgers. Pruyn served as a village trustee and backed the construction of the Sandy Hill, Fort Edward and Glens Falls Railway. Pruyn owned a home at the corner of Elm Street and Clinton Avenue (seen below), where he raised his three daughters, Charlotte, Mary, and Nellie.

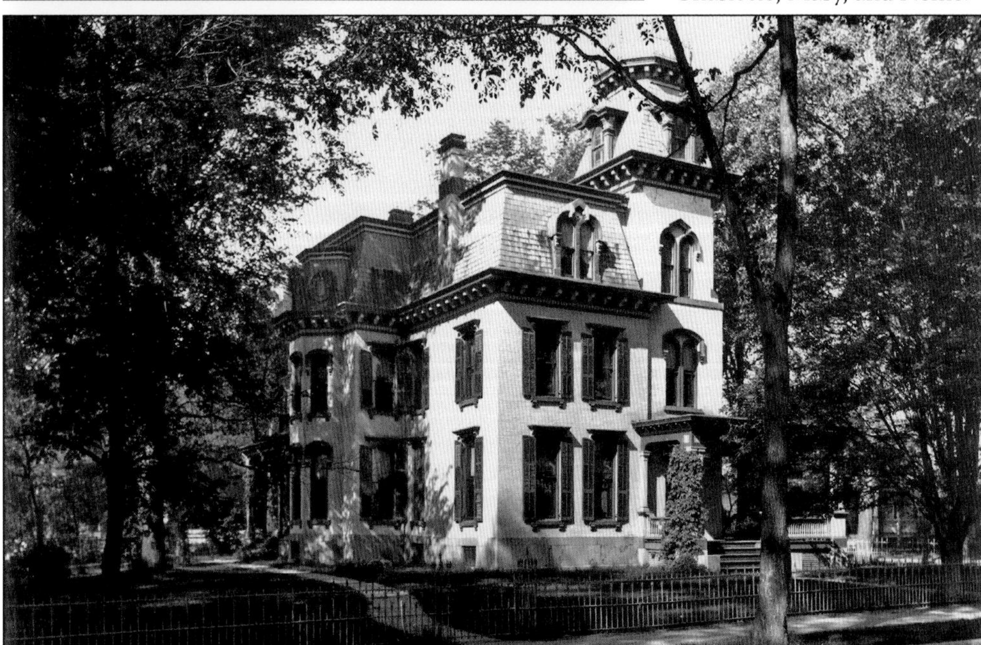

Seneca Ray Stoddard, 1844–1917, was born in Wilton and self-taught. His mother died when he was 7, and by age 10, he went to Troy to learn the trade of decorative painting. He worked for Eaton and Gilbert Company painting trolley and railroad cars. For over 50 years, he promoted the "glories of the great north woods" by the use of his camera.

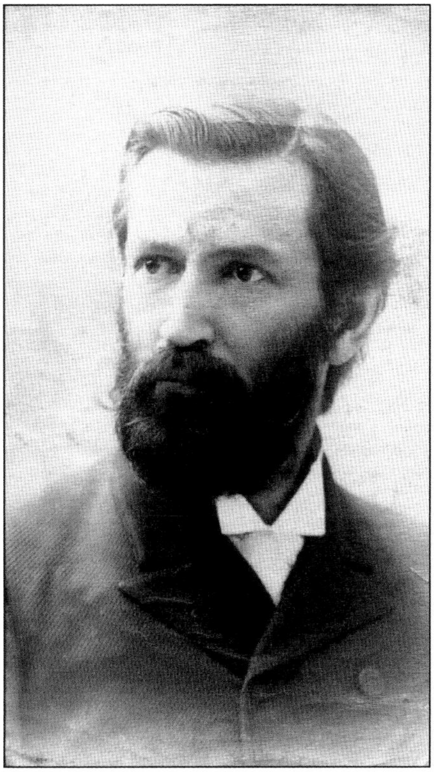

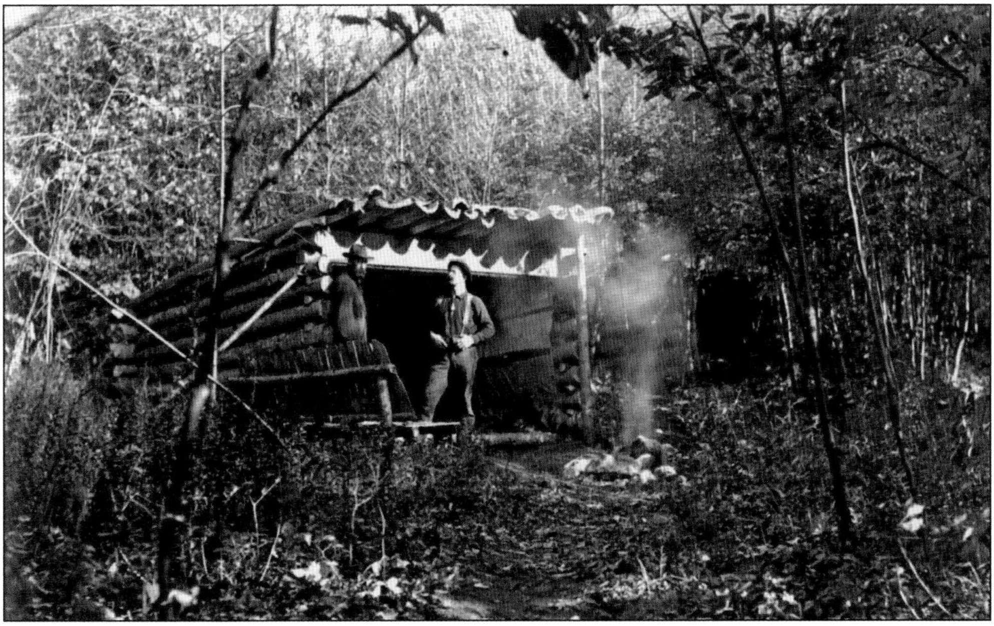

Stoddard began filming in the Adirondacks in 1872. While he is best known for his photography, he was also a painter, art teacher, cartographer, and environmental activist. He held two patents for the photographic equipment he invented. He made speeches in favor of preserving the Adirondacks. His impassioned speech to the New York State legislature led to the formation of the Adirondack Park to assure rustic camping would continue.

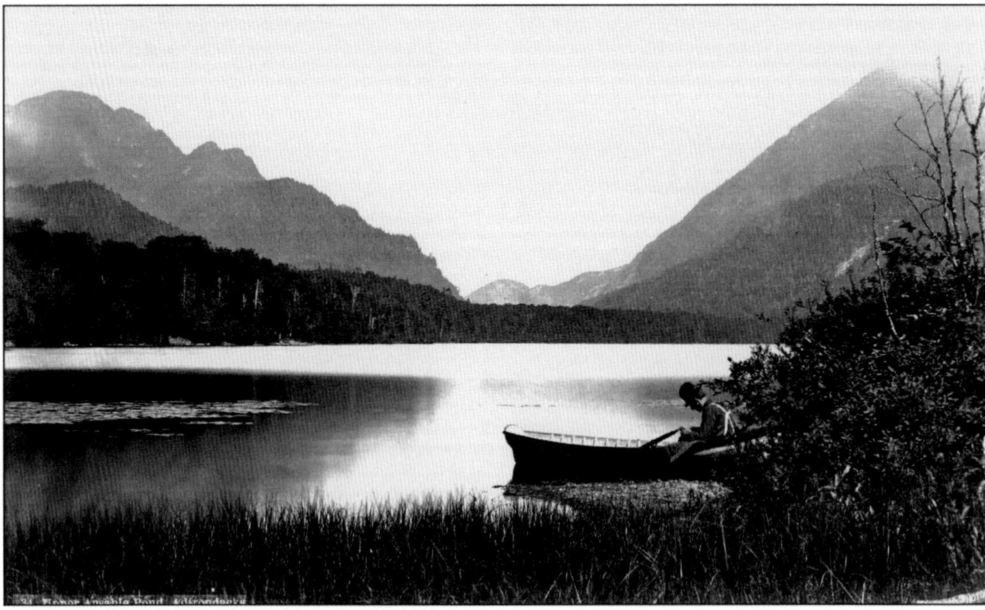

Stoddard married twice, first to Helen Potter with whom he had two children and then to Emily Doty. His home and studio was at 36 Elm Street. He wrote for local newspapers and produced his own magazine, *Stoddard's Adirondack Monthly*. He trained as a civil engineer and used these skills to publish maps of the Adirondacks. He produced 42 yearly guidebooks to the region.

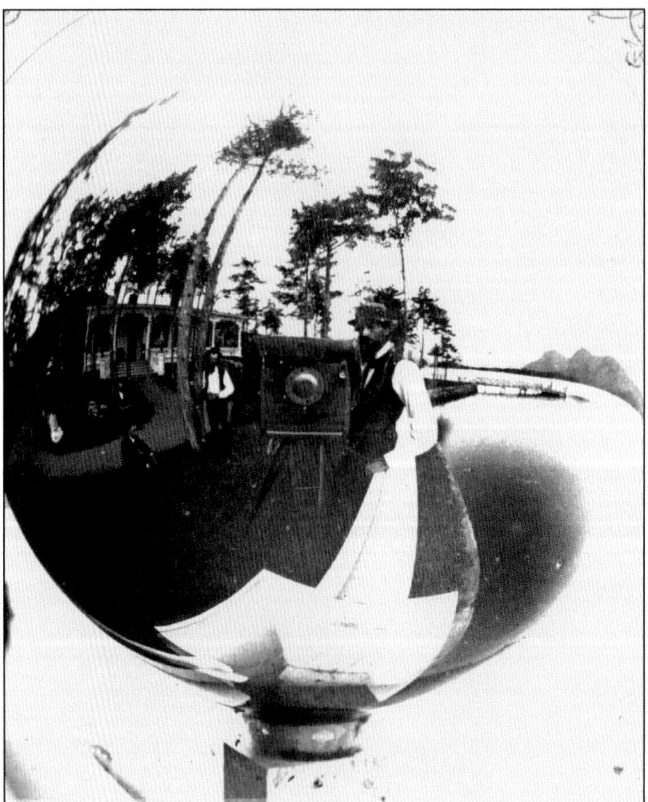

Although there exists large collections of his works in the Adirondack region reflecting his creativity as a photographer, Stoddard never became rich due to the large expense of photography at the time. He died in his final home on Harlem Street, Glens Falls, after two years of a lingering illness.

About the Chapman Historical Museum

The Glens Falls Historical Association began as the Old Glens Falls Club in December 1935. A meeting of older citizens met to reminisce about days gone by, and it was so rewarding, the group decided to continue meeting. As the number of members grew, they stopped meeting in private homes and convened at the Crandall Library. One of the early leaders was Marion Chitty, who is credited with extensive research of the area.

The group did not meet during the war years, but in 1947, under the leadership of Alexander Miller, superintendent of schools, the association met again in the library. It disbanded in the 1950s. In December 1963, Ralph Lapham and William Brown opted to reactivate the organization and search for a permanent home where a museum could be established. With a growing membership and the generous offer from Juliet Goodman Chapman, a Victorian home originally owned by Zopher and Catherine DeLong, at 348 Glen Street, became the Museum of the Glens Falls Historical Society.

The operation of the museum was run primarily from memberships. In 1973, the facility was formally named the Chapman Historical Museum in honor of Juliet and her husband, Frederick Braydon Chapman. Through its many donated artifacts and family biographies, the museum is a treasure of material from Glens Falls's past. The public is able to use the facilities during specified hours to conduct research. The archives are where the Corners Project has conducted its research to produce this book. The restored home is open for guided tours Tuesday through Sunday, together with changing exhibits in the Carriage House Gallery. A Web site can be accessed at www.chapmanmuseum.org.